I0811040

What early readers are saying about *Unrelenting Pursuit*

"All pastors, like me, long for everyone in their flock to walk intentionally as disciples of Jesus. How else can we enjoy and display the riches of Christ's grace, grow into godliness to reflect his image, and bear fruit in keeping with our calling! And yet so many Christians are lacking in this foundational pursuit. As if diagnosing and prescribing the perfect treatment for his pulmonary patients, Dr. Rose equips believers with the knowledge and tools to frame the salient issues pertinent to spiritual health. Page after page, with illustrations drawn from his career as a physician, Dr. Rose constantly leads the reader to God's truth, thus supplying ample confidence in the Lord's way to shape his readers into Jesus' faithful followers."

—Rev. Michael C. Sharrett, pastor
Presbyterian Church in America (PCA)

"A great discipleship tool combining a solid theological understanding of discipleship and the importance of disciple making. It is packed with powerful insights designed to help readers grow into spiritual maturity. Profitable for both laymen and ministers, it provides a great biblical approach to discipleship. It is Christ-centered and one hundred percent biblically sound. I love Doctor Rose's passion and love for our Lord and Savior, Jesus Christ, and for making disciples."

—Rev. Erick Kalenga, Senior Pastor
His Village Church, Culpeper, Virginia

"In his 40+ years in medicine, Ed cared for many people's physical needs, but he never forgot their spiritual needs. In this book, he diagnoses a specific spiritual pathology afflicting Christians in the 21st century. I particularly appreciated his emphasis on humility in surrendering to God's authority and in the oversight of others, especially the need for discipleship."

—**Rev. John Q. Hall**, pastor
Anglican Church in North America (ACNA)

"*Unrelenting Pursuit* is a lovingly written, concise, and thorough book on discipleship. The account of Mary seeking to be discipled by Jesus shows us that discipleship is necessary for every believer. Mary had the audacity to leave the kitchen and sit at the feet of Jesus. In a world where only men were allowed this privilege, Mary was welcomed and commended. This book will also give you the tools needed to disciple whomever God is calling you to, whether it's children, teens, or adults."

—**Carol Hill**, Women's Ministry leader,
former Children's Ministry Director

"The book details a logical path toward a relational disciple-making model that is understandable, practical, and complete. I expect that in my own attempts at disciple-making, contaminated by my own struggle with pride, I will return again and again to *Unrelenting Pursuit* as a template for disciple-making and thereby be better equipped to share the light, joy, and peace of Christ with a fallen world drowning in the whirling maelstrom of secular pride."

—**W. Gerald Teague, MD**
Professor of Pediatrics, University of Virginia

"In his treatise *Unrelenting Pursuit*, Ed shares his decades of experience and wisdom on fulfilling the Great Commission by believers. He has distilled the main points into a written and accessible format that Christians of all ages can grasp. I heartily commend this work to you as a guide to be read and regularly reviewed as you 'Go therefore and make the disciples' the Lord brings your way."

—**Michael S. Marsh, MD**, Family Practice
Port Republic, Virginia

"Many churches fall short of providing the tools and training to encourage the necessary development of more Christlike lives. This book is a needed addition to the current array of discipleship resources and is especially well-suited for individuals and small groups. It has been foundational and transformational in the spiritual growth for me and three other senior Christian men who meet regularly as a small group. I highly recommend the book to anyone seeking to grow in their faith, and especially those of us seeing the need to disciple others."

—**David L. Hill, PhD**
Professor Emeritus of Psychology, University of Virginia

"As a layman, I find *Unrelenting Pursuit* a sweet refresher on the basics of the Gospel. It reminds believers of our call to "make disciples of all nations" and provides an engaging format for readers to use in partnership with the Holy Spirit, who transforms us. Whether used in one-on-one discussion or in leading a small group, each brief chapter encourages the reader to seek spiritual truth, grow in the likeness of Jesus Christ, and bear fruit that glorifies God."

—**Bob Luck**, Retired Finance Executive
Charlottesville, Virginia

"Dr. Ed Rose's book is a beautifully written and concise resource to living a sanctified life. This book serves as a guide to enter into a renewed and glorious relationship with our Lord and Savior. Read it, take notes, and be prepared to dive headfirst into the challenge of living a sanctified life that honors our Lord."

—**Chester V. Oddis, MD**, Professor of Medicine
University of Pittsburgh School of Medicine

"In this powerful work, Dr. Ed Rose describes the path to sanctification through the Holy Spirit, the true essence of the gospel for every believer. It invites Christians to understand that grace, while freely given, calls for a life of transformation, sacrifice, and deep commitment. Readers will learn how to assess their progress in faith, allowing for continual growth and a deepening relationship with God. Whether you're new to faith or have walked with Christ for many years, this book serves as a roadmap for sanctification, leading toward a life marked by spiritual maturity and grace-filled transformation."

—**Hasnaa Jalou, MD,** Pediatric Pulmonology and Sleep
Medicine, Riley Children's Hospital, Indianapolis, Indiana

"While I have grown in my personal sanctification over the past four decades and have worked on many of the spiritual disciplines, I have often felt like I was treading water, stagnant, not really going anywhere. With *Unrelenting Pursuit,* Dr. Rose has unpacked these scriptural mandates in a thorough and organized manner. I feel better equipped and more inspired to be more like Jesus and become good soil that bears good fruit."

—**Richard L. Godine**, Doctor of Veterinary Medicine
Charlottesville, Virginia

"Dr. Ed Rose has written a book for all wonderfully steeped in The Holy Bible—scriptures drawn together from Old and New Testaments. *Unrelenting Pursuit* will nourish the soul of readers from youth, who may be just beginning to learn and explore their faith; to students hungry for deeper understanding of living the Christian life of discipleship. It is also a book for older experienced, faithful Christ-followers who will joy at the encouragement of their faith in Christ Jesus and the hope that is ours as we continue to run the race before us. *Unrelenting Pursuit* is a book for all."

—**Bill Porter**, Retired Civil Engineer
St. Louis, Missouri

Unrelenting Pursuit

Becoming God's Instruments in Making Disciples

C. Edward Rose, Jr., MD

Carpenter's Son Publishing

Unrelenting Pursuit: Becoming God's Instruments in Making Disciples

Carpenter's Son Publishing, Franklin, Tennessee
CarpentersSonPublishing.com

Good Soil Good Fruit Ministries, LLC, Charlottesville, Virginia
GoodSoilGoodFruit.com

ISBN 978-1-956370-77-5 (paperback)
Print and ebook formats available

Cover Image: The painting on the cover is a watercolor painting by Karren Rose derived from an original photograph by Giuseppe Peppe on Unsplash.com (https://unsplash.com/photos/people-riding-on-sailboat-on-sea-during-daytime-VylnmNlvmxc).

Edited by Bob Irvin

Cover and Interior Design by Suzanne Lawing

All profits from this book to the author will be directed to ministries which promote disciple-making.

Printed in the United States of America

Dedication

I am grateful to my wife Karren for her oversight, which began even before I came to know the Lord, and for her faithful encouragement throughout our marriage. Karren's input to this book has been significant. Throughout our life together, she has been and continues to be my most faithful and treasured resource for insight and encouragement.

This book is dedicated to Karren and to our children, Katie and Charlie, for their love and forbearance of an imperfect man who has sought to balance being a son of God, husband, father, and physician.

Acknowledgments

I would like to express my thanks and debt of gratitude to the following people who contributed greatly to the writing of this book.

Dr. Robert M. Carey for his discipleship by example through our forty-four years working together in Charlottesville.

Dr. Ken Elzinga for his input about the book and permission to include his principles for giving. Dr. Carey and Dr. Elzinga both suggested a chapter on humility, and Dr. Elzinga recommended Andrew Murray's book on humility.

Johan and Lida Gous of Hope Builders Ministry for their faithful encouragement in discipleship through teaching and by example.

Pastors John Q. Hall and Joseph F. "Skip" Ryan for their influence on my spiritual life and their suggestions in regard to this book.

Pastors Erick Kalenga and Robert McCready, who encouraged me as the book came together.

Dr. Frank Sutton for his discipleship and suggestions as I wrote this book, including his recommendation of Watchman Nee's book, *Let Us Pray.*

Jeanette Windle for her helpful editorial suggestions.

Wendall Winn, an elder who has discipled me through the years, who provided valuable insight as this book was being prepared.

C. Gary Young for his review of the manuscript.

Contents

PART THREE

Growing By Sanctification to Christ's Likeness to Produce Good Fruit

INTRODUCTION

A COSTLY GRACE

Fourth of July 2021 was a hot, humid Sunday afternoon at the tail end of the Covid pandemic. My wife Karren and I were among more than five hundred people attending an open-air revival service in Greene County, Virginia. The testimony of one speaker we heard at the revival underscores the reason for writing this book. After his initial faith experience, this particular speaker said, he didn't experience any substantial change in his life.

Several years later, the man made another profession of faith in Jesus. This time, he was discipled by mature followers of God. Only then did he begin growing spiritually, conquering life problems, and bearing spiritual fruit. My wife Karren and I were witnesses to that fruit at that revival service. This man was one of the spiritual counselors praying with and explaining the gospel to those who responded to the altar call.

The man's story is not uncommon. It is my own story. Many churches are simply not providing adequate discipleship so their flock can be sanctified. The issue is not new. Many prophetic voices have been crying out about complacency in disciple-making among institutional churches for nearly a century. Dietrich Bonhoeffer, A.W. Tozer, Chuck Colson, Dallas Willard, Francis Chan, and John Stott are just a few.

It is this critical need for top-notch disciple-making that led me, a physician who is not a pastor, to write a book on disciple-making. Shepherding other Christ-followers through the sanctification process by means of the grace God has provided should be the calling of every Christ-follower. Let me share my own spiritual journey to explain why this issue became such a burden on my heart.

I am the oldest of three children born to public school teachers. My father had a deep faith in God, but it was my mother who encouraged (and enforced!) our church life as a family. I regularly attended worship services in our local church and participated in church youth programs. At an early age, I knew I needed to accept Christ as my personal Savior. At age thirteen, I thought I did that.

There was just one problem. I misunderstood the gospel to be salvation by obedience to God's commandments. No one came alongside to disciple me. If they had, they might have discovered my misconception of the gospel. After multiple attempts and failures to follow God's commandments as given in Scripture, I gave up. My religious activities became limited to nominal attendance at weekly worship services.

This pattern continued through college and medical school. I met Karren Young from El Paso, Texas, in my third year of medical school. We were married six months before I became a physician. We soon found ourselves at the University of Alabama in Birmingham for my internal medicine and pulmonary disease training. Part of the pulmonary training involved rotating through the city-county Cooper Green Hospital. A week or two before my rotation, another doctor who had completed his own rotation there cautioned me that I could expect an invitation to an early-morning weekly meeting.

"It's weird!" my friend told me. "They pray!"

Otherwise, my peers in the program praised this particular rotation. The pulmonary specialist overseeing the rotation was Dr. Frank Sutton, an energetic, tall, fit man with a disarming personality. One look at him and you were sure he'd likely played basketball in college. Despite being prewarned, I was still caught off guard when Frank invited me to the morning Bible study he led each week with hospital personnel.

But I accepted the invitation and discovered the current Bible study was the Navigators' *Design for Discipleship*. At the first meeting, we came to the following passage.

> For by grace, you have been saved through faith; and that not of yourselves, it is the gift of God; not as a result of works, so that no one may boast (Ephesians 2:8, 9).

What? Could we read that again? Does this mean salvation is not by obeying God's commandments but by faith alone? My eyes had been opened. After hearing the true gospel for the first time at the age of thirty, in 1976, I repented, surrendered, and placed my faith in Jesus Christ.

After that, Frank and another Christian doctor in the pulmonary division faithfully discipled me until Karren and I left Birmingham in 1977. After two years of research training at the University of Colorado in Denver, I accepted a faculty position at the University of Virginia School of Medicine. In 1979 we moved with our children Katie and Charlie to Charlottesville, Virginia.

As with my initial misunderstanding that salvation is by good works, I had also misunderstood the vital importance of sanctification, i.e., growing into the likeness of Jesus Christ. As a family, we joined a vibrant evangelical church in Charlottesville. Through this wonderful church and the godly men God placed in my life, I began growing spiritually, albeit slowly. But I allowed the demands of being a clinician, teacher, and scientist to usurp my relationship with God, growth in sanctification, and roles as a husband and father.

In 2000, almost a quarter-century after I was born again, God began giving me a picture of my need for spiritual growth. Our church's lead pastor, John Hall, invited me and two other men to join him on a mission trip to India. In the two weeks we were there, we met many Christ-followers who gave medical care to people around them. Their equipment, medical supplies, and facilities were far inferior to what I worked with in the United States. Yet they were modeling Jesus in their lives much more faithfully and with much more joy than I was.

This trip brought me face to face with the realization that I was not following Jesus as I should. It seemed God used every subsequent mission trip to show me something deeper. For instance, He showed me my prideful heart through a visit to Santa Cruz, Bolivia, with an otolaryngologic surgical team. Several years after my trip to India, I became convinced that discipleship occurs relationally in a small-group setting. Jesus' design for discipleship was a relational model in which He lived His life with twelve men for three years. It is important to note that He devoted more intense discipleship with three of the disciples, Peter, James, and John.

I first led a group of men through Lynn Anderson's book on disciple-making, *They Smell Like Sheep* (West Monroe, LA: Howard Publishing Co., 1997). It was clear to me that Jesus' shepherding model for the growth of fellow Christ-followers in His likeness worked two thousand years ago and that it remained the best model for disciple-making. I had received this type of shepherding from my Christian brothers in Birmingham, and I was now privileged to come alongside other Christ-followers to encourage their sanctification. It is not just the people being shepherded who grow spiritually. With every discipleship encounter, I also have grown.

Many in the church today live a substantial part, if not the entirety, of their lives after coming to faith in Jesus with complacency about becoming like Him and producing the fruit for which God created us. Jesus is the Chief Shepherd. He calls every Christ-follower to evangelize those who have not yet been born again. He also calls us to be His under-shepherds in discipling those who receive Him so that they may grow into His likeness. This is what is often called the Great Commission. The Father, Son, and Holy Spirit have given us the means. All they ask us to do is be faithful.

I retired from my position as a professor of medicine in 2021. Retirement from one's lifetime vocation is a milestone that, for me at least, caused a look back over the course of my life. In doing so I recognized God's hand in my spiritual growth through many people and circumstances. I felt God's leading to write a book on the importance of sanctification in every Christ-follower. This is the backdrop for the material you are about to read, written not by a seminarian but from the perspective of a professor who has taught the practice of medicine for more than four decades.

The first part is for anyone who has not yet placed their faith and trust in Jesus Christ and outlines the basic gospel, i.e., the steps to be born again. The remainder of the book is meaningless until that happens. Growth into Christ's likeness will only occur through the indwelling of His Spirit, which happens through faith. Even if you've already been born again, please don't skip this section because even born-again Christ-followers can misunderstand the true gospel. Yes, salvation is by faith alone. But it also costs everything. We must completely surrender "self" if we are to follow and serve the Lord Jesus Christ. The true gospel is a gospel of "costly grace."

The book's second part focuses on the means of grace God gives the Christ-follower so we can grow to be like Him. This includes allowing the Holy Spirit to indwell and transform us, correctly using God's Word, and praying. Part three focuses on using these means of grace to grow in sanctification. Putting sin to death. Forgiving unconditionally. Growing in affliction. Growing through giving. This is good fruit.

As a Christ-follower grows more like Him, he or she begins to produce mature fruit of His likeness that glorifies the Father and Son. This includes evangelism, i.e., sharing the good news of the gospel with others. This is making disciples who in turn make other disciples. And it is faithfully following the "one another" commandments and other good works.

This book has been written for several types of readers. Perhaps you are not yet born again but are seeking spiritual truth. Or perhaps you are new in your faith in Jesus. In either case, your next step should be to join a local church that believes in God's Word, the Bible, and endeavors to follow it. Identify yourself as a seeker or new in faith and ask for a mature Christ-follower to come alongside and guide you in your growth in His likeness.

Or you may already be a mature Christ-follower with the desire to disciple other Christ-followers to spiritual maturity. Maybe you are a pastor or leader in a local church seeking the right platform to fulfill your church's primary purpose of discipling congregants to spiritual maturity so they in turn can become disciple-makers. The self-evaluation questions at the end of each chapter will provide metrics for evaluation of your congregation and an assessment of progress in your church's disciple-making program.

One caveat about this book: it is not self-help. It is Holy Spirit help. Immersing yourself in the chapters of the book alone will not cause you to grow in the likeness of Christ. These chapters are intended to direct you to seek God and discipline yourself to be transformed through the Holy Spirit and the means of grace God provides to bear good fruit. For you will only bear fruit that glorifies Him through "Christ in you, the hope of glory" (Colossians 1:27).

PART ONE

Born Again Through Faith to Grow into Christ's Likeness

CHAPTER ONE

FAITH ALONE IN CHRIST ALONE

"To accept Christ in anything like a saving relation is to have an attachment to the person of Christ that is revolutionary, complete, and exclusive."[1]
A.W. Tozer

According to Pew polling, the number of adults who identify as Christian in the United States is 63 percent.[2] This percentage is decreasing decade by decade.[3] Similarly, there are countries all over the globe that were once considered Christian nations but today have a shrinking percentage of the population that still identifies as Christian. Regrettably, even the most current polling numbers don't indicate that this is the percentage of adults who have faith that provides salvation.

The term "Christian" was first used for followers of Jesus Christ[4] in Antioch (see Acts 11:26). Over time, the word itself has become increasingly nonspecific. It can refer to someone actually following the Messiah but also to someone raised in a Christian family or who attended church at some point or even as a default when someone is asked to identify their religion. In the twenty-first century, it is an imprecise word that includes people with little or no interest in following Jesus Christ.

I was recently speaking with an acquaintance about one of the prevailing social issues.

"That is the great thing about Christianity," he responded. "It's a big tent."

This notion is contrary to the words of Jesus we read in the Gospel of Matthew.

> "For the gate is small and the way is narrow that leads to life, and there are few who find it" (Matthew 7:14).

The word for "church" in the original Greek in which the New Testament was written is *ecclesia*, meaning God's called-out ones, or authentic followers of Jesus who have salvation. The late pastor and seminary president Dr. Edmund Clowney[5] beautifully frames Jesus' church as "a new community, joined in a common faith and life . . . a colony of heaven. . . . The church is found when the saints are found, and where they are fulfilling their calling from Christ."[6]

But in modern parlance, there has been a drift in the meaning of the word "church" from the definition given by Dr. Clowney. Like "Christian," it has come to be nonspecific, representing a local group of people meeting regularly, only some of whom may be faithful followers of Jesus. From the outset, humans have attempted to alter the gospel message. It is human nature to reduce the gospel to terms that serve our own desires and minimize changing our lives to conform with following Jesus (see Jude 1:4). The result is a watered-down gospel message. In many churches today, any person who attends weekly with regular financial contributions receives a figurative stamp of approval. These people are now "in." With their salvation seemingly secured by church attendance or perhaps membership, they mistakenly believe they can live however they see fit.

Far from being set apart from the world, these people remain unchanged. They may practice what they think is a holy life one day of the week, but their lives are indistinguishable the remainder of the week from the outside world. Their lives blaspheme Jesus, whose power is intended to transform lives and bring the kingdom of God to earth. The Bible describes this as "holding to a form of godliness, although they have denied its power" (2 Timothy 3:5). Such people may not have the salvation they think they have.

The early church had similar problems, as we see in the New Testament epistles and letters to the churches in Revelation. Lukewarm spirituality is the outcome of having no interest in growing into the likeness of Jesus Christ (i.e., to spiritual maturity). Jesus rebuked the churches of Ephesus, Pergamum, Thyatira, Sardis, and Laodicea for being asleep or lukewarm (see Revelation 2:1–3:18). The following profile that we see in much of the institutional church today would undoubtedly receive a similar rebuke.

- Absence of love for God.
- Indifference for God's will to be done.
- Lack of love for other Christ-followers with no effort to maintain the unity of the Spirit in the bond of peace.
- Compromise on the inerrancy and absolute truth of Scripture in favor of moral relativism.
- Continuation in besetting sin—or failing to warn others of it.
- Participation in or support of the pagan practice of child sacrifice through abortion.
- Unwillingness to risk persecution by speaking God's truth against prevailing societal evils.
- Stinginess with resources of compassion, time, and finance.
- No interest in evangelizing others or making disciples.
- Rank complacency about growing to spiritual maturity in order to bear the good fruit for which we were created.

In His rebuke, Jesus exhorted the five churches to wake up and "remember what you have received and heard; and keep it, and repent" (Revelation 3:2, 3). He exhorted those in these churches to buy from Him "gold refined by fire" (Revelation 3:18). These admonitions speak of growth to spiritual maturity and a harvest of good fruit by persistence and endurance in the midst of trials and hardship. The starting place is the gospel.

Samuel Wilberforce was the Bishop of Winchester in the Church of England during the nineteenth century. He was the son of the legendary William Wilberforce, who led the campaign in British Parliament to abolish the slave trade. In his sermons, Samuel Wilberforce preached "man's life ruined by sin," and the "glory of redemption, that it restores us to the state from which Adam by transgression fell."[7] He said, "The gift of regeneration is the restoration of the supernatural grace of God's indwelling."[7] Being born again through redemption and the process of regeneration by which we grow in Christ's likeness through the power of His Spirit are linked. You can't have one without the other.

RUIN

God created us in His perfect design to enjoy fellowship with Him forever. When our original ancestors, Adam and Eve, broke God's commandment, sin entered the world (see Genesis 2:16, 17, 3:1-13). God punished this rebellion, and all creation, including humankind, fell from what it was intended to be (see Genesis 3:14-24). Sin ruined Adam and Eve and every generation that followed.

So how do we define sin? Sin is missing the mark in carrying out God's imperatives for relating to Him and fellow humans. It is frank rebellion against God. The psalmist notes:

> For the wicked boasts of his heart's desire, and the greedy man curses and spurns the Lord. The wicked, in the haughtiness of his countenance, does not seek Him (Psalm 10:3, 4).

The prophet Jeremiah portrays human rebellion against God.

> For I solemnly warned your fathers in the day that I brought them up from the land of Egypt, even to this day, warning persistently, saying, "Listen to My voice." Yet they did not obey or incline their ear, but walked, each one, in the stubbornness of his evil heart; therefore, I brought on them all the words of this covenant, which I commanded them to do, but they did not (Jeremiah 11:7, 8).

This stubborn, evil heart is in every human being. Whereas humanity once had fellowship with God, who is the true light, sin broke that relationship and cast everyone in utter darkness. In consequence, God pronounced a curse on Adam and Eve, expelled them from the perfect garden He had made for them, and cursed the world (see Genesis 3:14-19). Scripture describes clearly how extensive that darkness is and its impact on our relationship with God.

- God is a light shining in the dark (see 2 Peter 1:19) and warns us by the examples of others (see Psalm 19:11; 1 Corinthians 10:11).
- God is holy and "there is no unrighteousness in Him" (Psalm 92:15).
- God is a righteous judge who cannot overlook evil and wickedness (see Habakkuk 1:13); therefore, sin separates us from God (see Isaiah 59:2).
- As a righteous judge, God must punish sin (see Romans 1:18).
- God's just punishment for sin is eternal death (see Isaiah 1:28; Ezekiel 18:20; Romans 6:23); not just physical death, but spiritual death (see Ezekiel 18:4).

In contrast to God's righteousness, Scripture makes clear that every descendant of Adam and Eve is guilty of sin and therefore under sentence of death (see Isaiah 53:6; Romans 6:23). No human being can free us of this dilemma. Even if a mortal human offered to take the punishment for another person's sins, this would not satisfy God's justice because that human is also guilty of sin and under a death sentence. We are trapped, dead in our sins, and unable to save ourselves (see Ephesians 2:1). Which brings us to the gospel. What is the gospel? The original Greek word is *euangelion* (see Matthew 4:23). It means good news. Because of God's love for us, He has provided redemption and regeneration through His Son Jesus Christ to those who would receive Him. Why? For us to serve and glorify Him and be with Him forever.

REDEMPTION THROUGH FAITH ALONE

God loves us and creates us to have a relationship with Him. Throughout Scripture, He proclaims His desire to dwell among His people and be their God (see Leviticus 26:12; Jeremiah 7:23, 24:7; Ezekiel 36:28, 37:27; Zechariah 8:7, 8; 2 Corinthians 6:16). This desire will be fulfilled in the new heaven and new earth (see Revelation 21:1-3). Despite our sins and rebellion, His love endures from generation to generation (see Jeremiah 31:3).

Because He loves us, God sent His only Son Jesus to save us (see John 3:16). Jesus was deity fused with human flesh, and He never sinned (see Hebrews 4:15; 1 Peter 2:22), making Him an acceptable sacrifice for the sins of all humankind. God's plan of salvation was that Jesus would redeem us (i.e., buy us back from our death sentence). He did this by *substitutionary atonement* whereby God attributes our sins to Jesus and accepts Jesus' death on the cross as payment in full for our sins (see 2 Corinthians 5:21; 1 John 2:2). At the moment a person places his or her faith in His Son, God declares that person righteous, or *justified*, which is a legal term. The apostle Paul describes this in his epistle to the Roman church.

> This was to demonstrate His righteousness, because in the forbearance of God He passed over the sins previously committed; for the demonstration, I say, of His righteousness at

> the present time, so that He would be just and the justifier of the one who has faith in Jesus (Romans 3:25, 26).

Justification is a judicial act by a righteous God to declare righteous any person who has faith in Jesus Christ. We receive forgiveness of our sins through the atoning sacrifice of Jesus Christ by faith alone.

> For by grace you have been saved through faith; and that not of yourselves, it is the gift of God; not as a result of works, so that no one may boast (Ephesians 2:8, 9).

But what exactly is this faith through which God forgives our sins and we are reconciled to Him? First, it involves *repentance*. Repentance is grief for our sins that sent Jesus to the cross, godly sorrow that leads to confession and salvation (see 2 Corinthians 7:10). It involves recognizing one's sin and abandoning self-defense or self-justification. Some have defined repentance as turning away from sin. This is true, but it is more than that. It is turning from sin toward the true light, Jesus Christ.

Second, faith *believes* that Jesus was the Son of God and Messiah and that His death on the cross paid the penalty for our sins. It trusts and embraces that Jesus Christ is the all-sufficient and only mediator between humans and God who can bring forgiveness and reconciliation (see 1 Timothy 2:5). The Bible defines faith as "the assurance of things hoped for, the conviction of things not seen" (Hebrews 11:1).

Humility is a third and vital component of faith that has been neglected but is emphasized by well-known nineteenth-century South African author, pastor, and theologian Andrew Murray.[8] Jesus admonished people who were attacking Him, such as in this passage.

> "How can you believe, when you receive glory from one another and you do not seek the glory that is from the one and only God?" (John 5:44)

Speaking of this admonition, Murray wrote, "Faith and humility are at root one, and we can never have more of true faith than we have of true humility."[8]

Humility brings us to empty self and become a usable vessel for His work in us. This results in His working through us (see 2 Corinthians 4:7). It is, therefore, surrender. We can summarize that the components of a faith that saves are humility that brings repentance, trust, and complete surrender to becoming empty of self.

God provided us a way out from the human predicament of sin because He is a God of kindness, love, mercy, and grace (see Isaiah 30:18; Ephesians 2:4; Titus 3:4-7; Hebrews 4:16). He is a God of mercy in providing a way for us to avoid something we deserve—death for our sins. This is because He is a God of grace giving us something we don't deserve: unmerited favor. This is not because of anything we have done but because of who He is.

What do we make of the concept of free will in salvation? There are a number of Scriptures that support that salvation is a choice offered to every person, and God wants no one to perish.

> "I call heaven and earth to witness against you today, that I have set before you life and death, the blessing and the curse. So choose life in order that you may live, you and your descendants" (Deuteronomy 30:19).

> "Do I have any pleasure in the death of the wicked," declares the LORD God, "rather than that he should turn from his ways and live?" (Ezekiel 18:23)

> This is good, and pleases God our Savior, who wants all people to be saved and to come to a knowledge of the truth (1 Timothy 2:3, 4, NIV).

> The Lord is not slow about His promise, as some count slowness, but is patient toward you, not wishing for any to perish but for all to come to repentance (2 Peter 3:9).

Yet Scripture also states that God has predestined those who will be adopted into His family (see Ephesians 1:4, 5). Jesus said, "No one can come to Me unless the Father who sent Me draws him" (John 6:44). The Apostle Paul wrote "No one can say 'Jesus is Lord,' except by the Holy Spirit" (1 Corinthians 12:3). Transformation to Christlikeness (i.e., regeneration) is through the power of the Holy Spirit (see 2 Thessalonians 2:13; 1 Peter 1:2).

A spectra of beliefs have arisen. One end of the spectra holds to a belief that absolute free will is present over every aspect of salvation. This is called libertarianism. On the other end is the belief that God's sovereignty is absolute and draws the elect to salvation. There is no free will. This is referred to as determinism. Problems may occur with both doctrines. On the one hand, libertarianism can result in denial of the role of the Holy Spirit in our ability to confess Jesus as Lord and in our transformation to Christ's likeness. On the other, determinism, with its belief that salvation is totally under God's sovereignty, can lead to passivity in following and serving Jesus Christ. This is a mindset that can lead to complacency, one that believes that if I am supposed to do it, God will make me do it. It is being paralyzed by a misunderstanding of grace.

Dr. Donald J. Barnhouse (1895-1960) was pastor of the Tenth Presbyterian Church in Philadelphia. Both pastors James Montgomery Boice[9] and Philip Graham Ryken,[10] themselves also subsequent pastors at the same church, describe an illustration Dr. Barnhouse used to provide insight into free will and pre-election. He portrayed the cross of Jesus Christ as having a door on it with a sign that proclaimed Revelation 22:17:

> And let the one who hears say, "Come." And let the one who is thirsty come; let the one who wishes take the water of life without cost.

For those who entered through the door of the cross and received salvation, on glancing back at the door through which they had entered, the sign now stated: "He chose us in Him before the foundation of the world, that we would be holy and blameless before Him . . . " (Ephesians 1:4).

The mystery of salvation is that both are true. We choose to come to Jesus Christ for salvation, and yet our choice is predetermined. The apostle Paul was no stranger to these issues, writing to the Ephesians about pre-election (Ephesians 1:4, 5) and to the Corinthians on the central role of the Holy Spirit in salvation (see 1 Corinthians 12:3). But Paul exhorted everyone not to rest in the doctrine of pre-election. He was fervent in exhorting every Christ-follower to do their part in their salvation.

> Not that I have already obtained it or have already become perfect, but I press on so that I may lay hold of that for which also I was laid hold of by Christ Jesus (Philippians 3:12).

> Work out your salvation with fear and trembling; for it is God who is at work in you, both to will and to work for His good pleasure (Philippians 2:12, 13).

REGENERATION

The first thing that occurs through Jesus' work on the cross is that when God looks at a person who has placed his faith in Jesus, resulting in justification, He now sees the righteousness of Jesus instead of the person's unrighteousness. This is the *positional holiness* of the new believer. The second thing that happens at the moment of faith is that the new believer receives the promised Holy Spirit, who directs *transformational holiness*. This is regeneration, also known as sanctification (see Acts 2:38; Ephesians 1:13, 14; Titus 3:5-7).

Sanctification begins with the transformation of our will. The entirety of our actions follows a Christlike will. We receive salvation to bring glory to God (see John 15:8; 1 Corinthians 6:20; 1 Peter 4:11).

We do this by performing the good works God created in advance for each of us to do, which in turn glorifies Him (see Ephesians 2:10).

Some may point to the thief on the cross as an example of salvation without corresponding good works (see Luke 23:40-43). That is true. At the moment he placed his faith in Jesus, the thief was dying. There was no time for sanctification to produce good fruit in his life. The only thing he could offer Jesus was his faith. For this faith, he received salvation. The same can't be said for most of us who have been given additional time to grow in the likeness of Christ and bear fruit before we take our last breath.

Some might also ask whether a requirement for spiritual maturity and good works is a form of legalism that adds good works to faith for salvation instead of faith alone. The answer is no. The new birth is by faith alone. There is no good work that can reconcile us to God (see Romans 3:20). The apostle Paul makes this clear.

> He [God] saved us, not on the basis of deeds which we have done in righteousness, but according to His mercy, by the washing of regeneration and renewing by the Holy Spirit, whom He poured out upon us richly through Jesus our Savior (Titus 3:5, 6).

The instant you repent and place your faith in Jesus, you are declared righteous by God, your guilt is removed, and you become a member of His family (see John 1:12; Ephesians 2:8, 9). It is an act by a righteous Judge whereby you are declared righteous and acquitted (see Acts 13:38, 39; Romans 3:24; 1 Corinthians 1:30; 2 Corinthians 5:21). Good works do not save us. We are saved by faith in Jesus (see Ephesians 2:8, 9). But while we do not receive salvation *by* good works, we receive salvation to *do* good works through the working of the Holy Spirit.

> For we are His workmanship, created in Jesus Christ for good works, which God prepared beforehand so that we would walk in them (Ephesians 2:10).

If we have faith and repentance that leads to salvation, we will be captured by the Holy Spirit. Through God's Spirit, God's Word, and prayer, we become able to conquer sin in our lives and increase in obedience. This leads to doing good works that are an outward sign of the inward process of repentance and faith. James put it this way.

> Someone may well say, "You have faith and I have works; show me your faith without the works, and I will show you my faith by my works" (James 2:18).

CHAPTER ONE APPLICATION

DISCUSSION QUESTIONS

- What is the faith that saves?
- What is justification and what does it mean?

SELF-EVALUATION

- Examine the components of faith discussed earlier. Do you believe you are a sinner? Have you repented of your sin and placed your faith and trust in Jesus Christ alone for the forgiveness of your sins through His death on the cross?
- Do you believe doing good works are not a part of being born again, that this comes only through faith in Jesus Christ?

If any of your answers to the questions above are not affirmative, you should consult a mature man or woman who is a Christ-follower, or a pastor of a church that holds to the inerrancy and truth of Scripture.

MEMORY VERSES

> For by grace you have been saved through faith; and that not of yourselves, it is the gift of God; not as a result of works, so that no one may boast. For we are His workmanship, created in Christ Jesus for good works, which God prepared beforehand so that we would walk in them (Ephesians 2:8-10).

CHAPTER TWO

THE FULL GOSPEL MESSAGE

"Whoever desires to come after Me, let him deny himself, and take up his cross, and follow Me."
MARK 8:34 (NKJV)

Some people do not receive the washing of regeneration (see Titus 3:5, 6) because they have never understood the gospel clearly. For this reason, a complete gospel presentation is more likely to produce faith that brings salvation because it is an informed faith. Faith is an inward change in our minds that leads to conviction, repentance, decision, and commitment. This necessitates embracing the full gospel message. *An informed faith that brings salvation encompasses the following factors.*

- **Conviction**: This includes being convicted of God's love for us (see Jeremiah 31:3), our alienation from God because of sin (Romans 3:23; Colossians 1:21), the punishment for sin of eternal death (see Romans 6:23), that Jesus was God's Son, and that the only means for forgiveness of sin and reconciliation to God is through Jesus' death on the cross and resurrection (Acts 4:12; Colossians 1:13, 14, 21, 22).

- **Repentance**: This involves sorrowful recognition of our sins against God and turning away from them toward God in repentance (see Acts 2:38).
- **Humility**: We must understand there is nothing we can do through good works to earn salvation (see Romans 3:20; Galatians 2:16; Ephesians 2:9).
- **Decision**: We must receive this free gift God offers through faith alone in Jesus alone, trusting our eternal destiny with God to Jesus Messiah, alone, as the mediator for our redemption and reconciliation (see John 1:12, 13; Ephesians 2:8, 9).
- **Commitment**: Faith that brings salvation is a commitment to wholeheartedly follow Jesus for the remainder of our lives, endeavoring to model Him, serve Him, and bear fruit (see John 15:1-8) in a ministry of reconciliation that brings others to the Savior (2 Corinthians 5:19, 20).

A partial response to the gospel is not optional. Nineteenth-century Anglican clergyman Harvey Goodwin said:

> Faith implies a revelation, and men of faith are just those who feel that a revelation must not be trifled with, must not be set aside, must not be condemned, but must be adopted as the law of life.[1]

The gospel message is also not a promise of prosperity. Many who follow Him will suffer and go through trials. Jesus exhorted everyone to count the cost before choosing to follow Him. It is a narrow path, and suffering and hardship will likely be involved (see Matthew 7:14; Luke 14:27-35). It cost God His only Son to reconcile us. It cost Jesus His life on the cross to pay the penalty for our sin, as the apostle Peter points out.

> Knowing that you were not redeemed with perishable things like silver or gold from your futile way of life inherited from your forefathers, but with precious blood, as of a lamb unblemished and spotless, the blood of Christ (1 Peter 1:18, 19).

It is also costly to the follower of Christ, including full submission (i.e., surrender) to His lordship over every compartment of their life (see Mark 8:34, 35). This is a lifelong commitment. Christ calls us to deny ourselves, take up our cross, and follow Him (Matthew 16:24, 25). American pastor, church planter, and missionary Jack Miller framed it this way.

> Often we do not take the trouble to explain to people that "choosing Christ" is not an act of human autonomy but a surrender of human autonomy.[2]

Early twentieth-century German theologian and anti-Nazi dissident Dietrich Bonhoeffer called this commitment "costly grace."[3] Every Christ-follower must renounce all past sins and endeavor with all of their heart to live for Him. We must strive to overcome sin with increased obedience for the rest of our lives (see 2 Timothy 2:19). This may mean giving up friends, relationships, or even jobs as we make Christ the most important entity in our life.

Conversely, life with Jesus will never be boring, dull, or onerous. He promises that if we follow Him, He will provide us with life to the full (see John 10:10), one with great joy. He tells us that His yoke is easy and His burden is light (Matthew 11:28-30). He will take His followers into salvation. The motive that drives such discipleship is a love for Jesus, which makes following Him and becoming like Him the top priority of our lives. In a letter to a woman fearful of going on the mission field, Pastor Jack Miller wrote:

> What you discover is that there is no permanent joy in Christ apart from a willingness to deny ourselves, take up our cross, and follow Him. Your life cannot have any power in it or even

salvation if you refuse to be like a grain of wheat that must fall to the ground and die in order to bring forth much fruit.[4]

THE GOOD SOIL

In the Parable of the Sower, Jesus explained different responses to the Gospel (see Matthew 13:1-23; Luke 8:5-15). A farmer cast seed broadly. Some fell alongside a path, some on rocky ground, some among thorns, and some on good soil. In this parable, the seed represents God's Word, the gospel.

The *seed by the path* is stepped on and eaten by birds, and this represents the evil one taking away the word from the hearers (see Luke 8:12). They are blinded by the evil one, and say, "I am not interested in that kind of thing." Some will deny they have sinned against God and need forgiveness and reconciliation. Others believe in salvation by their good works, i.e., legalism. Any attempt to gain merit with God by keeping the law is strongly condemned by Scripture (Romans 3:20). None of us can keep the whole law, and breaking a single law renders us guilty of all of the law (James 2:10). Moreover, the apostle Paul states that if righteousness were through the law, then there was no purpose in Christ's death (Galatians 2:21). Still others take their faith in Christ as a license to sin exuberantly. This is *antinomianism.*

The *seed falling on the rocky soil* represents people who hear the Word, then fall away during hard times because they have no roots (Luke 8:13). This can happen to followers of the "prosperity gospel," a belief that people of faith will be richly blessed with health and financial prosperity. Their faith is exploded in hard times, and they fall away.

The *seed falling among thorns* represents people who fall away because of the care and concerns of life. The cares of this world choke out the gospel (see Luke 8:14). Take, for example, "woke" social causes. God cares about social issues including poverty, racial injustice, and oppression. Scripture commands God's followers to engage in the battle against these things (Isaiah 58:1-7). But we do not receive our salvation or sanctification through our involvement in social issues. To believe so is legalism, which is a false gospel.

While we are called to fight social evils in our culture, the true solution will always be hearts transformed by the gospel of faith in Jesus. This includes the hearts of those committing acts of injustice, the hearts of the unjustly treated, and the hearts of Christ-followers called to engage in relieving these forms of injustice and oppression. It always has been and always will be.

When the Holy Spirit works, transformed hearts no longer commit acts of injustice. Those unjustly treated can forgive and harbor no resentment or bitterness—nor commit other sinful actions in response to their mistreatment. When God's people, *ecclesia*, by leading of the Holy Spirit, engage in their calling of true fasting (see Isaiah 58:1-7), "Justice [will] roll down like waters and righteousness like an ever-flowing stream" (Amos 5:24). Social injustice is a heart problem. That problem is resolved only when those hearts are transformed by the gospel and the Holy Spirit.

Only in hearts which are the *good soil* will the gospel seed flourish. These are people who "heard the word in an honest and good heart, and hold it fast, and bear fruit with perseverance" (Luke 8:15). We are reconciled to God for a relationship with Him in order to increase in holiness, encounter His presence, and worship Him. The good soil is a heart devoid of pride, and this allows the seed to grow the taproot of humility. The first fruit of a gospel-transformed heart is the grace of humility. Only then can the seed of the gospel fully germinate and grow. What results are the good works God has prepared in advance for us to do (see Ephesians 2:10). This is the good fruit the Christ-follower is prepared to bear. Matthew writes:

> "The good soil . . . is the man who hears the word and understands it; who indeed bears fruit and brings forth, some a hundredfold, some sixty, and some thirty" (Matthew 13:23).

From the standpoint of the Bible, what are "fruit"? Fruit are actions of the Holy Spirit in a person through which, inwardly and outwardly, they reflect the likeness of Jesus Christ. The apostle Paul describes inward changes as fruit of the Spirit.

> But the fruit of the Spirit is love, joy, peace, patience, kindness, goodness, faithfulness, gentleness, self-control; against such things there is no law (Galatians 5:22, 23).

The apostle Peter describes this fruit as faith, moral excellence, knowledge, self-control, perseverance, godliness, brotherly kindness, and love (see 2 Peter 1:5-7). These inner virtues induced by the Holy Spirit result in outward changes in a person's attitudes, demeanor, and actions. Holy Spirit-led fruit of our actions as Christ-followers are the "good works" we were created to do (Ephesians 2:10).

NO OTHER ROUTE TO GOD

A host of human-derived dead religions attempt to reconcile humanity to some alternate god or belief instead of the God of the Bible and His Son Jesus Christ. Deists, for example, believe in a God but refuse to accept His Son Jesus Christ as the provision for their forgiveness of sins and spiritual maturation. The apostle Peter stated to the religious leaders in the Sanhedrin that Jesus was the cornerstone which they had rejected and that no other name under Heaven provided salvation (see Acts 4:11, 12). The apostle John stated that the person who has the Son has life and the person who does not have the Son of God does not have life (1 John 5:12). Jesus Himself stated clearly that He is the only way to the Father and no one comes to the Father except through Him (John 14:6).

Many will bristle and say there are many pathways to God. But leaders of other religious paths were not like Jesus. Mohammed lived and died. Buddha lived and died. They cannot offer anything to our predicament of sin other than human instruction. In contrast to

Mohammed and Buddha, God raised Jesus from the dead, and He sits at God's right hand in Heaven and intercedes for His followers (see Romans 8:34). Jesus will always live in Heaven as our High Priest to make intercession for us.

> Therefore He is able also to save forever those who draw near to God through Him, since He always lives to make intercession for them (Hebrews 7:25).

There is no doubt that many followers of these other religions are sincere in their faith. However, the object of our faith matters. God sent Jesus, not Mohammed or Buddha, to rescue us. Jesus is alive, and to those who believe in Him, His Spirit transforms them into His likeness to bear fruit. Even when sincere, faith cannot provide salvation unless that faith is in the One who can provide salvation. Make no mistake: unless we place our faith and trust in Jesus, we will be accountable for the penalty of our sins and undergo a second death. A spiritual death. There are only two places your sin burden can be placed—either on Jesus, for which He died and paid the penalty when He was crucified two thousand years ago, or on you. If your sin is on you, you will be declared guilty and suffer the penalty when you come to judgment at the end of your life (see Revelation 20:11-15). If someone chooses any alternative other than Jesus for the forgiveness of their sin, the consequence is spiritual death.

Early in my medical practice when I was prescribing penicillin tablets for Group A Streptococcal pharyngitis, I emphasized to every patient they complete the ten-day course. Some patients stopped the antibiotic on the third or fourth day when their sore throat resolved, putting them at risk for heart or kidney complications. They had been prescribed what they needed but didn't follow the treatment. Jesus, the Great Physician, the "author and perfecter of our faith" (Hebrews 12:2), has prescribed what we need. We need to be born again in Him, and we need Him in order to grow to spiritual maturity so we may accomplish the assignments He has given us to bear good fruit. The question is: do we trust Him to do this?

CHAPTER TWO APPLICATION

DISCUSSION QUESTIONS

- What is meant by an informed faith?
- What is *positional* versus *transformational* holiness?
- What is meant by Bonhoeffer's phrase "costly grace"?
- Why are the "prosperity" and "woke" gospels false gospels?

SELF-EVALUATION

- After understanding the benefits and costs of placing your faith in Jesus, did you unreservedly receive Him as Savior and commit to follow and serve Him?
- Since your faith decision, have you been baptized? If not, you should be.

If any of your answers to the questions above are not affirmative, you should consult a mature brother or sister who is a Christ-follower or the pastor of a church that holds to the inerrancy and truth of Scripture.

MEMORY VERSE

> Then Jesus again spoke to them, saying, "I am the Light of the world; he who follows Me will not walk in the darkness, but will have the Light of life" (John 8:12).

PART TWO

God's Means of Grace for Growing into Christ's Likeness

CHAPTER THREE

TRANSFORMATION THROUGH THE HOLY SPIRIT

"Put on the new self, which in the likeness of God has been created in righteousness and holiness of the truth."
EPHESIANS 4:24

When the prophet Isaiah encountered Jesus, he exclaimed:

> Woe is me, for I am ruined! Because I am a man of unclean lips, and I live among a people of unclean lips; For my eyes have seen the King, the LORD of hosts (Isaiah 6:5).

The apostle John, one of the closest disciples to Jesus during His ministry on earth, encountered the risen Christ toward the end of his life on the island of Patmos. Notice his reaction.

> Out of His [Jesus'] mouth came a sharp two-edged sword; and His face was like the sun shining in its strength. When I saw Him, I fell at His feet like a dead man (Revelation 1:16, 17).

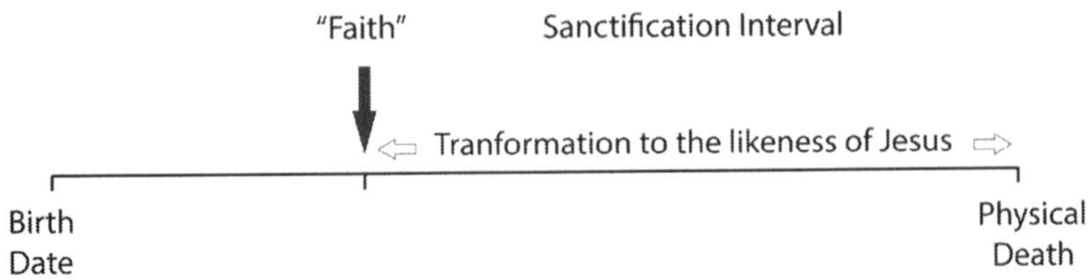

At the end of time, Jesus will return in His glory to judge every person for what they have done, separating them into sheep and goats (see Matthew 25:31-46). The sheep, representing Christ's followers, will be with Him for eternity. The goats, representing those who reject Christ, will be condemned to eternal punishment.

A false Jesus is being preached in the world today. He is incorrectly portrayed as someone who overlooks all sin, who just wants people to be happy and prosperous. It is incorrect to assume this false teaching applies only to the unsaved outside the organized church who have never expressed faith in Jesus. It is also held by a faction within the organized church today. The figure displayed above represents a person's life who comes in "faith" to Jesus Christ (at the point of the arrow), resulting in justification. Some believe they have secured their salvation and can continue to live according to their own desires and wishes without change. Everything afterward is optional.

They are wrong. God's grace and the transformational work of the Holy Spirit run throughout the fabric of salvation from the faith moment that initiates our salvation until our last breath on earth as a Christ-follower. Salvation is a call to follow Jesus and be sanctified to become like Him. The writer to the Hebrews proclaimed that the person of faith is called to a life of holiness.

> Pursue peace with all men, and the sanctification without which no one will see the Lord. See to it that no one comes short of the grace of God (Hebrews 12:14, 15).

In his second letter to the Corinthians, the apostle Paul proclaimed:

> Behold, now is "the acceptable time"; behold, now is "the day of salvation" (2 Corinthians 6:2).

What Paul meant is that salvation begins during our life here on earth. Every follower of Jesus Christ will have opportunities God may not present again. Paul follows this with clarification of what this looks like.

> Giving no cause for offense in anything, so that the ministry will not be discredited, but in everything commending ourselves as servants of God, in much endurance, in afflictions, in hardships, in distresses, in beatings, in imprisonments, in tumults, in labors, in sleeplessness, in hunger, in purity, in knowledge, in patience, in kindness, in the Holy Spirit, in genuine love [*agape*[1]], in the word of truth, in the power of God; by the weapons of righteousness for the right hand and the left, by glory and dishonor, by evil report and good report; regarded as deceivers and yet true; as unknown yet well-known, as dying yet behold, we live; as punished yet not put to death, as sorrowful yet always rejoicing, as poor yet making many rich, as having nothing yet possessing all things (2 Corinthians 6:3-10).

What Paul is referring to is that a sanctified life will bear fruit now, not just in eternity. Every Christ-follower is called to this if they have truly been born again. Like many terms in the church, *sanctification* has become increasingly misunderstood or ignored. The remainder of this book is about sanctification. It is therefore essential that several terms be defined.

- **Holiness**: to be holy refers to God's attributes, nature, and whole Being, that they are strikingly different from the world. God calls all to holiness: "You shall be holy, for I the Lord your God am holy" (Leviticus 19:2). To be holy is to be set apart to represent the purity of God.

- **Righteousness**: to be righteous is to conform to God's standard of holiness. The Father, Son, and Holy Spirit are righteous.
- **Sanctification**: Sanctification is the process by which the Holy Spirit, with God's additional means of grace, transforms a Christ-follower into increasing holiness throughout their life (see Romans 15:16; Ephesians 3:16-19; Titus 3:5). Jesus is our supreme example of holiness, and it is the power of His Spirit that mediates and enables our increase in holiness. Jesus was the Lamb of God (John 1:29, 36) who demonstrated perfect holiness in His life (Hebrews 4:14, 15). Therefore, the goal of sanctification is to become increasingly like Jesus Christ in every way: Christlikeness.

As we saw in the previous section, when God looks at a person who has received Jesus through faith, He sees the cloak of righteousness of His Son (see Isaiah 61:10; 1 Corinthians 1:30). This is referred to as *declarative* or *positional* righteousness. Some people think this is the completion of their salvation and that there is nothing more to do. But under that cloak of the Messiah, the new Christ-follower still has sin that was present in their lives before placing faith in Him.

At the moment of faith, the Holy Spirit comes into the believer and launches the process of spiritual maturation (see Acts 2:38; 2 Corinthians 1:22; Ephesians 1:13)—what is termed *transformational holiness*. There is much to do by the new person of faith in Jesus Christ. They must engage with all their being and work with the Holy Spirit in the process. This is a process that occurs over the remainder of a Christ-follower's life here on earth. Positional holiness does not in any way obviate the requirement for increasing holiness in the Christ-follower.

Another word for transformational holiness is *sanctification*. This is the process of growth in holiness from the time of faith until the death of the Christ-follower, which is each believer's "sanctification interval." In contrast to justification, sanctification requires active participation (works) by the Christ-follower. As we will see, it is a battle for our own heart, and this battle will continue until our last heart contraction. Sanctification is not optional (see Hebrews 12:14, 15; 1 Peter 1:14-16).

THE SUPREME DISCIPLE-MAKER

In Jesus' ministry and in the early church after His ascension into Heaven, the Greek word *mathetes* was used to refer to people who followed Jesus (see Matthew 26:20). The English word *disciple* was used to represent this word. A disciple is a learner—but he or she is more than that. A disciple is more like an apprentice. This concept has faded somewhat in current understanding. But in past times, a person who wanted to learn a profession came alongside and worked with someone in the trade to learn the profession. These were called apprentices.

Disciples were men and women who counted the cost and chose to follow Jesus' call to "follow Me." They were His apprentices. They literally followed Jesus during His ministry on earth. On counting the cost, these disciples recognized they were not just accompanying a rabbi of the time. They were following the promised Messiah.

Jesus taught those accompanying Him that His body was true spiritual food and drink. He announced that some were there who did not believe and that no one would come to Him unless it had been granted by the Father (see John 6:47-66). As a result, many followers abandoned Him. Scripture says they "withdrew." Jesus then asked the twelve disciples if they would also abandon Him. The apostle Peter's statement of faith is one of the most poignant proclamations in all of Scripture.

> "Lord, to whom shall we go? You have words of eternal life. We have believed and have come to know that you are the Holy One of God" (John 6:68).

After Jesus returned to Heaven, His disciples were led by the Holy Spirit. In biblical context, a disciple is someone totally resolved to follow Jesus as a lifelong apprentice in pursuit of being transformed by Him in union with His Spirit. *Discipleship* is the process of being discipled. The goal of discipleship is for the person to become like Jesus so that they serve others and bear fruit by which the Father is glorified (see John 15:8). Discipleship to the likeness of Jesus Christ is sanctification.

A *disciple-maker* comes alongside a Christ-follower to guide and encourage that person to grow into the likeness of Christ. Jesus was the supreme disciple-maker during His ministry on earth. His model for disciple-making is presented in the four Gospels: Matthew, Mark, Luke, and John. Jesus took eleven ordinary men and discipled them to holiness. They lived with Him, learning His wisdom and how to pass it on to others. They learned how to faithfully replicate His actions on every occasion, becoming like Jesus in every part of their being. Jesus then used His model to launch His church.[2]

When Jesus ascended into Heaven, there were at least one hundred and twenty disciples (see Acts 1:15). These disciples launched the most incredible movement in human history. To understand discipleship, we must look at how Jesus did it since He is the ultimate disciple-maker.

First and foremost, He chose ordinary people, those not viewed by the world as having exceptional value. He didn't call people acclaimed by the world with high social standing. The religious establishment had already recruited the "elite." Jesus took the leftovers, ordinary men, to shame the wise and demonstrate that the disciple's transformation came from God, not human ability. This put to rest any boasting (see 1 Corinthians 1:26-29).

Second, when Jesus said "Follow Me," He required those who accepted this call to give up everything. His disciples needed to live with Him and give Him their full attention. Discipleship would be ineffective if their lives were full of distractions.

Third, they spent a great deal of face-to-face time with Jesus. They ate meals together, traveled together, and shared all their resources.

Jesus engaged His disciples to assist in His ministry. They spent three years as His apprentices at His side. What did they see and learn?

They saw a carpenter full of love, compassion, and humility. Jesus looked at every person as an image-bearer of God worthy of His love and consideration. He forgave sin (see Luke 5:20), healed the sick and demon-possessed (Matthew 15:29-31; Mark 5:1-20), fed the hungry, and comforted the downtrodden (John 4:7-26). A person didn't have to be among the world's highly esteemed to be Christ's follower. Indeed, Jesus condemned the worldly, those who were acclaimed for their religiosity and false piety (Luke 18:9-14). He rebuked many for their neglect of justice, mercy, and faithfulness (Matthew 23:23).

Jesus did seemingly scandalous things. He spent time in the company of tax collectors, prostitutes, and others condemned by the religious leaders of the time as "sinners" (see Mark 2:16, 17; Luke 7:37-48). When a woman caught in adultery was brought to Him by the crowd for judgment and stoning, He instead rendered mercy and forgiveness (see John 8:3-11).

The disciples also saw someone who displayed exemplary faithfulness to God in everything He did. Jesus identified that His purpose was to be perfectly obedient to God's will in order to bring glory to God (see John 17:4, 5). He came to save the lost (Luke 19:10). He was faithful in submission to baptism (Matthew 3:15-17), prayer (Matthew 14:23), and Scripture. He affirmed God's Word in both teaching and absolute perfect obedience. In Him, there was no sin (2 Corinthians 5:21). Jesus had complete knowledge of Scripture when He taught (Luke 4:14-21). He readily quoted Scripture when tempted by the evil one (Matthew 4:1-11). Jesus perfectly demonstrated His obedience, including His willingness to suffer and die on the cross (Matthew 26:39-42).

Jesus' disciples also witnessed His unwavering dedication to spreading the gospel—i.e., the good news that the kingdom of God was near and that salvation was through repentance and belief in Him. He referred to Himself as the Light of the world (see John 8:12) and declared that He alone was the way to eternal life (John 11:25, 26, 14:6). He invited all to "follow Me," but warned that this would require sacrifice and servant leadership (Mark 9:35; Luke 14:25-35). He emphasized that to truly live we must first lay down our life and take up our cross (Matthew 10:38, 39; Luke 9:23, 24). He also promised that His yoke was light and that He would provide rest for the weary (Matthew 11:28-30).

Those discipled by Jesus heard Him condense a life of following Him into a sold-out love for the Father and other people. Such love for each other would show the world they were His disciples (see John 13:34, 35). Jesus maintained obedience to the law, teaching His disciples that obeying His commandments demonstrated their love for Him (John 14:21). Jesus taught that He chose every one of His followers to bear good fruit to glorify the Father (John 15:8, 16). Producing such fruit was a sign of repentance (Matthew 3:8), salvation (Matthew 7:16-23), and that they were His disciples (John 15:8). He cautioned that they could only bear fruit through attachment to Him, the true Vine, for apart from Him they could do nothing (John 15:1-7).

The disciples heard Jesus prepare them for His departure (see John 13:33). He promised that the Holy Spirit would teach them all truth and grow them in holiness after He was gone (John 16:5-14). They often heard Him say it was necessary for Him to suffer and die but that He would be raised from the dead. They heard Him warn that they would be scattered, persecuted, and tried, but that they should take heart for He had overcome the world. He promised His disciples that the Holy Spirit would lead them in their persecution and that they need have no anxiety (Luke 12:11, 12). He prayed for the protection of His disciples from the evil one (John 17:15).

The disciples heard Jesus teach that the path to salvation was narrow and few would find it (see Matthew 7:13, 14). They heard Him warn about the dangers of unbelief, being ashamed of Him, unforgiveness, and religiosity (Matthew 6:1-6, 10:32, 33; Mark 11:25, 26; Luke 16:19-31). He taught them of the danger of wealth, love of money, and storing up possessions on earth (Matthew 6:19-21; Luke 12:15-21, 16:13). They witnessed Jesus rebuke people for valuing glory from the world rather than God (John 5:44). They heard parables about servants trusted to develop talents while their lord was away and the terrible consequences for those servants who squandered their opportunities (Matthew 25:14-30; Luke 12:42-48).

Jesus' disciples were asked to preach repentance and heal while He watched. When He thought they were ready, He sent them out two by two for the ministry (see Mark 6:7-13; Luke 10:1-20). Jesus grew the disciples to spiritual maturity so they could bear fruit.

The biggest lesson the disciples learned from Jesus was observing Him give up His life in humble obedience to the Father. They saw His agony in considering the cross, yet He remained faithful to the will of the Father. They witnessed His unbearable suffering on the cross. They heard the sickening sound as soldiers positioned the cross upright into a large, deep hole, a thud that caused intense pain as Jesus' flesh was torn by the spikes in His hands and feet. They observed Jesus slowly smothering to death as His weight on the cross overburdened His respiratory muscles to the point He couldn't take an adequate breath. They saw Him die, the Light of the world, the hope of humankind, a man beaten beyond recognition with no breath or pulse.

Jesus' execution left His followers bewildered and confused. They had heard Him proclaim that He came to save the lost. He had told them He needed to suffer and die. But they didn't understand. Immediately after His crucifixion, they had dashed hopes, thoughts of unfulfilled promises, and rampant fear that the same might happen to them. Then on the third day came news of an empty tomb. Reports spread that Jesus had been seen alive. His appearance to His disciples removed all doubt.

Before He left them, Jesus commissioned the disciples to go to the ends of the earth and make disciples, baptizing these disciples in the name of the Father, Son, and Holy Spirit, and teaching them to follow everything He had commanded them (see Matthew 28:19, 20). They saw Jesus restore Peter to fellowship and exhort him to show his love for Jesus by feeding and shepherding His flock (John 21:15-17). They heard Him promise power from the Holy Spirit to enable them to be His witnesses to the ends of the earth (Acts 1:8).

CHAPTER THREE APPLICATION

DISCUSSION QUESTIONS

- What is holiness? Is it different from sanctification?
- What is the difference between *positional* holiness and *transformational* holiness in a Christ-follower?
- What is the relationship of sanctification to salvation?
- How is sanctification different from justification?

SELF-EVALUATION

- After understanding the benefits and costs of placing your faith in Jesus, have you unreservedly received Him as Savior and committed to follow and serve Him?
- Having come to repentance, faith, and trust in Jesus Christ, do you now endeavor to fully submit to His lordship to grow in spiritual maturity in order to bear the fruit He created you to bear?

MEMORY VERSE

> But if the Spirit of Him who raised Jesus from the dead dwells in you, He who raised Christ Jesus from the dead will also give life to your mortal bodies through His Spirit who dwells in you (Romans 8:11).

CHAPTER FOUR

THE CHARACTERISTICS OF A DISCIPLE

"By this all men will know that you are My disciples, if you have love for one another."
John 13:35

Jesus' discipleship profoundly affected these men. Before His return to Heaven, the disciples had feet of clay. Peter denied Jesus three times on the night of His arrest (see Matthew 26:69-75). James and John wanted to call down lightning on inhabitants of a town that refused to welcome Jesus (Luke 9:51-56). The disciples argued about who among them would be the greatest in Heaven (Luke 22:24).

When the Holy Spirit came on them at Pentecost, everything changed (see Acts 2:1-12). After that, they were in union with Jesus through the Holy Spirit. Led by the Spirit, Peter boldly proclaimed the gospel to a crowd that likely included many who just weeks before had screamed "crucify Him!" to Pontius Pilate during Jesus' trial (Acts 2:14-41). The remainder of the book of Acts narrates the crucial acts of the apostles as the Holy Spirit guided them to establish His church.

By now, I trust it is crystal clear to every reader that it is God's will for each of us to grow into the likeness of Jesus Christ through sanctification after we have placed our faith in Him (see Matthew 5:48; 1 Thessalonians 4:7, 8). The apostle Paul wrote to the Romans:

> For those whom He foreknew, He also predestined to become conformed to the image of His Son, so that He would be the firstborn among many brethren (see Romans 8:29).

To the Corinthians, Paul proclaimed:

> But we all, with unveiled face, beholding as in a mirror the glory of the Lord, are being transformed into the same image from glory to glory, just as from the Lord, the Spirit (see 2 Corinthians 3:18).

Why? So that every child of God will be the image of Jesus Christ to others, manifesting "the sweet aroma of the knowledge of Him in every place" (see 2 Corinthians 2:14). A Christ-follower becomes an ambassador for Jesus to the world, one who is placed in a ministry of reconciliation. Being obedient to the Great Commission to evangelize and disciple others is that ministry of reconciliation.

> Now all these things are from God, who reconciled us to Himself through Christ and gave us the ministry of reconciliation, namely, that God was in Christ reconciling the world to Himself, not counting their trespasses against them, and He has committed to us the word of reconciliation. Therefore, we are ambassadors for Christ, as though God were making an appeal through us; we beg you on behalf of Christ, be reconciled to God (2 Corinthians 5:18-20).

In summary, we are called to grow into the likeness of Jesus Christ for the purpose of advancing God's kingdom on earth through a ministry of reconciliation by producing good fruit and doing works of righteousness assigned to us to bring glory to the Father and the Son as the apostle Paul expressed in his letter to Philippians.

> Having been filled with the fruit of righteousness which comes through Jesus Christ, to the glory and praise of God (Philippians 1:11).

How do we know that we are maturing into Christ's likeness? Again, Jesus is our supreme example. He obeyed and pleased the Father and never sinned (see Hebrews 4:15). None of us will ever reach His perfection, but over the remainder of our lives, in all aspects, we are to become more like Jesus. One of the most significant battles for every person is to take the focus of our hearts away from ourselves and set it on Jesus. Only then will we be transformed in our union with Him through the Spirit to develop the love with all our heart, soul, and mind for Him and people that results from spiritual maturation (Mark 12:29-31).

How can we have confidence we are Jesus' disciples? There are a number of characteristics that give evidence of being a disciple of Jesus.

- **Fruit of the Holy Spirit:** the apostle Paul identified the evidence of the Holy Spirit in someone's life as the presence of His fruit—love (agape), joy, peace, patience, kindness, goodness, faithfulness, gentleness, and self-control (see Galatians 5:22, 23). *Agape* is particularly important. Jesus said *agape* for one another would identify them as being His disciples (John 13:35).

- **Humility**: Andrew Murray frames the most valid sign of holiness in a Christ-follower as humility, which is a first fruit of holiness.[1] When Christ-followers have emptiness of self, the Spirit of Jesus Christ creates a servant's heart to put others above himself or herself.

- **Continuing in God's Word**: Jesus said, "If you continue in My word, then you are truly disciples of Mine; and you will know the truth, and the truth will make you free" (see John 8:31, 32). Throughout our lives, we must be ardent students of God's Word, the Scriptures. We must apply it diligently to recognize, overcome, and delete sin from our lives. By keeping God's Word, we show our love for the Father and the Son (John 14:15; 1 John 2:3-6, 5:3).

- **Outward Fruit of Good Works**: when the Holy Spirit begins transforming the person who comes to faith, He gives them the ability to do good works consistent with salvation (see Matthew 5:13-16). Jesus warned that we are not to be deceived by false prophets.

> "You will know them by their fruits. Grapes are not gathered from thorn bushes nor figs from thistles, are they? So every good tree bears good fruit, but the bad tree bears bad fruit" (Matthew 7:16, 17).

Without faith, a person cannot be subject to the transforming power of the Holy Spirit, which results in the fruit of the Spirit. Faith with transformational holiness will always bring about outward actions as well as inward change. This inward change will transform the motive for which the person is doing good works from self-glory to *agape* for God and people. The Pharisees did plenty of good works, but they displayed no *agape* (see John 5:42).

How were the Pharisees and other religious leaders so deceived? One explanation is that they misunderstood the gospel, believing that good works reconciled them to God. This misconception continues today. In my own experience in sharing the gospel, the most common answer people give when asked how they are reconciled to God is "by the good things I have done." The absence of good works in our lives should concern us about our faith. But we must not use good works as the sole criterion for faith. Many have been deceived by their good works in thinking they had salvation when they did not. Such were the Pharisees.

Another trap is misinterpreting an emotional feeling as the faith which saves. Emotions are involved in coming to faith in Jesus, but emotions alone do not save. A third possibility is faith based on wrong motives. Some people have a "faith moment" out of fear of eternal damnation rather than wonder and awe of God and love for Him. Thinking they have completed the transaction, they fail to follow and serve the One who was pierced, bled, and died for them. They are not, in actuality, regenerated.

The improper motive of prosperity lurks in devotees of the prosperity gospel. When they are not blessed, they become disillusioned. A person once told me they were giving up on following God because He had not resolved the financial problems in this person's life.

Many in the church today believe a putative faith moment in Jesus resulted in their salvation, but they've never engaged in regeneration to an end point of good works under the power of the Holy Spirit. Dietrich Bonhoeffer called this "cheap grace."[2] American pastor and author A.W. Tozer referenced this impending spiritual blight in the church as "the easy acceptance of Christ."[3] Rather than following Jesus and being regenerated to glorify God through good works, such people decide on their own what they will believe and do. Nineteenth-century pastor Charles Spurgeon rebuked any notion in a person that their faith moment is an end in itself for salvation.

> We mistake if we think that the pardon of sins is God's ultimatum. No, no; it is but a beginning, a means to a further purpose. He forgives our sins with a design of curing our sinfulness. We are pardoned that we may become holy. God forgives the sin that He may purify the sinner.[4]

The story is told of a company that realized its product was substandard and not what it intended. Accordingly, business leaders hired an outside consultant. After thoroughly investigating the manufacturing process, the consultant told them, "Your manufacturing process is perfectly designed for the product you are getting. Your problem isn't an inferior product. It is an inferior process."

We discussed in a previous chapter how an incomplete understanding of the gospel results in unregenerated church members. The solution is, therefore, the presentation of the complete gospel, one that emphasizes saving faith as the starting point rather than the end point. Salvation is a life of obedience with humble surrender to Jesus' lordship.

If we had to target the main reason for so many unregenerated people in the church today, it is an unwillingness to make more than a nominal commitment to Jesus Christ. Many people are interested in being saved from the prospect of eternal damnation, but few are willing to completely submit to the lordship of Jesus. After warning that a tree would be known by whether it produced good or bad fruit, Jesus asked, "Why do you call Me, 'Lord, Lord,' and do not do what I say?" (Luke 6:46)

The "cheap grace" cohort in today's churches largely represent those with an unwillingness to surrender their lives in obedience to Jesus Christ's lordship. When the cost goes beyond nominal commitment, such people say, "No thanks." They have reduced life's most important decision, one that affects their eternal destiny, to that of ordering a hamburger at a fast-food restaurant. Instead of "no lettuce or onions, please," it is, "just my faith alone for salvation, please. Hold the growth to become like Jesus Christ to do good works for which He created me!"

In contrast, the presence of an inner faith that saves brings about outer actions that others can see (see Philippians 2:12; James 2:14-26). These acts are signs of true repentance (Acts 26:20).

Pride in the unregenerated crowd leads to taking offense to any appeal to be sanctified and bear fruit. Instead, these people stir up discord to get the pastor fired. This occurs frequently enough that some pastors become reluctant to speak the truth regarding growth to spiritual maturity. The apostle Paul prophetically warned:

> For the time will come when they will not endure sound doctrine; but wanting to have their ears tickled, they will accumulate for themselves teachers in accordance with their own desires (2 Timothy 4:3).

In many churches, living out a brand of nominal spirituality goes unchallenged by pastors and church leaders. This is particularly true in larger churches that do not provide oversight of their flock with assignments to grow others with the help of a spiritual mentor or small group. Some of these churches may have an active evangelism program but are complacent about growing new converts to maturity. They may hope it happens through an appeal from the pulpit, small groups, or outside ministries, but they don't have a program designed to develop shepherds and then assign them to disciple their flock to maturity.

In the absence of such programs, I have been surprised by how *clericalism* is given priority in many churches today over spiritual maturation in the members. New members are rapidly assimilated into the "needs" of the church to perpetuate the organization, many or most of which have nothing to do with spiritual maturation. Perhaps even worse, some churches that have caved to the social/woke gospel are quick to siphon off immature believers to charge the quixotic windmills of prevailing social and political causes.

Whether unintentionally or intentionally, many churches are designed for the existence and tolerance of the lukewarm in their congregations. They represent a component of the organized church that believes a person can have salvation without putting on the humility of Jesus Christ and growing in His likeness. Such lives fail to heed numerous warnings in Scripture. These are potential talents God has given each local church that are being squandered. They are lives that never reach spiritual maturation to accomplish their high calling for the kingdom.

The worst part is that these people think they have salvation when, in fact, they may not. After teaching that a good tree will be known by its fruit, Jesus said:

> "Not everyone who says to Me, 'Lord, Lord,' will enter the kingdom of heaven, but he who does the will of My Father who is in heaven will enter" (Matthew 7:21).

John the Baptist reiterated this truth when he stated:

> "Indeed the axe is already laid at the root of the trees; so every tree that does not bear good fruit is cut down and thrown into the fire" (Luke 3:9).

Jesus' condemnation of religious leaders in His time remains a warning for those who would allow people in today's church to be comfortable with the view that they have salvation without actually following Jesus.

> "Woe to you, scribes and Pharisees, hypocrites, because you shut off the kingdom of heaven from people; for you do not enter in yourselves, nor do you allow those who are entering to go in" (Matthew 23:13).

In 2019, a study was undertaken by Discipleship.org and Exponential to evaluate the degree of disciple-making in Protestant churches across the United States.[5] The study found that 73 percent of churches surveyed either "don't help others make disciples" or "don't seek to intentionally influence others for spiritual growth." Astoundingly, less than 5 percent of churches in the study were identified as "seeking to actively equip and coach their members to make disciples." The study found that only 15 percent of pastors interviewed indicated an existing model in their church "to equip their members to make disciples and a framework or metric for measuring their success at doing so." This study outlined the attributes of a robust disciple-making church.[5]

What is the primary purpose of Jesus' church, the *ecclesia* on earth? Edmund Clowney clearly describes it.

> The Great Commission is not a theme float for mission in a long parade of cultural triumphs. It is the marching orders of the Lord for His church. The Lord of the harvest calls us to call to Him to thrust forth labourers into His harvest. He must send, but he moves us to pray and leads us to go. The church's primary task is to make disciples. To this task the gifts of the Spirit are directed.[6]

If local churches are to fulfill the Great Commission (Matthew 28:18-20), their leadership must correctly identify and agree to this mission. Once this has been accomplished, the leadership must state the mission to the church members, then prioritize resources to accomplish it. They must be faithful to keep their eye on the ball despite changing leadership and membership. A local church's noblest mission is to be a vehicle through which people come into a saving relationship with Jesus Christ, and then, trained to be personal disciple-makers, grow to spiritual maturity to evangelize and make more disciples!

CHAPTER FOUR APPLICATION

DISCUSSION QUESTIONS

- Why is every Christ-follower called to be sanctified?
- What are Bible verses that identify characteristics of someone who is one of Jesus' disciples? Name those characteristics. Read *Discipleship: What It Truly Means to Be a Christian*, by A.W. Tozer,[3] which goes into great detail about the calling and characteristics of Jesus' disciples.

- What is cheap grace? Is it an option?

SELF-EVALUATION

- Do you understand that every Christ-follower is to grow in spiritual maturity, which means becoming more like Jesus Christ?
- Are you committed to this and willing to grow in the means of grace God has given you for sanctification, which includes pursuing His Word, the Bible, prayer, and other means of grace He provides?
- Are you in a church that provides oversight for your spiritual growth in Christlikeness?

MEMORY VERSE

"My Father is glorified by this, that you bear much fruit, and so prove to be My disciples" (John 15:8).

CHAPTER FIVE

GROWING IN CHRISTLIKENESS

"Since we live by the Spirit, let us keep in step with the Spirit."
GALATIANS 5:25 (NIV)

So how, specifically, do we grow in the likeness of Jesus Christ? Following are some key steps summarized from the apostle Paul's admonitions to the Roman church (see Romans 6:3-14) for doing our part to collaborate with the Holy Spirit and discipline ourselves to God's means of grace.

Know who you are and what Jesus Christ has done for you in justification. Before faith in Jesus, we were unregenerate, guilty of sin, and headed for eternal death. At the moment of faith in Jesus Christ, we were baptized into His death on the cross and buried with Him in death (see Romans 6:4). The old man or woman was crucified with Jesus Christ so that its body of sin could be done away with and we would no longer be in bondage to sin (Romans 6:6). We were raised as a "new man" or "new woman" from death with Jesus Christ so we might walk in newness of life, being united with Him "in the likeness of His resurrection" (Romans 6:4-6). Union with the Spirit of Jesus

Christ, who never sinned, has now freed us from sin's dominion and enables the Christ-follower to resist and overcome sin (Romans 8:13).

Many people don't realize they have this freedom. An analogy can be found in my experience with putting out a humane cage trap to identify animals destroying vegetables in our garden. One morning, I discovered a sad raccoon in the cage. With protective gloves, I carried the cage to the edge of our woods, opened the door, and tilted it so the animal landed gently on the ground outside the cage. But the animal didn't immediately scamper off. Only with prodding did he move a short distance as it gradually occurred to him that he was free. Then he scurried off with a few choice glares at for me as he put distance between me and the garden.

The Holy Spirit led the apostle Paul to give Christ-followers who don't recognize their freedom in Christ a similar prodding (see Romans 6:6, 7; Galatians 5:1). We are free from the penalty of sin and its dominion. We can resist sin. Remember the words of Jesus to the man He healed, and to the woman caught in adultery: "Go. From now on sin no more" (John 5:14, 8:11). Through justification, God declared us righteous. Now He enables us to become righteous through sanctification by His means of grace. He calls each of us to "Go. From now on sin no more."

Put on the "new self." Knowing our new position as crucified with Christ, raised in newness of life, and freed from sin's dominion, we are to "put on the new self, which in the likeness of God has been created in righteousness and holiness of the truth" (Ephesians 4:24).

Have faith. Justification is by faith alone (see Ephesians 2:8, 9), but sanctification is by faith and obedient action (Romans 6:12, 13). The apostle Paul proclaimed, "For we walk by faith, not by sight" (2 Corinthians 5:7). Faith brings us to an overwhelming conviction of the magnitude of the Father's and the Son's love for us (Jeremiah 31:3; Romans 8:38, 39; Ephesians 3:17-19). It is faith that brings us to a realization that God wants only the very best for us and that to pursue Him and have a relationship with Him is far better than any other choice for joy, contentment, and our eternal destiny (John 10:10). It is faith that carries the Christ-follower through intense struggles to overcome sin, making him or her assured that the Holy Spirit can enable this overcoming, and confident that God will not abandon them midstream (Romans 8:29-37; Philippians 1:6).

Surrender fully to the work of the Holy Spirit. This involves a decision on our part. We must be willing to wholeheartedly seek God and His Kingdom and abandon any notion of dabbling in worldly pursuits. Our primary ambition can no longer be success in or acclaim by the world in some way, but rather to grow in the likeness of Jesus Christ, which in turn means becoming a nonconformist with the world, as the apostle Paul so clearly instructs.

> Therefore, I urge you, brothers and sisters, in view of God's mercy, to offer your bodies as a living sacrifice, holy and pleasing to God—this is your true and proper worship. Do not conform to the pattern of this world, but be transformed by the renewing of your mind. Then you will be able to test and approve what God's will is—His good, pleasing, and perfect will (Romans 12:1, 2, NIV).

Keep in step with the Spirit (see Galatians 5:25, NIV). Sanctification comes through the power of the Holy Spirit (2 Thessalonians 2:13). But the Holy Spirit's mediation of transformational holiness in the individual Christ-follower can be limited by complacency, stubbornness, and sin that both resist and grieve the Holy Spirit. Just because a Christ-follower has been anointed with the indwelling of the Holy Spirit upon being born again doesn't mean the Holy Spirit will overcome an uncooperative, stubborn will that won't follow His leading or grieves Him through willful sin (Ephesians 4:30). How then can a Christ-follower fully benefit from the transformative power of the Holy Spirit?

- **Agape**: First, we must grow in our love (agape) for the Father and Son as we seek them with all our heart, soul, and mind (see Mark

12:29, 30). Moses proclaimed, "You will seek the LORD your God, and you will find Him if you search for Him with all your heart and all your soul" (Deuteronomy 4:29). We must also grow in an out-of-control love (agape) for the people they care about. Who are these people? Everyone around us (see Mark 12:31).

- **Devotion to God's Word:** The Holy Spirit uses God's Word to sanctify us (see John 17:17). It is one of the ways He teaches us truth (John 16:13). Every Christ-follower must diligently immerse themselves in the study of and meditation on Scripture. The Word of God is the sword of the Holy Spirit (Ephesians 6:17). It is better than any imaging device ever developed by human hands. It images the soul of the Christ-follower and discerns its thoughts and intentions (Hebrews 4:12). If we sufficiently quiet our hearts by meditating on the words God inspired in the Bible, we can hear His voice (Joshua 1:8; Psalm 1:1, 2, 19:14, 119:78, 97-99, 148).
- **Prayer**: Every Christ-follower must increasingly grow in the Spirit in communing with God through prayer (see Romans 8:26, 27).
- **Asking**: Jesus taught that the Father would give the Holy Spirit to those who asked (see Luke 11:9-13). As above, every Christ-follower was given the promised Holy Spirit at the time of faith. The prayer of the Christ-follower should be for God to reveal to him or her ways in which they can increase the transformative power of the Holy Spirit in their lives. Moreover, this request must always be for the right motives (James 4:3).
- **Acting to Overcome Sin**: The transformative action of the Holy Spirit will be diminished by the presence of willful sin in the Christ-follower since the Holy Trinity[1] cannot abide sin. Among the things that grieve the Holy Spirit are pride, arrogance, unforgiveness, anger, and bitterness for trials God places in our lives to grow us, and seeking acclaim from the world. Resistance

to the still, quiet voice of the Holy Spirit in our lives is another. Scripture explains clearly the adverse effects of grieving and resisting the Holy Spirit (see Isaiah 63:10; Acts 7:51; Ephesians 4:30; 1 Thessalonians 5:19-22). Putting sin to death in the Christ-follower's life is critical to keeping in step with the Spirit. Overcoming sin is a work every Christ-follower must do in their own sanctification.

> Consider yourselves to be dead to sin, but alive to God in Christ Jesus. Therefore do not let sin reign in your mortal body so that you obey its lusts, and do not go on presenting the members of your body to sin as instruments of unrighteousness; but present yourselves to God as those alive from the dead, and your members as instruments of righteousness to God (Romans 6:11-13).

> Work out your salvation with fear and trembling; for it is God who is at work in you, both to will and to work for His good pleasure (Philippians 2:12, 13).

As the Holy Spirit reveals areas of your life needing to be transformed, obey and do not resist Him. The presence of continued willful sin will diminish His power, which is critical for overcoming sin. The Holy Spirit will give the Christ-follower this ability as we submit to Him. To fully benefit from the Holy Spirit requires learning to recognize His voice, growing in communion with Him, and walking with Him (see Galatians 5:25, 26). As we discipline ourselves by these means of grace that God has provided, we learn to commune with the Holy Spirit and hear His voice. As we grow in this process, we increasingly become a temple the Holy Spirit can occupy and use to bring glory to God (1 Corinthians 6:19, 20). This is what is meant by the admonition of Paul to "keep in step with the Spirit" (Galatians 5:25, NIV). The Christ-follower is to become a "slave to righteousness, resulting in sanctification" (Romans 6:19).

Whether lay person or lead pastor, recognize you need to be discipled by a more mature Christ-follower your entire life. As some grow in the likeness of Christ, they become deceived, thinking they have outgrown the need to be discipled and are now only called to make disciples. Jesus reflected the full righteousness of the Father. In contrast, every Christ-follower is vulnerable to our flesh nature, the world, and the evil one—until we pass into the next life.

The path of serving God is strewn with the lives of "acclaimed" people of God who fell from their calling due to sin. This isn't to say they lost their salvation, but many have disqualified themselves from the elevated positions of service in which God had placed them. In his farewell at Ephesus, the apostle Paul appealed to the elders to watch over themselves as well as God's flock entrusted to them (see Acts 20:28). Every Christ-follower must first and foremost keep watch over themselves.

Win the battle for your own heart. When we were born again through faith in Jesus, the old man or woman died with Jesus, and the new man or woman rose with Jesus in newness of life (see Romans 6:4-7). Our spirit is now in fellowship with the Holy Spirit and amenable to transformation. Both the old and new man or woman reside within the outer shell, which is still the old "Adamic" flesh. This old Adamic flesh will continue battling with the regenerated spirit over sin. The apostle Paul vividly describes the conflict.

> I find then the principle that evil is present in me, the one who wants to do good. For I joyfully concur with the law of God in the inner man, but I see a different law in the members of my body, waging war against the law of my mind and making me a prisoner of the law of sin which is in my members (Romans 7:21-23).

What is the solution? Paul also proclaimed, "The law of the Spirit of life in Christ Jesus has set you free from the law of sin and of death" (Romans 8:2). This is every person's first battle. A battle for our own heart (see 1 Peter 2:11). Every Christ-follower must be vigilant in this or we will be deceived. It is a lifelong battle we must continuously win through the power of the Holy Spirit.

Put on the full armor of God (see Ephesians 6:10-18, NIV). In his letter to the Ephesians, the apostle Paul reminds the Christians in the city of Ephesus that their battle is not against flesh and blood, but against the "rulers, against the authorities, against the powers of this dark world and against the spiritual forces of evil in the heavenly realms" (Ephesians 6:12, NIV). For this reason, he exhorts them—and us—to put on the full armor of God so that we will withstand these forces in our journey. We are to attach the belt of truth and breastplate of righteousness (Ephesians 6:14), have our feet bound with the gospel of peace (Ephesians 6:15; Romans 10:13-15), take up the shield of faith (Ephesians 6:16), protect our minds with the helmet of salvation, arm ourselves with the sword of the Holy Spirit which is God's Word (Ephesians 6:17), and pray in the Spirit (Ephesians 6:18).

What is the full armor? In his letter to the Romans, Paul encourages his readers to "put on the armor of light" (Romans 13:12). He then adds an incredible statement. "But put on the Lord Jesus Christ, and make no provision for the flesh in regard to its lusts" (Romans 13:14). In other words, the full armor of God is Jesus Christ in us. To avail ourselves of this full armor is to grow in His likeness, i.e., sanctification.

Over the timeline of our life in Christ, our sanctification interval, our likeness to Jesus Christ, should steadily increase. While there may be brief downturns in this process, continuing in chronic sin after a profession of faith is strongly condemned (see Romans 6:1-14; Ephesians 5:1-5; 2 Timothy 2:19; 1 John 2:4, 3:6; 3 John 11) and should be cause for someone to examine if they are genuinely born again.

Following Christ means discipline. It means training ourselves as runners do for a race to improve our obedience and likeness of Him through spiritual discipline (see 1 Corinthians 9:24-27). It means removing sin from our lives. Sin grieves the Holy Spirit (Ephesians

4:30), so how can we be discipled by the power of the Spirit when we knowingly have sin in our lives we are not overcoming? Rather than grieving the Spirit or quenching His power (1 Thessalonians 5:19), we are to keep in step with the Holy Spirit (Galatians 5:16).

Being in step with the Spirit doesn't just mean obedience to "thou shalt not" commandments. It also means obeying the positive imperatives. Go and make disciples. Evangelize. Do good one to another. The essential positive commandment is boundless love (agape) for God and others.

Some may think such exhortations are just for pastors, teachers, and church leaders. After all, they have been trained, and many are being paid for their ministry. If you think this, reread Ephesians 4:11-16. These verses indicate that the main work of ministry doesn't rest on the shoulders of paid professionals but on every member of the body of Christ (i.e., the saints). Those in top leadership such as prophets, evangelists, pastors, and teachers are called, in turn, to equip the saints, which includes every Christ-follower, and each is tasked with the main work of building the body of Christ (see Ephesians 4:12).

Imagine walking in the shoes of a pastor whose congregation thinks it is the duty of the pastors, elders, and leaders to do all discipleship, evangelism, teaching, exhortation, counseling, and visitation of the sick. This is "cheap grace" thinking. Such people show up expecting to be entertained by worship, music, and the message from the pulpit (sound familiar?). Sadly, they are an increasing constituency of today's churches, or what has been termed "consumer Christians." They are often the ones most critical of their pastors and local church.

We must go back to the pattern given us by Jesus and His apostles of discipling others, who in turn disciple others, and so on. Sanctification is a process that every follower of Jesus Christ must unwaveringly pursue for the entirety of our lives. There is no retirement from that process. Nor should Christ-followers ever reach a point where we are content with our level of spiritual maturity. It doesn't matter what we've accomplished so far in our lives. We must wholeheartedly press on in sanctification as the apostle Paul expressed so succinctly.

> I do not regard myself as having laid hold of it yet; but one thing I do: forgetting what lies behind and reaching forward to what lies ahead, I press on toward the goal for the prize of the upward call of God in Christ Jesus (Philippians 3:13, 14).

CHAPTER FIVE APPLICATION

DISCUSSION QUESTIONS

- What does it mean that surrender is required for sanctification?
- What are aspects of keeping in step with the Holy Spirit?
- What is the full armor of God and how is it acquired? Why is it important?

SELF-EVALUATION

- Are you committed to discipleship, meeting with someone who is discipling you to maturity, and growing in obedience and good works?
- Are you in turn discipling someone else with the goal of bearing fruit in every opportunity God provides you?
- While you are saved by repentance and faith alone, it is vital you understand that faith leading to salvation involves sanctification to the likeness of Jesus. For this to happen, you must be in fellowship with mature Christ-followers. If your current church has not assessed your spiritual maturity and plugged you into a discipleship group to grow to become like Jesus, you need to consider

finding a church that does. Your eternal destiny may depend on it.

MEMORY VERSES:

Now the Lord is the Spirit, and where the Spirit of the Lord is, there is liberty. But we all, with unveiled face, beholding as in a mirror the glory of the Lord, are being transformed into the same image from glory to glory, just as from the Lord, the Spirit (2 Corinthians 3:17, 18).

CHAPTER SIX

CORRECTLY USING GOD'S WORD

"A new world will arise out of the religious mists when we approach our Bible with the idea that it is not only a book which was once spoken, but it is also a book which is now speaking."[1]

—A.W. Tozer

What is truth? Is everything we see, taste, smell, hear, touch, and love the result of an accidental assembly of atoms in a primordial soup on a massive ball of dirt with a molten center hurtling through space at sixty-seven thousand miles per hour around a sun in a solar system traveling nearly one-half million miles per hour through a galaxy?[2] Or is there another dimension we can't see or hear that has an intelligent Creator? One who created everything, loves us, and wants a relationship with us?

We may find answers to these questions in two ways. First, the Creator of everything that exists, i.e., God, has revealed Himself to us in His creation. This is called general revelation.

But God has done much more than that. God and His Son Jesus Christ have revealed themselves by speaking to us through the writings of forty men over approximately fifteen hundred years. This is called specific revelation. These writings in Hebrew, Aramaic, and Greek were not a collection of musings. They were written through the inspiration of the Holy Spirit in the context of time, culture, and language (see 2 Timothy 3:16; 2 Peter 1:20, 21). In addition, Jesus Christ came among us and spoke, and faithful men recorded His words.

> God, after He spoke long ago to the fathers in the prophets in many portions and in many ways, in these last days has spoken to us in His Son, whom He appointed heir of all things, through whom also He made the world (Hebrews 1:1, 2).

These writings were assembled from ancient manuscripts into what we know today as the Bible or Holy Scriptures. It comprises many literary styles, including laws and commandments, history, chronicles, narratives, poetry, proverbs, prophecies, parables, teaching, genealogies, sermons, and letters. In the Bible, God tells us about Himself; the origin, fall, and curse of humankind and all creation; and of His restorative plan through His Son Jesus Christ. The purpose of God's inspired Word is for every man and woman to be reconciled to God through Jesus Christ and to grow to be like Christ so they may glorify God and His Son and fellowship with them forever.

A fundamental problem in many churches is a flawed concept of who God and His Son Jesus Christ are. The apostle Paul said of Jesus:

> He is the image of the invisible God … For it was the Father's good pleasure for all the fullness to dwell in Him, and through Him to reconcile all things to Himself, having made peace through the blood of His cross (Colossians 1:15, 19, 20).

Jesus said, "I and the Father are One" (John 10:30). He taught His disciples that when they saw Him, they were also seeing the One who sent Him (see John 12:45). Those who knew Him also knew the Father.

> "From now on you know Him, and have seen Him … Believe Me that I am in the Father and the Father is in Me" (John 14:7, 11).

ATTRIBUTES OF GOD AND HIS SON JESUS CHRIST

We see revealed in Scripture the following attributes of God and His Son Jesus Christ.

Name: God told Moses His Hebrew name, *Yahweh* (see Exodus 3:15). In English-language Bible translations, the terms "God" and "Lord" are used for our Creator. But when the original Old Testament text uses God's Hebrew name Yahweh, you will see this represented by the word "LORD" in small caps.

Transcendency and Infiniteness: Jesus is the Creator of all things (see John 1:3; Colossians 1:15, 16). God the Father is transcendent, meaning He is outside the boundaries of time and physical laws which limit human beings (2 Peter 3:8). Scripture declares that God lives forever, which means He is eternal (Isaiah 57:15). Jesus is "before all things, and in Him all things hold together" (Colossians 1:17). So both the Father and Son are limitless.

Omnipotence: There is no greater power than God, and that power is infinite. The following Scriptures capture God's all-powerful nature.

> "Ah LORD God! Behold, You have made the heavens and the earth by Your great power and by Your outstretched arm! Nothing is too difficult for You" (Jeremiah 32:17).
>
> By the word of the LORD the heavens were made, and by the breath of His mouth all their host (Psalm 33:6).

Preeminence and Self-existence: God is the only God. God the Father, and through the Father, His Son Jesus Christ, are self-existent. I.e., they are not dependent on an outside source for existence as humans are dependent on their Creator.

> "To you it was shown that you might know that the Lord, He is God; there is no other besides Him" (Deuteronomy 4:35).

> "For just as the Father has life in Himself, even so He gave to the Son also to have life in Himself" (John 5:26).

Omnipresence: God is present everywhere, as King David declared in the psalms.

> Where can I go from Your Spirit? Or where can I flee from Your presence? If I ascend to heaven, You are there; if I make my bed in Sheol, behold, You are there (Psalm 139:7, 8).

Omniscience: Scripture reveals that God is all-knowing about all things. This includes everything around us since He created all things from subatomic particles and atoms to DNA and every living creature. He also numbers the hairs on our head (see Luke 12:7). He knows our thoughts and what we will say even before we speak a word (Psalm 139:2-4). God told the prophet Jeremiah that He knew Jeremiah even before forming him in his mother's womb (Jeremiah 1:5).

Wisdom: God is more than all-knowing. He is all-wise. Wisdom is the application of knowledge in rightness, judgment, and actions. The apostle Paul exclaims:

> Oh, the depth of the riches both of the wisdom and knowledge of God! How unsearchable are His judgments and unfathomable His ways! (Romans 11:33)

Holiness and Righteousness: Scripture tells us that God is holy: "Who is like You among the gods, O Lord? Who is like You, majestic in holiness?" (Exodus 15:11). God's holiness indicates that He is set apart from everything else. His holiness is the essence of His being—His truth, love, eternal nature, mercy, and grace. His determination of right and wrong represents His holiness. Righteousness, on the other hand, indicates conformance to the standard of God's holiness.

Jesus was also without sin, holy, and righteous (see 1 Corinthians 1:30; Hebrews 7:26).

Justice: God embodies truth, holiness, and rightness. He is the author of all truth, the sole determiner of right and wrong, good and evil, and therefore what is just. God judges all peoples with equity according to His righteousness.

> "I, the LORD, speak righteousness, declaring things that are upright" (Isaiah 45:19).
>
> The judgments of the LORD are true; they are righteous altogether (Psalm 19:9).
>
> Righteousness and justice are the foundation of His throne (Psalm 97:2).

Sovereignty: God is the supreme power and answers to no one. For this reason, He will not alter His sovereign will, as the prophet Daniel exclaimed.

> All the inhabitants of the earth are accounted as nothing, but He does according to His will in the host of heaven and among the inhabitants of the earth; and no one can ward off His hand or say to Him, "What have You done?" (Daniel 4:35)

Goodness: The Bible repeatedly tells us that God is good.

> You [God] are good and do good (Psalm 119:68).
>
> "For the LORD will again rejoice over you for good, just as He rejoiced over your fathers" (Deuteronomy 30:9).
>
> O taste and see that the LORD is good; how blessed is the man who takes refuge in Him! (Psalm 34:8)

God's goodness extends to those who seek and obey Him. But to those who rebel, God shows severity (see Romans 11:22).

Love: God is love, as the apostle John expresses repeatedly.

> God is love ... We have come to know and have believed the love which God has for us. God is love, and the one who abides in love abides in God, and God abides in him. By this, love is perfected with us, so that we may have confidence in the day of judgment; because as He is, so also are we in this world (1 John 4:8, 16, 17).

The Greek word John uses for God's love is *agape*. This is a sacrificial, serving form of love. The Holy Spirit empowers such *agape* for God and fellow humans in us (see Galatians 5:22). Jesus was the incarnate manifestation of *agape*, most profoundly expressed when He died on a Roman cross for our sins (John 15:13).

Mercy: Every person on this planet is a recipient of God's mercy, beginning in the Garden of Eden when Adam and Eve sinned by violating the one commandment God gave them. He would have been fully justified in destroying humanity. Instead, God showed us mercy. The ultimate expression of mercy was when Jesus did something humanity did not deserve. Though He never sinned, He died on the cross to pay the penalty for the sins of anyone who believed in Him (see John 3:16).

Grace: Instead of giving us what we deserved—i.e., His wrath—God gave us what we didn't deserve, His grace. His ultimate grace was sending Jesus Christ to be the sacrificial Lamb of God through whom all who repent have redemption and forgiveness of sins.

> Blessed be the God and Father of our Lord Jesus Christ, the Father of mercies and God of all comfort (2 Corinthians 1:3).

> The Lord is compassionate and gracious, slow to anger and abounding in lovingkindness. He has not dealt with us according to our sins, nor rewarded us according to our iniquities (Psalm 103:8, 10).

> Being justified as a gift by His grace through the redemption which is in Christ Jesus; whom God displayed publicly as a propitiation in His blood through faith (Romans 3:24, 25).

Immutability and Faithfulness: God's attributes do not change, which is good news for humanity. It means that God remains faithful to His covenant of grace through Jesus Christ for those who will receive it.

> God said, "For I, the LORD, do not change; therefore you, O sons of Jacob, are not consumed" (Malachi 3:6).

> "Know therefore that the LORD your God, He is God, the faithful God, who keeps His covenant and His lovingkindness to a thousandth generation with those who love Him and keep His commandments" (Deuteronomy 7:9; see also Exodus 34:6, 7).

> Let us hold fast the confession of our hope without wavering, for He who promised is faithful (Hebrews 10:23).

Personal and Jealous for a Relationship with Us: Dr. Edmund Clowney was teacher-in-residence for many years at a church in Charlottesville that Karren and I attended. We were blessed to sit under the Bible teaching of this humble pastor and theologian. Dr. Clowney emphasized the presence of Jesus Christ in all of Scripture, as well as the continuous theme throughout the entirety of Scripture of God's desire for a personal relationship with His people (see Exodus 29:45, 46; Leviticus 26:12; Jeremiah 7:23; Ezekiel 14:11; Zechariah 8:8). This will be fulfilled in Heaven.

> Behold, the tabernacle of God is among men, and He will dwell among them, and they shall be His people, and God Himself will be among them (Revelation 21:3).

However, God is a jealous God who will punish those who go after false gods as Moses warned the Israelites.

"For the Lord your God is a consuming fire, a jealous God" (Deuteronomy 4:24, see also Deuteronomy 6:15).

"It shall come about if you ever forget the Lord your God and go after other gods and serve them and worship them, I testify against you today that you will surely perish" (Deuteronomy 8:19).

GOD'S PLAN FOR US

Scripture reveals that humanity is fallen and estranged from God (see Genesis chapter 3). This is in stark contrast to His original intention for creating us in His image to fellowship with Him in a perfect world (Genesis chapters 1-2). It wasn't just our ancestors who sinned. Each of us without exception is guilty of sin before a holy God (Romans 3:23). The Holy Spirit works through Scripture to convict us of sin (John 16:8, 9; Hebrews 4:12). Because of God's love, mercy, and grace, He sent His only Son to be the atonement for our sins and redeem us (Isaiah 53:1-5; Luke 24:44-49; John 1:1-14; 1 John 4:8-10). There is no other name for salvation (see John 14:6; Acts 4:12).

Scripture also outlines what God requires to restore humanity to His original intention. We are saved by reconciliation to God through faith in Jesus Christ (see Ephesians 2:8, 9) so that we may glorify the Father and the Son through good works (Psalm 115:1; Isaiah 43:7; John 15:8; Ephesians 2:10; 1 Peter 1:6, 7). To do this, we must be sanctified. Through sanctification, we grow to the likeness of Jesus Christ by being attached to Him, the true Vine, through the Holy Spirit and the Word (John 15:5, 17:17; 2 Thessalonians 2:13).

God wants all people to love Him and seek Him with all their hearts (see Deuteronomy 4:29, 6:4). We are to fear Him and be obedient to His commandments (Deuteronomy 5:29, 10:12, 13). King Solomon declared:

> The fear of the LORD is the beginning of wisdom, and the knowledge of the Holy One is understanding (Proverbs 9:10).

God wants us to remember what He has done for us (see Deuteronomy 6:12). He wants no one to perish but for all to be saved and come to the knowledge of the truth (Deuteronomy 30:15-20; Ezekiel 18:23; 1 Timothy 2:4). This brings us to the primary purpose of Scripture, which is our transformation. First, by leading us to Jesus so we can be reconciled to God. Then, through communion with God's Spirit so we may grow in Christ's likeness to bring glory to the Son and the Father.

GOD'S VITAL ARMOR FOR THE SPIRITUAL BATTLE

We discussed previously the urgency of being dressed in the full armor of God (see Ephesians 6:12-18). Scripture tells us that our life is a battle, not just against human flesh but against spiritual forces of darkness. While many parts of the armament such as the shield and helmet are defensive, the sword of the Spirit, which is God's Word, and prayer are offensive weapons (Ephesians 6:17, 18).

How is this helpful to the Christ-follower? Jesus demonstrated this in repelling the three temptations of Satan while He was in the wilderness (see Matthew 4:1-11). Jesus repelled each attack by speaking Scripture to Satan. Don't think this wasn't a significant challenge for Jesus, because after Satan gave up and left, angels came and ministered to Jesus (v. 11). Similarly, when Christ-followers encounter the evil one—and we will—the armor of God, including God's Word in the Bible, will allow us to stand our ground and resist evil as Jesus did (Ephesians 6:13).

CHAPTER SIX APPLICATION

DISCUSSION QUESTIONS

- What is general revelation? What is specific revelation?
- What is the chief purpose of God's inspired Word, the Bible?
- Describe the attributes of God. Why are they important?

SELF-EVALUATION

- Do you believe God continues to speak to humanity in the present time through His Word in the Bible?
- Are you willing to conform your life to the commandments and mandates in the Bible?

MEMORY VERSES

"If you continue in My word, then you are truly disciples of Mine; and you will know the truth, and the truth will make you free" (John 8:31, 32).

CHAPTER SEVEN

PRINCIPLES FOR INTERPRETING SCRIPTURE

"They received the word with great eagerness, examining the Scriptures daily to see whether these things were so."
ACTS 17:11

As Christ-followers, we may not all be seminary graduates with formal instruction on interpreting Scripture. Thankfully, there are excellent resources on interpreting the Bible that we can turn to for in-depth information,[1] including online resources like Bible Hub or Olive Tree Bible Software, print commentaries and study guides, small group Bible studies, and many classic and new books on the topic. As we study God's Word, there are some important principles to keep in mind.

The Holy Spirit is a necessity for understanding Scripture. We cannot effectively understand Scripture and apply it to our lives without the work of the Holy Spirit (see 1 Corinthians 2:12-16). We receive the indwelling of the Holy Spirit by faith in Jesus Christ (Ephesians 1:13). Therefore, to properly understand Scripture, it is necessary to be born again. In Christ-followers, unaddressed sin grieves the Holy Spirit and hampers the Spirit's power to help us interpret Scripture (Ephesians 4:30). As we obey the truths the Holy Spirit shows us, more is revealed. Keeping in step with the Holy Spirit is essential (Galatians 5:25, NIV).

Scripture is the means to bring us into God's presence. It is easy to adopt a mindset that Scripture is to teach us conformity to God's commandments, which is true. However, Scripture has a much higher purpose: bringing the Christ-follower into the very presence of God. Once we understand this, it becomes clear why stilling our hearts, praying, and meditating on the Scripture passage we are reading is so important.

We must embrace essential truths to be under the authority of Scripture. If we are to be under the authority of God's Word and have it play its proper role in helping us grow into Christ's likeness, we must embrace four essential truths about Scripture.

- The Bible is the literal word of the Supreme Being, the living God, speaking to us (see 1 Thessalonians 2:13).
- God's words are true and without error. The Bible is self-validating; i.e., it testifies to its own origin and proclaims that it is truth. Since God is incapable of lying (see Titus 1:2; Hebrews 6:18) and Scripture is God's words given to men through the inspiration of the Holy Spirit (2 Timothy 3:16), we know His words in Scripture are truth (2 Samuel 7:28). The Bible consistently proclaims its inerrancy (see Psalm 119:160), and the apostle Paul refers to the gospel as the message of truth (Galatians 2:5; Ephesians 1:13; Colossians 1:5).
- Scripture is eternal. It will last forever, as the prophet Isaiah states: "The grass withers, the flower fades, but the word of our God stands forever" (Isaiah 40:8). This means there is no "use by" date beyond which God's precepts and commandments expire.

- God's words are immutable; i.e., they are unchanging. God's words do not sway to accommodate shifting winds of cultural "morality." When Jesus was teaching the crowd, He upheld the immutability of Scripture: "Do not think that I came to abolish the Law or the Prophets; I did not come to abolish but to fulfill" (Matthew 5:17).

All humanity is under the authority of Scripture. Authority refers to someone or something in a position to influence the mind (thoughts and opinions) and behavior (actions) of someone. When I drive, a speed limit sign expresses the authority of county and state governments to control my maximum speed on that particular stretch of road. Scripture is an expression from the Supreme Being of His authority over each of us regarding our thoughts, opinions, and actions. No authority on earth takes precedence over God's Word, and certainly our wills do not.

Christ-followers are to submit to the absolute authority of Scripture over every aspect of their lives. In the maelstrom of moral relativism, many claim that the Bible is an antiquated book of writings with no relevance in today's world. They are dead wrong. God's Word in Scripture became flesh and dwelt among us in the incarnate Jesus Christ (see John 1:14).

That said, obeying God's commandments in Scripture doesn't earn salvation or additional favor from God. To believe that falls into the trap of legalism. But while faith alone provides salvation, we show our love for Jesus by doing what He commands (see John 14:15). A.W. Tozer viewed the authority of Scripture this way.

> It is one thing to believe the Bible but something else altogether to allow the Bible, through the ministry of the Holy Spirit, to impact and change your life.[2]

Use the M-M-O-R-E approach to interpret and apply Scripture. While embracing essential truths about Scripture is critical, this must be coupled with correct interpretation of Bible passages. Physicians use acronyms as mnemonics to remember things that are important in treating patients. When it comes to the Bible, the correct interpretation and faithful application of Scripture can be approached using the mnemonic M-M-O-R-E: meditate, mind-change, obey, recall, and export. Let's look at these elements individually.

M = Meditation and Mind-change: It is essential that the Christ-follower meditate on Scripture. For this to occur, distractions from the world must be shut out. J.I. Packer wrote an excellent definition of this.

> Meditation is the activity of calling to mind, and thinking over, and dwelling on, and applying to oneself, the various things that one knows about the works and ways and purposes and promises of God. It is an activity of holy thought, consciously performed in the presence of God, under the eye of God, by the help of God, as a means of communion with God.[3]

As a Christ-follower studies a Scripture passage, he or she must consider its context since it was written in different cultures, socio-political conditions, and time periods than the present day. What was written? Why was it written? To whom was it written? Was it written just for the people of the time, or does it transcend time and apply today? Do the verses preceding or following the passage provide insight? For each verse, do you agree to its truth and that it applies to your life? In meditation, the Holy Spirit guides this process and convicts the Christ-follower through passages that are authoritative for his or her life.

O = Obey: Once we agree a passage is true for our lives, we must obey it. We must be "doers of the word, and not merely hearers who delude themselves" (James 1:22). The Hebrew word *shema* means "to hear." The hearing that brings salvation and spiritual transformation is more than the mechanical vibration of tympanic membranes creating electrical signals traveling to our brains. True *shema* means to come under the conviction that the teaching revealed by the Holy Spirit in a Scripture passage is God's valid will for us and to submit to it in practice (see Deuteronomy 6:4). This entails repenting, asking for forgiveness, and submitting to the command. In doing this, we are submitting to the authority of the lordship of Jesus.

R = Recall: The importance of memorizing Scripture must be emphasized. In this era of electric vehicles, the different modes of charging can be seen as an analogy of the value of knowing Scripture by memory. Reading, meditating, mind-changing, and obeying can be equated to level 1 and 2 charging stations for electric vehicles. They are effective (if you can find one) but take time. Memorizing Scripture doesn't replace these steps but speeds up the process—something like a level 3 charging station.

Having God's Word readily available in your mind and on your tongue brings additional benefits. It provides greater insight into and understanding of the "Word" that became flesh, Jesus Christ (see John 1:14). As we've already discussed (Matthew 4:1-11), this is vital in overcoming sin and dealing with temptation. The psalmist exclaims, "Your word I have treasured in my heart, that I may not sin against You" (Psalm 119:11).

E = Export: Lastly, we should export God's Word to others. This part is instrumental in evangelism and making disciples. Memorizing Scripture enhances this. The people I've known who are the greatest disciple-makers have a vast knowledge of Scripture internalized.

Scriptural examples are not commandments. Examples and narratives in Scripture should not be considered authoritative in our lives unless associated with a specific command. God often gave narratives as examples of what not to do. Moses disobeyed God by striking a rock rather than ordering water to come out. King David committed adultery and murder. These passages contain no command that we are to follow their example. Even when commands are given in Scripture, they may have been for a specific person or nation at one time and are not applicable today. This is why it is vital to interpret Scripture in context.

An example is when God commanded Abraham to sacrifice Isaac as an offering on Mount Moriah (see Genesis 22:2). God did this to test Abraham's faith. Abraham was ready to do this, fully confident that God could raise Isaac back to life (Hebrews 11:17-19). But let's be very clear that this was a test only for Abraham. Throughout Scripture, God has made it clear that sacrificing children is an abomination (Leviticus 18:21, 20:2-5; Deuteronomy 12:31; 2 Kings 16:3; Jeremiah 7:31, 32:35).

Likewise, Jesus never married, and yet Scripture blesses the institution of marriage. In contrast, Jesus was known for His love, and that aspect of His life is indeed associated with a direct command in Scripture for His followers to follow His example in loving others (see John 13:34).

Promises are not available to all people at all times. The belief that all promises in Scripture are always available for all believers has been a source of great error, especially in the counterfeit prosperity gospel, or "name it and claim it." This error comes about through taking Scriptures, such as the following, out of context.

> "Bring the whole tithe into the storehouse, so that there may be food in My house, and test Me now in this," says the LORD of hosts, "if I will not open for you the windows of heaven and pour out for you a blessing until it overflows" (Malachi 3:10).
>
> You do not have because you do not ask ... The effective prayer of a righteous man can accomplish much (James 4:2, 5:16).

Followers of a prosperity gospel have misinterpreted these passages to claim that financial blessings and physical healing from disease are always available to all people of faith who tithe correctly, pray the "correct" way, or have "the right kind of faith." The prosperity gospel doesn't take into account that we live in a broken world with broken bodies, and bad things still happen to people, including those who follow Christ.

Years ago I heard the story of a woman in Charlottesville who misunderstood the promises in Scripture and incorrectly counseled a patient dying of cancer that she wasn't being healed because she didn't have the right faith. In an illness in any given person, we can never know the cause of the disease. The condition could be to bring glory to God (see John 9:2, 3) or that God is ending their life on earth as He did for the prophets and kings (2 Kings 13:14). Consider the apostle Paul's thorn in the flesh (2 Corinthians 12:7-10). Paul was a mature, faithful servant of God, yet God didn't heal him in response to Paul's pleas to remove the thorn. Instead, God told Paul that He was using the affliction to grow Paul spiritually.

We should also take caution before assuming an affliction is due to sin. Job's friends did this, and they were wrong. Jesus asked the crowd whether the Galileans murdered by Pilate and the people killed in Siloam when a tower fell were more guilty than others around them. He made clear they were not, but added: "unless you repent, you too will all perish" (Luke 13:5, NIV). The book of Hebrews describes how some of God's people were jeered, mocked, and brutally executed, yet Scripture commended them for their faith and said that the world was not worthy of them (see Hebrews 11:36-40). We can find clarity on this issue in the following verse.

> This is the confidence which we have before Him, that, if we ask anything according to His will, He hears us (1 John 5:14).

In other words, God has given us His promises in accordance with His sovereign will. We turn these promises around when we try to get God to do *our* will. We reject His sovereignty when we think we can somehow manipulate God into healing by some quality in our faith or prayers. He is not our servant. We are His servants. Does this mean we should not plead with him for healing? Not at all! But our attitude must always be that of Jesus (i.e., "not My will but Yours be done"; see Luke 22:42).

Many promises are available to God's church today, including salvation through faith in Christ (see Romans 10:9-13) and God's peace by praying (Philippians 4:6, 7). Other promises do not apply to present times because they were made in context. Referring to pestilence, the psalmist writes:

> A thousand may fall at your side and ten thousand at your right hand, but it [pestilence] shall not approach you (Psalm 91:7).

The many deaths that occurred during the COVID-19 pandemic included followers of Jesus Christ. Does that mean they didn't have salvation, or something had been wrong with their faith? Not at all. The error in the "name it and claim it" mentality involves interpretation of Scripture out of context, claiming promises made to a group of people, of which they are not a part, or putting faith in faith rather than in God and His sovereignty! We are always to pray for our needs and the needs of others. But by no means are we promised prosperity or freedom from disease, persecution, calamity, or suffering.

No authority overrules Scripture. Many church denominations have strayed from the authority, inerrancy, and absolute truth of Scripture and are increasingly embracing moral relativism. Such churches condone what Scripture describes as evil. For example, some churches now condone practices of sexual immorality that are described in the Bible as unrighteous acts that are unworthy of God's kingdom (see 1 Corinthians 6:9, 10; Ephesians 5:5). Sexual immorality, same-sex marriages, and the transgender movement represent beliefs that one's personal truth can override God's commandments (Genesis 1:27; Matthew 19:4-6; 2 Timothy 2:19; Revelation 21:8). The Bible calls people who justify evil and condemn God's righteous saints who uphold the truth of Scripture an abomination to the Lord (Proverbs 17:15). No one is exempt from God's commandments in His Word or His wrath for not obeying them.

Induced abortion was practiced in ancient times. One of the tenets of the Oath of Hippocrates (460-370 BC) taken by physicians was to provide no deadly medicine or contraceptive device to a woman that could cause an abortion. Today, medically induced abortion is legal across most of the planet. Among militant pro-abortion movements are many who identify themselves as "Christian."

Scripture does not explicitly prohibit the practice of induced abortion. But I believe God has spoken in His Word sufficiently to allow His followers to determine His will on this practice, including the following Scriptures. The psalmist proclaims that God formed and ordained both King David and the prophet Jeremiah in their mothers' wombs.

> For you created my inmost being; you knit me together in my mother's womb … Your eyes saw my unformed body; all the days ordained for me were written in your book before one of them came to be (Psalm 139:13, 16, NIV).

> "Before I [God] formed you in the womb I knew you, and before you were born I consecrated you" (Jeremiah 1:5).

Were these words just for King David and the prophet Jeremiah, or does God consecrate and ordain all the days of every fetus before a life is born? In the past, God's wrath was unleashed against Israelites who sacrificed their own children.

> They even sacrificed their sons and their daughters to the demons, and shed innocent blood, the blood of their sons and daughters, whom they sacrificed to the idols of Canaan; and the land was polluted with the blood. Therefore, the anger of the LORD was kindled against His people and He abhorred His inheritance (Psalm 106:37, 38, 40).

Hands that shed innocent blood are an abomination to God (see Proverbs 6:17). Today, globally, the innocent blood of more than seventy million fetuses is shed to the god of "self" every year. God's

Word is supreme. His commandments cannot be overruled by local or national governments, church denominations, or constantly shifting "personal truth."

Scriptural poetry, metaphors, and anthropomorphisms should not be interpreted literally. Take, for example, the following poetic expression from Psalms.

> The pastures of the wilderness drip, and the hills gird themselves with rejoicing (Psalm 65:12).

Obviously, these beautiful words are not a literal description of pastures and hills but a proclamation that our Creator is so worthy of praise that even nature can be imagined praising Him. Likewise, Scripture often uses metaphors to emphasize a point. An example is when Jesus states: "I am the door; if anyone enters through Me, he will be saved" (John 10:9). Jesus is using "door" as a metaphor for the truth that He is our only entrance into salvation (John 14:6).

Scripture also contains anthropomorphisms, which are human characteristics ascribed to God to make God and His words more comprehensible to human beings confined to physical bodies. For instance, in Moses's final discourse to the Israelites, he wasn't saying that God reached down into Egypt with a literal hand and arm to free the Israelites.

> "You shall remember that you were a slave in the land of Egypt, and the LORD your God brought you out of there by a mighty hand and by an outstretched arm" (Deuteronomy 5:15).

Some narratives are allegorical. Scripture may be more than documentation of the history of human relationships; it also works through allegories that represent principles of God's sovereignty. For example, God chose Jacob over Esau "so that God's purpose according to His choice would stand, not because of works but because of Him who calls" (Romans 9:10-12). Every parable represents an allegory.

The lives and actions of people are used to illustrate biblical truths about faith, salvation, and sanctification.

Use Scripture to interpret Scripture. Scripture is like a well-designed strong fortress that supports itself. Each structure in the fortress is not independent of the others. Other Scripture verses are often instrumental in arriving at the proper interpretation and application of a particular verse or passage. Sometimes these verses are in context of the passage being studied. But they may also be in one or more other sections of Scripture.

For instance, Jesus commanded His disciples to love one another, and He went on to say that their love for each other would be a sign to others that they were His disciples (see John 13:34, 35). If this verse was interpreted completely on its own, one could mistakenly conclude we are to love only brothers and sisters in the family of God. But other Scripture passages reveal that Jesus exhorts His followers to love their neighbors (Matthew 22:39), love foreigners and strangers (Leviticus 19:34; Deuteronomy 10:19), and even their enemies (Luke 6:27), which includes loving an entire spectrum of people outside the body of Christ.

This illustrates how Scripture helps interpret Scripture. One verse may illuminate a precept or a command with a single spotlight. Additional verses illuminate the passage from different angles so we are better able to understand and apply it to our lives as God intends.

Every Christ-follower is called to approach Scripture with persistent diligence. American preacher A.W. Tozer once opined that the problem with people in the church was not a lack of Bibles or available translations.

> Does it not seem strange that the generation with the most advanced technology and the easiest-to-read Bible translations is the weakest generation of Christians in the history of our country?[2]

God's Word, the Bible, is one of the essential means God gives us to know Him and mature spiritually. We must learn to use Scripture correctly and be persistent in diligently studying it. Diligence is intense concentration and focus on interpreting and applying the whole of scriptural truth to our lives. Persistence is refusing to give up. It is an ongoing process throughout our lives.

Christ-followers shouldn't be frustrated when they encounter passages they don't understand. Persons of faith often express how the Holy Spirit shows them something they haven't seen before as they reread Scripture. This is one value of having a reading plan that comprehensively covers the Bible every twelve to twenty-four months. Even with discipline in the study and application of Scripture, there will be verses and concepts a Christ-follower will never understand completely until we are in Heaven with God. The apostle Paul describes it this way.

> For now we see in a mirror dimly, but then face to face; now I know in part, but then I will know fully just as I also have been fully known (1 Corinthians 13:12).

Every Christ-follower is responsible to the best of his/her ability to correctly interpret and apply scriptural truths to their life. Since the journey of faith is not solo, any misinterpretation of Scripture can untowardly influence others as well as themselves. Paul encouraged his son in the faith, Timothy:

> Be diligent to present yourself approved to God as a workman who does not need to be ashamed, accurately handling the word of truth (2 Timothy 2:15).

Choose a good Bible translation. The original languages of the Bible were Hebrew (Old Testament) and Greek (New Testament) with some Aramaic (Daniel, Ezra). It is important to know that the original Hebrew texts of the Pentateuch, the first five books of the Old Testament, were translated into Greek in the third century BC.

This was the Septuagint—meaning: "seventy"—which references seventy-two translators, six from each of the twelve tribes of Israel. The Septuagint is the oldest example of translating Scripture from its original language into another. Eventually, the entire Old Testament canon was incorporated into the Septuagint, which was used widely by early Gentile Christians who spoke no Hebrew.

In the post-exilic period, use of Hebrew as a language declined. Aramaic became the common language of the Jewish people after their return from captivity, and under Alexander the Great and his successors, Koine Greek became the common language throughout much of the known world. By the time of Christ, there were more Jews living throughout the Greek and Roman empires than in Israel itself, which factored prominently in the quick spread of the gospel through diaspora Jewish communities and synagogues during the early church period (see the book of Acts).

Many of these expatriate Jews spoke no Hebrew at all. Thus, a Greek translation from the Hebrew text was helpful in maintaining familiarity with the Old Testament among the Jewish people inside and outside of Israel. Nevertheless, most available Bible translations today are based on ancient Hebrew manuscripts for the Old Testament and ancient Greek manuscripts for the New Testament.

When we use a translation from these ancient manuscripts converted into our own language, we have already entered into scriptural interpretation since the translators have interpreted Scripture to some extent in converting it from the original language to English. Translation methods range across a spectrum from formal to informal. The more formal translations focus on word-for-word translation. To make the language more relatable to current times, translators have also employed more informal methods by paraphrasing; i.e., giving the overall meaning of a phrase rather than translating each word in order.

If you've studied a foreign language or even watched a dubbed movie, this will be a familiar process since the order and conjugation of words in one language can produce a very different meaning or even gibberish if the same word order and conjugation is used in a translation. So even formal word-for-word translations may be adjusted to make sense in the new language, a reason why skilled scholarship and knowledge of both languages is necessary.

English-language translations go from more formal to less formal, such as from the King James Version (KJV), New King James Version (NKJV), New American Standard Bible (NASB), English Standard Version (ESV), to the New International Version (NIV). No one translation can be singled out as ideal or the only one that should be read. But consideration might be given to getting a study Bible that provides additional resource information. An excellent choice would be the *ESV Study Bible* by Crossway.

That said, every person should find a translation with which they are most comfortable. Obtaining two translations, one in the formal group and one from the informal group, might also be considered. When encountering a challenging passage, it is often helpful to compare the verses in multiple translations. Parallel Bibles offer the advantage of providing verse-to-verse comparisons between translations. Electronic Bible apps allow easy, rapid comparisons between multiple translations.

There are also numerous free online resources that can be very useful. Bible Hub is an excellent resource with a myriad of features.[4] For a given section of Scripture, an English Greek/Hebrew Interlinear Bible feature provides the Hebrew or Greek words in a verse with their English translation. Clicking on the Hebrew or Greek word of interest provides detailed information on the definition of the word, other verses that also use the word, and the total times the word is used. The commentary function provides valuable commentaries by a number of authors on most verses or sections of Scripture.

One word of caution. Avoid any translation purporting to be a Bible version that departs significantly from the ancient Hebrew and Greek manuscripts used for the translations above and/or has added extraneous non-biblical text. The most common of these are the Bible of the Church of Jesus Christ of Latter-day Saints, or the Book of Mormon, and the New World Translation, which was written specifically for Jehovah's Witnesses. Both can be extremely misleading.

CHAPTER SEVEN APPLICATION

DISCUSSION QUESTIONS

- Name and discuss the four foundational truths which must be embraced to be under the authority of the Bible.
- Why is merely reading the Bible insufficient for growth to Christlikeness?
- How can you determine which commandments in the Bible apply to you now?
- How can you determine which promises in the Bible apply to you now?
- Can a person's beliefs, church doctrine, or a government overrule God's Word in the Bible?

SELF-EVALUATION

- How often do you read and meditate on Scripture? At least fifteen minutes daily with a reading plan, meditation, and journaling? Usually daily but not more than fifteen minutes? Two to four times a week? Infrequently? Mainly in times of trouble? Never? List your most common plan or plans.
- Is your study and meditation of the Bible leading to recognizing and overcoming sin in your life?

- What steps are you willing to take to improve your personal Bible study? List them.

MEMORY VERSE

For the word of God is living and active and sharper than any two-edged sword, and piercing as far as the division of soul and spirit, of both joints and marrow, and able to judge the thoughts and intentions of the heart (Hebrews 4:12).

CHAPTER EIGHT

THE SACRED TRUST OF GOD'S WORD

"Guard what has been entrusted to you."
1 Timothy 6:20

Regarding the study and application of Scripture in the life of the Christ-follower, allow me to make a few additional points.

Defending Scripture: In the early church, the apostles often had to address false gospels that arose, including legalism and antinomianism. The apostle Paul urged Timothy to guard the treasure of sound gospel and teaching entrusted to him (see 2 Timothy 1:14). He states why he is so passionate about defending the gospel.

> For I am not ashamed of the gospel, for it is the power of God for salvation to everyone who believes, to the Jew first and also to the Greek (Romans 1:16).

The assault on the gospel and God's Word continues to the present era. Counterfeit gospels swirling in our culture include legalism, antinomianism, the prosperity gospel, and the gospel of social and woke causes. Christ-followers are called to represent the truth of the gospel of Jesus Christ to all. In a culture increasingly in rebellion against God, we are neither to be ashamed nor afraid of doing so. God's Word is the timeless absolute truth for humanity.

Small-group Bible studies: Among the benefits of taking part in a small-group Bible study is hearing the Holy Spirit's guidance on the meaning and interpretation of Scripture through fellow Christ-followers. The weekly small-group Bible study that started in my office in the medical center continues to meet after my retirement. We use a simple format. Anyone can share and interpret Bible verses that have spoken to them in recent weeks. One person will share a verse and discuss what it means to them. Others will add insight or point the group to relevant passages.

Some may consider this an unstructured format. But, in fact, the format lends itself to focusing on Scriptures various members have found helpful, and hearing how the Holy Spirit guided them in its interpretation and application (see Colossians 3:16). We have done this over the years and continue to be amazed at the insights we've obtained.

The power of God's Word: One morning in a bustling clinic at the University of Virginia, I reached for the otoscope on the wall to examine my patient's ears. The light wouldn't come on. I went to the nurse's station, retrieved a new bulb, rushed back into the room, and replaced the old bulb. The light still wouldn't come on. Only then did I follow the power cord to the wall outlet, which was out of view behind the exam table. The otoscope was not plugged into the power source.

It isn't good to practice medicine in the dark. Likewise, it isn't good to live our lives in darkness. Jesus uses another metaphor in describing Himself.

> "I am the Light of the world; he who follows Me will not walk in the darkness, but will have the Light of life" (John 8:12).

Jesus' light is transmitted to us by the Holy Spirit and God's Word, the Bible. God's Word is one of the significant sources of power He has given us. Jesus, the Word who became flesh, said:

> "If you continue in My word, then you are truly disciples of Mine; and you will know the truth, and the truth will make you free" (John 8:31, 32).

While training in pulmonary medicine, I made rounds of hospital patients with my professor. One afternoon we walked into a room to find the patient there crying. He told us he believed he would die. Nothing in our evaluation led us to the impression the man was at risk of imminent death. But we remembered the medical axiom: when a patient expresses premonitions of death, they should be taken seriously.

My professor noticed a Bible on the table next to the patient. He asked if he could read from the book. The patient nodded affirmatively. My professor read the following passage.

> Be anxious for nothing, but in everything by prayer and supplication with thanksgiving let your requests be made known to God. And the peace of God, which surpasses all comprehension, will guard your hearts and your minds in Jesus Christ (Philippians 4:6, 7).

As my professor read these verses, we saw the Holy Spirit of peace pass over the patient. His tears dried up.

Returning to see this patient the next day, we found an empty bed. He had died during the night.

I have used these verses in Philippians countless times through the years in my practice. I have sometimes written them on a prescription and given the verses to a patient. Countless times I have seen the peace of God pass over my patients as this Scripture blesses them. It was through this I learned that God's Word has power, just as God spoke through the prophet Isaiah.

"So will My word be which goes forth from My mouth; It will not return to Me empty, without accomplishing what I desire, and without succeeding in the matter for which I sent it" (Isaiah 55:11).

PRACTICAL SUGGESTIONS FOR PERSONAL BIBLE STUDY

- **Read the Bible in solitude to block out the world's noise**—cell phones, conversations, media, and anything else that might distract you. My treasured times in the Bible have been with a good cup of coffee in the early morning before the hustle and bustle of phones and pagers begins. As I read and meditate on God's Word, I frequently hear the voice of the Spirit interpret meaning and application.
- **Be well-rested and alert.**
- **Begin with prayer and ask God's Spirit to prepare your heart and speak to you as you read.** Confess any sins that might quench the voice of the Holy Spirit. Pray that your study and meditation over His Word will bring you into His presence.
- **Don't be in a hurry.** Go at a pace that allows you to meditate and reflect on what you read.
- **Consider a plan to read the Bible systematically within a certain time frame—so long as it doesn't cause you to rush to keep up,** thereby preventing you from meditating on God's Word and hearing the Spirit. There are many such plans. One plan can be obtained through the app from World Outreach Church (Pastor Allen Jackson, Murfreesboro, Tennessee). The plan guides your reading at a comfortable pace, but results in reading the entire Bible every 12 months.

- **Don't accept what someone else tells you the Bible says.** Read it and determine for yourself. If you have questions, consult a mature Christ-follower.
- **In regard to using a printed Bible versus a downloaded Bible app, use what works best for your own focus and meditation.** Many electronic Bible apps are available, and these allow flexibility in which translation to read. These include the Olive Tree Bible,[1] YouVersion,[2] Bible Hub,[3] and the Blue Letter Bible.[4]
- **Written notes through journaling or tags in an electronic Bible are also quite helpful for future reference.** The Olive Tree Bible app has a tag function that allows you to create folders with which you can categorize verses for future reference.
- **Internalizing Bible verses through memorizing is an excellent way to have them readily accessible for use in your life and in sharing your faith with others.** A helpful app for this is Fighter Verses.[5] It suggests crucial verses for memory and allows the creation of a personalized list of verses to memorize. An added feature is an option to place a verse you are memorizing on the lock screen of your phone.
- **Get involved in a Bible study that focuses on God's Word.** A small-group Bible study can be valuable if it allows sharing the meaning of Bible passages. This provides two things. First, thc Holy Spirit speaks through other Christ-followers on the meaning of Scripture. Second, the interaction often allows exposure to other Bible translations besides your own.

CHAPTER EIGHT APPLICATION

DISCUSSION QUESTIONS

- What is meant by the statement that God's Word is a sacred trust?
- What are methods of assault on God's Word today? What is the role of the Christ-follower in opposing these attacks?
- Why is it important to share God's Word with others, both Christ-followers and those who have not yet come to faith in Him?

SELF-EVALUATION

Are you putting into practice the Practical Suggestions for Personal Bible Study given just above in this chapter? If not, consider implementing one, several, or all. Start with just one or two you haven't yet implemented, and as those become a part of your daily routine, add others until you are completing the entire list.

MEMORY VERSES

> All Scripture is inspired by God and profitable for teaching, for reproof, for correction, for training in righteousness; so that the man of God may be adequate, equipped for every good work (2 Timothy 3:16, 17).

CHAPTER NINE

TALKING TO GOD IN PRAYER

"Prayer does not equip us for greater works—
prayer is the greater work."[1]
Oswald Chambers

Prayer isn't a vending machine from Heaven for material blessings that allow us to enjoy worldly lives. It isn't just a spiritual 911 number when we encounter crises. Prayer is much more. It is a means of grace given to us by a loving Father so we can talk to Him and collaborate with Him in works of His will on earth and in Heaven. It is a means by which God transforms us to the likeness of Jesus through the Holy Spirit. Chinese preacher and church leader Watchman Nee describes the work of prayer.

> The central purpose of prayer is to prepare for Christ a glorious church that is conformed to Him.[2]

Prayer is not optional. We pray because God exhorts us repeatedly in His Word to call to Him.

> "Call to Me [God] and I will answer you, and I will tell you great and mighty things, which you do not know" (Jeremiah 33:3).

> "Keep watching and praying that you may not enter into temptation; the spirit is willing, but the flesh is weak" (Matthew 26:41).

> "Ask and it will be given to you; seek, and you will find; knock, and it will be opened to you" (Luke 11:9).

The apostle Paul urged Timothy that "entreaties and prayers, petitions and thanksgivings, be made on behalf of all men" (1 Timothy 2:1). He instructed the Colossians to be devoted to prayer (see Colossians 4:2). To the Thessalonians, Paul said, "Pray without ceasing" (1 Thessalonians 5:17). James proclaimed that Christ-followers should pray for one another so they would be healed (James 5:16).

Prayers of the righteous are a delight to God (see Proverbs 15:8). The apostle John glimpsed the prayers of the saints in God's heavenly throne room.

> The twenty-four elders fell down before the Lamb, each one holding a harp and golden bowls full of incense, which are the prayers of the saints (Revelation 5:8).

As people humbly offer their prayers to God, bowing to His authority and sovereignty, they come into God's presence, and His presence changes them. They begin to see people, circumstances, and things through God's eyes. They begin to have a broken heart for what breaks God's heart. They begin to love people the way God loves them. Worldly values are transformed into God's values and kingdom perspective.

Prayer is not just a one-way communication from us to God. A physician colleague recently said to me, "When I pray, I always come away changed!" Seventeenth-century English preacher Thomas Watson had this to say about prayer.

> A godly man is a praying man. .... As soon as grace is poured in, prayer is poured out. ... Prayer is the soul's traffic with heaven; God comes down to us by His Spirit, and we go up to Him by prayer.[3]

Jesus provided the supreme example of prayer. His prayers were often in solitary places (see Mark 1:35). If we are to be engaged in the great spiritual battle for God's kingdom against the evil one and his minions, that battle must begin with prayer. While the Great Commission is one of the highest callings of a Christ-follower, Jesus emphasized that this must be preceded by and bathed in prayer (Matthew 9:37, 38).

COMPLACENCY IN PRAYER

Sadly, prayer is, for many, the most underutilized means that God has given us for spiritual maturation and kingdom work. Neither will happen if prayer is only employed infrequently. I see three main reasons for widespread complacency about prayer in the church today.

Self-sufficiency: Prideful, stubborn independence is at the top of the list. To say, "I've got this," is only too common. In contrast, prayer takes humility. It means saying, "I've not got this at all!" It means surrender, which is the opposite of self-reliance, revealing our absence of control and need for God to help. Even among people of faith, we too often pray most frequently during crises.

Busyness: A second reason for complacency in prayer is a busy, frenetic life. There is no justification in Scripture for being too busy to pray. On the contrary, this is the very time we should pray. Prayer transforms our self-centered busyness and stubborn independence from God. In the Psalms, we are reminded that we must seek God for help, not trust in ourselves.

> For I will not trust in my bow, nor will my sword save me. But You have saved us from our adversaries, and You have put to shame those who hate us (Psalm 44:6, 7).

Church planter and missionary Jack Miller wrote:

> God-given prayer and praise have as their essence a waiting on God, a willingness to be wrought upon by the hammer and the fire of the Almighty, until the chains of self-centered desires fall away from the personality, and the love of Christ becomes the deepest hunger of the inner life.[4]

Apathy: A third reason for complacency in prayer is thinking it won't make any difference. Ironically, this is the opposite of disbelief. It leads to a misconception that God's sovereignty is so insuperable that our prayers are superfluous. A view that outcomes depend on prayer may seem to conflict with God's attributes of omniscience, omnipotence, and sovereignty. In fact, we see God's sovereignty and response to prayer in play simultaneously throughout Scripture. This view is referred to as *compatibilism*. Scripture urges us to call on God in prayer and ask for what we need. Our response shouldn't be a debate on how our prayers impact God's actions but simple obedience.

One way to convince yourself that prayer makes a difference is to keep a prayer journal with a regular review of your requests to see how God has answered. Like the Israelites, we often quickly forget God's blessings, including answers to prayers. Reviewing past prayer requests reminds us of God's answer to those prayers.

COMPATIBILISM AND PRAYER

Scripture teaches that we do not have because we do not ask (see James 4:2). Yet God is sovereign and will do nothing outside His will even if we ask in prayer. Watchman Nee, imprisoned for his faith, wrote of the "mystery of prayer."[2] Indeed, prayer is a mystery. But two principles help clarify the compatibility between God's sovereignty and our supplications.

First, God's Holy Spirit changes us so that our prayers align with God's will. As we mature spiritually, our prayers become transformed from our own selfish petitions to prayers aligned with God's will. In its purest, most holy expression, prayer is a Christ-follower speaking God's will to Him. American Bible teacher and theological author Warren Wiersbe wrote:

> The same God who ordains the end also ordains the means to the end, and prayer is an important part of that means. When God wants to accomplish something, He raises up a man or a woman, or perhaps a group of believers, to pray about that very matter, and through their prayers He accomplishes His work.[5]

Watchman Nee explains further that a fundamental principle for God working on earth is through the prayers of His people.

> He [God] will perform [it] only after His people show their sympathy in prayers.[2]

The corollary is that complacency in prayer leads to things left undone that God intends to do. Let that sink in. Can it be that apathy in prayer by Christ-followers attenuates God's intervention in the world? Will God allow Satan and his minions to prevail temporarily if the people of God are negligent in cooperating with Him in prayer? Considering Jesus' teaching below, is the opposite true of Christ-followers who neglect binding the evil one in prayer?

> "Truly I say to you, whatever you bind on earth shall have been bound in heaven; and whatever you loose on earth shall have been loosed in heaven" (Matthew 18:18).

Second, within His sovereignty God can and does answer specific and personal prayers. We see in Scripture examples where God appears to change a seemingly intended action in response to prayer. When God told Moses of His intention to destroy the Israelites for their apostasy in making and worshiping the golden calf, Moses implored God to have mercy. Scripture tells us that God didn't destroy the Israelites, and their pilgrimage continued through the desert.

> The Lord changed His mind about the harm which He said He would do to His people (Exodus 32:14).

Similarly, when God sent the prophet Isaiah to tell King Hezekiah he would die of illness, Hezekiah prayed earnestly to God. God sent Isaiah back to the king to say that He had heard Hezekiah's prayers and would extend his life by fifteen years (see 2 Kings 20:1-6). Could it be that God's will and eternal purposes are broad, but so long as His general purposes prevail, God grants our petitions on specific details? An example might be my recent drive from Charlottesville to Richmond, Virginia. I could have taken various routes. The most direct route is by Interstate 64. Or I could enter Interstate 295 off Interstate 64 near Richmond and arrive at my destination from the north. I could avoid the interstate altogether and take the historic "Three Chopt Road," which would be more scenic but prolong the travel time. If God's sovereign will for me is to travel from point A (Charlottesville) to point B (Richmond), He can grant my prayer for safe travel along any of these routes without compromising His will.

We've already seen that God does not change (see Malachi 3:6). While God may change an action, He does not change His will. Jesus perfectly exemplifies this compatibility between God's sovereignty and our petitions when He prayed just before His crucifixion:

> "Father, if you are willing, remove this cup from Me; yet not My will, but Yours be done" (Luke 22:42).

Jesus taught us to pray always that God's will be done. But with that sincere acknowledgment, we should feel free to ask for things in our hearts.

THE HIGH COST OF PRAYER

We must never take prayer lightly. Our reconciliation to God through which we have access to Him in prayer came at a high cost, the precious blood of His Son. Before Jesus died on the cross, only high priests, once a year, could enter the inner Most Holy Place of the Temple to offer sacrifices on behalf of the people (see Leviticus chapter 16; Hebrews 9:7). After Jesus' sacrifice on the cross, He became our High Priest (Hebrews 4:14-16). Through His blood, we were given access in prayer to make our petitions directly to God (Hebrews 10:19-22). Our access to God through prayer is a sacred privilege, and unwillingness to pray cheapens Jesus' sacrifice. Our appropriate response is to praise and glorify God through a robust prayer life in submission to His lordship.

HOW JESUS TAUGHT US TO PRAY

The response of Jesus when His disciples asked Him to teach them to pray is among the most memorized, repeated collection of words in human history. When prayed sincerely, these words have the power to change the human condition.

> "In this manner, therefore, pray: Our Father in heaven, Hallowed be Your name. Your kingdom come. Your will be done on earth as it is in heaven. Give us this day our daily bread. And forgive us our debts, as we forgive our debtors. And do not lead us into temptation, but deliver us from the evil one. For Yours is the kingdom and the power and the glory forever. Amen" (Matthew 6:9-13, NKJV).

We see in this passage a model of the crucial components of prayer. The mnemonic G-R-A-C-E-D is another useful tool for bringing these elements in prayer before the throne of grace (see Hebrews 4:16), and it is fitting because the Father, Son, and Holy Spirit have graced every person.

G = Glorify: The psalmist proclaimed, "Sing for joy in the Lord, O you righteous ones; praise is becoming to the upright" (see Psalm 33:1). Praising and blessing God in our prayers gives Him the glory He deserves (see Psalms 27:6, 29:1-2, 33:1-3, 34:1-3, 113:2-3). Praying that God's name be glorified can take the selfishness out of our prayers, reminding us that we should be about His glory and not our own (Psalm 115:1).

R = Remember: Take time in prayer to remember with thanksgiving what God has done, what He is doing, and what He will do in our lives (see Deuteronomy 8:2; Psalm 78:42, 106:21, 22).

A = Arrogance: If we are to grow in Christ's likeness, our arrogance and pride in "self" must be put to death. We must pray regularly that God through His Holy Spirit will remove every form of pride and arrogance in our hearts and replace them with the meekness and humility of Jesus Christ.

C = Confess: We must repent from our sins by confessing them to God and asking for forgiveness. If we do, He will forgive us and cleanse us (see 1 John 1:9). We must also forgive others their offenses against us (Matthew 6:14, 15) and confess our own offenses to others and ask for their forgiveness.

E = Entreat: We must entreat God for our own needs and those of others. This should come after the previous components and with caution as, too often, self-interests predominate our prayers. A.W. Tozer once commented: "Prayer among evangelical Christians is always in danger of degenerating into a glorified gold rush."[6] God certainly wants us to bring our requests to Him, but we shouldn't allow the needs of self to monopolize our prayer life, and we are to make our requests with thanksgiving (see Philippians 4:6). When we do this, God promises us the peace that passes all understanding which will guard our hearts and minds in Jesus (Philippians 4:7).

D = Defend: We should complete our prayers by pleading the blood of Jesus and asking God to defend us from Satan and his evil forces.

ADDITIONAL SUGGESTIONS

- Don't delay in praying once you sense the Holy Spirit is giving you a burden to pray about something.

- Have dedicated times for prayer every day in solitude behind a closed door with your Bible. Make sure all electronics are silenced.
- Journal your prayer requests so you can be reminded of God's answers to your prayers.
- Quality is more important than duration. Take your time, relax, and listen for the voice of the Spirit to lead you in your prayer. As you grow in your ability to pray in the Spirit, the duration of your prayers may increase. But the quality of the prayer and your coming into God's presence is essential.
- Pray specifically that God will reveal the assignments He has for you, open the door for them, and give you the strength and courage to complete them (see 1 Corinthians 16:9; 2 Corinthians 2:12; Colossians 4:3).

CHAPTER NINE APPLICATION

DISCUSSION QUESTIONS

- What are three reasons for complacency in prayer? Why is each one not valid?
- How does God use the prayers of His people to accomplish His will?
- How can God be sovereign and still answer prayer? Discuss.
- What are the essential components of prayer (G-R-A-C-E-D)?

SELF-EVALUATION

- Do an inventory of a week of your prayer life. Are you regularly praying daily, or do you mainly pray in crisis?
- Are your prayers covering the same requests every day?

MEMORY VERSES

Rejoice always; pray without ceasing; in everything give thanks; for this is God's will for you in Christ Jesus (1 Thessalonians 5:16-18).

CHAPTER TEN

UNANSWERED PRAYER

"I implored the Lord three times that it might leave me. And He has said to me, 'My grace is sufficient for you, for power is perfected in weakness.'"
2 CORINTHIANS 12:8, 9

If you have followed Jesus for any time, you know God doesn't answer every prayer the way you want it. The apostle Paul, no stranger to deep prayer in the Spirit, pleaded for healing from an affliction he called "a thorn in the flesh." God didn't heal him. Instead, God told Paul that His grace was sufficient for him and that His power was made complete through weakness (see 2 Corinthians 12:7-9). God may answer our prayers with a "yes," but he may answer with a "no" or a "not yet." There are also reasons why God may not respond at all. Let's examine these varying responses individually.

DELAYED ANSWER TO PRAYER

We live in an age that expects quick service. Fast food, instant coffee, overnight delivery of items ordered online—these are just a few examples. And we want equally quick answers to our prayers. Human nature hasn't changed much from what we see in the Psalms.

> Hear my prayer, O LORD! And let my cry for help come to You. Do not hide Your face from me in the day of my distress; Incline Your ear to me; In the day when I call answer me quickly (Psalm 102:1, 2).

But God operates in a dimension unlike our concept of time. He is in the past, present, and future and can see all things in this framework. He loves us too much to give us everything we ask for. If you are a parent, you know that many things your child asks for are not suitable for them. If we were to give them everything they request, it would not be wholesome. God parents us in the same way. If God's answer is no, we must accept it, remembering that He will hear anything we ask that is according to His will (see 1 John 5:14). God's answer may also be delayed a few days, weeks, months, or even years according to His timetable. Or He may answer differently from what we asked. King David outlined two truths to hold on to as we wait for an answer to our prayers.

> I remain confident of this: I will see the goodness of the LORD in the land of the living. Wait for the LORD; be strong and take heart and wait for the LORD (Psalm 27:13, 14, NIV).

Notice first that while we are waiting, we must remain confident we will see God's goodness "in the land of the living." If we genuinely believe in God's amazing love for us and that He wants only the very best for our lives (see Psalm 37:4-11), we can be at peace while we wait, trusting that God is using the situation to benefit us as would not happen were He to grant our request. Jesus' promise of abundant life (John 10:10) is not a promise that God will give us everything we ask. We must instead trust that God has good plans to give us hope and a future (Jeremiah 29:11).

Second, we must be strong and courageous as we wait. Watchman Nee explains that God's answer may be delayed because He awaits the prayers of a significant number of Christ-followers before responding.[1] Or there may be delay due to particular constraints requiring more prolonged, intense prayer to overthrow opposition from the evil one.[1] We see this when the prophet Daniel prayed for understanding of things to come in end-times. God responded on the first day, but there was a delay of three weeks before an angel delivered God's answer due to intense spiritual opposition from the demonic prince of the kingdom of Persia (see Daniel 10:12-14).

UNANSWERED PRAYER DUE TO SIN

Unrepented, unconfessed sin is another reason for unanswered prayer. The prophet Isaiah states that unforgiven sin is an obstacle that separates us from God so that "He does not hear" (Isaiah 59:2; see also 2 Chronicles 6:24-31; Psalm 66:18; Proverbs 15:29). God told the prophet Zechariah that He does not listen to those who reject His call.

> "When I called, they did not listen; so when they called, I would not listen," says the Lord Almighty (Zechariah 7:13, NIV).

Scripture goes further, saying of the person who refuses to listen to God's law that his very prayer "is an abomination" (Proverbs 17:15). A number of specific sins are mentioned in Scripture as a barrier to prayer. These include unbelief, unforgiveness, disunity, improper motives, and hypocrisy. Let's examine these individually.

Unbelief: It's impossible to please God without faith (see Hebrews 11:6). James wrote the following about petitioning God in prayer.

> But he must ask in faith without any doubting, for the one who doubts is like the surf of the sea, driven and tossed by the wind. For that man ought not to expect that he will receive anything from the Lord, being a double-minded man, unstable in all his ways (James 1:6-8).

As we discussed previously, this must be placed in context, as the "name it and claim it" prosperity gospel adherents will diagnose all unanswered prayer as being a faith problem.

Unforgiveness: In the two verses following Jesus' instruction on prayer, He exhorts His followers to forgive others so that God will forgive them (see Matthew 6:14, 15). The location of these verses on forgiveness just after Jesus' instructions on how to pray strongly implies that a bitter spirit of unforgiveness against others will be a barrier to our prayers.

Looking at the context in other Scripture passages, there are two thoughts on this. First, we are told to forgive as we have been forgiven by God in Christ Jesus (see Ephesians 4:32). God forgives repented sin, not the unrepentant sinner. Second, we are told to forgive those who ask forgiveness no matter how many times that person has repeated the same sin against us. The disciples thought forgiving someone seven times was generous, but Jesus told them that even if the person committed the same offense seventy times seven and asked forgiveness, they were still to forgive. The context is the parable of the unmerciful debtor, a man who had been forgiven a huge debt but then threw in prison another debtor who owed him only a small amount, though the person pled for mercy (see Matthew 18:21-35).

Disunity: Discord with others is a barrier to prayer that can certainly occur in the church. Jesus urged anyone who remembered disunity with another brother or sister while offering a gift to God to lay down their gift, go to the other person, and be reconciled before coming back to present their offering (see Matthew 5:22-24). Anger and contempt for others are barriers to prayer, giving a foothold for the evil one in our hearts (Ephesians 4:26, 27). Scripture also exhorts husbands to treat their wives with understanding and honor "so that your prayers will not be hindered" (1 Peter 3:7).

Improper motives: God knows the underlying motive for every prayer. When the motive is self-centered and not in line with God's will, He will not answer (see James 4:3). One scriptural example is when the mother of James and John asked Jesus that her two sons sit on His right and left in His kingdom (Matthew 20:20-23). Nowhere did her petition indicate, "if it is your will, Lord." In her own will, possibly for pride, she wanted a special blessing for her sons. We all struggle with deceitful hearts (Jeremiah 17:9) and are easily tripped up by improper motives. Only the transformation of our hearts by the Holy Spirit will generate the right motivation for prayer.

Religiosity and hypocrisy: God has clarified that hypocrisy blocks prayers (see Isaiah 58:2-9). We need look no further than the parable in which the Pharisee prayed out of arrogance and contempt for others, not realizing his own spiritual poverty (Luke 18:10-14). God didn't hear the Pharisee's prayer. In contrast, the tax collector recognized his sin, pled humbly for mercy, and went home justified.

THE POWER OF PRAYER

On multiple occasions in my clinical practice, I have encountered patients who had recurrent lung infections for reasons that were unclear. Often I asked and was given permission to pray by the patient. I prayed that God would give me wisdom to identify the problem. As is my practice, I closed the prayer in Jesus' name. I have been amazed at how often God has led me to the correct diagnosis with prayer. On arriving at the diagnosis, I instituted the appropriate treatment and the lung infections resolved.

THE BLESSING OF BEING IN GOD'S PRESENCE

The greatest blessings we receive from prayer aren't getting the things we pray for but being in God's presence. He is the gift! The psalmist expresses the joy of God's presence.

> Then I will go to the altar of God, to God, my exceeding joy;
> And upon the lyre I shall praise You, O God, my God (Psalm 43:4).

CHAPTER TEN APPLICATION

DISCUSSION QUESTIONS

- What are two truths we should hold to while awaiting an answer to prayer?
- What are the causes for delay in an answer to prayer?
- What are the areas of sin that can result in unanswered prayer?

SELF-EVALUATION

- How do you respond when there is unanswered prayer? Frustration? Anger? Decreased prayer? Are these responses biblical?
- Have you identified an area of sin that might have led to an unanswered prayer? How do you plan to address it?

MEMORY VERSE

This is the confidence which we have before Him, that, if we ask anything according to His will, He hears us (1 John 5:14).

CHAPTER ELEVEN

PRINCIPLES FOR PRAYER

"Call to Me and I will answer you, and I will tell you great and mighty things, which you do not know."
Jeremiah 33:3

Prayer is a learned discipline led by the Holy Spirit. When I began earnestly praying after coming to faith, I approached God's throne of grace with a sense of anticipation, fear, and yet peace. Thankfully, God isn't looking for professional prayers. The power of prayer isn't in the person praying, but in God. He is pleased when His children humbly approach His throne and cry, "Abba, Father" (see Romans 8:15-17), a term of parental affection.

As we mature spiritually, our prayers also mature. We grow in our faith and love for God by seeking Him (see Matthew 21:22; Hebrews 11:6) and by increasingly abiding in God's Word (John 15:7). Scripture tells us that "the prayer of the upright is His [God's] delight" (Proverbs 15:8). As we pray, there are several principles we need to consider.

Pray in the name of Jesus. Jesus is our great High Priest who provides us access to the throne of grace through His atonement on the cross for our sins (see Hebrews 10:19-22). Jesus instructs His followers to pray to the Father in His name and promises that what we ask in His name will be heard and answered by the Father.

> "Whatever you ask in My name, that will I do, so that the Father may be glorified in the Son" (John 14:13).
>
> "You did not choose Me but I chose you, and appointed you that you would go and bear fruit, and that your fruit would remain, so that whatever you ask of the Father in My name He may give to you" (John 15:16).
>
> "Until now you have asked for nothing in My name; ask and you will receive, so that your joy may be made full" (John 16:24).

It is only in the name of Jesus and through His work on the cross that we have access to God's throne. For this reason, we should offer our prayers in His name.

Learn to pray in the Spirit. In our flesh, we would never be able to pray as we should. Not only is Jesus our provision for prayer, He enjoins us with the Holy Spirit who guides us in how to pray.

> In the same way the Spirit also helps our weakness; for we do not know how to pray as we should, but the Spirit Himself intercedes for us with groanings too deep for words; and He who searches the hearts knows what the mind of the Spirit is, because He intercedes for the saints according to the will of God (Romans 8:26, 27).

The Holy Spirit is available to lead and guide our prayers, interceding on our behalf for things we don't even know to ask for. To accomplish this, we must silence our hearts and minds in a solitary, isolated environment to hear His voice. Prayer lists are helpful, but if we go through them mechanically, it is easy to miss the Spirit's voice. This is why we should put our lists away for at least part of our prayer. Invite the Holy Spirit to lead your prayer after you have silenced your heart and mind. Then listen. He will begin to put people and priorities in your heart. As He does, pray for them. This is Spirit-led prayer. We are encouraged at all times to pray in the Holy Spirit to stay in the epicenter of God's love.

> But you, beloved, building yourselves up on your most holy faith, praying in the Holy Spirit, keep yourselves in the love of God, waiting anxiously for the mercy of our Lord Jesus Christ to eternal life (Jude 1:20, 21).

This is why we are called to be suitable vessels for occupancy by the Holy Spirit (see Ephesians 4:30), not quenching the Spirit's power (1 Thessalonians 5:19), so we can "with all prayer and petition pray at all times in the Spirit" (Ephesians 6:18).

Pray with right motives. Through the Holy Spirit, our will is aligned with God's will. Then we can pray sincerely for His will on earth to be done. For each of us, it is God's will that we accomplish the assignments He has given us. When we view prayer this way, the following Scripture becomes clear.

> Whatever we ask we receive from Him, because we keep His commandments and do the things that are pleasing in His sight (1 John 3:22).

God is delighted to enact His will but often waits on the prayers of His people before taking action. Scripture is also clear we shouldn't pray for worldly desires that will enhance our comfort or pleasures (see 1 John 2:16, 17) or things that have become idols of our heart (1 Corinthians 10:14), including praise from humans (Proverbs 27:21; John 12:43). When threatened by the Sanhedrin for sharing the gospel, the apostles didn't pray for protection but that God would empower them to speak God's Word boldly (Acts 4:24-31). Regarding this, nineteenth-century American clergyman and author Phillips Brooks (1835-1893) wrote:

> O do not pray for easy lives. Pray to be stronger men! Do not pray for tasks equal to your powers. Pray for powers equal to your tasks! Then the doing of your work shall be no miracle. But you shall be a miracle.[1]

Pray for protection from Satan and his minions. One summer while at her family's ranch in Texas, Karren had a close encounter with a diamondback rattlesnake coiled under a bush. It is only by God's grace she wasn't bitten. Karren was shaken at the close call, and with more bravado than wisdom, I decided to kill the snake. Experts never recommend this since it often results in snakebite. As I dropped rocks on the viper, it began biting indiscriminately at everything within striking range. This was a life-or-death conflict!

We face a similar situation with Satan. Few regularly pray for protection from the enemy. In many English language translations, including the NASB, the Lord's Prayer contains the phrase "deliver us from evil" (Matthew 6:13). The NKJV and *Aramaic English New Testament* translate the phrase, "Deliver us from the evil one." When we pray in God's will, we engage on God's side in the great spiritual conflict between God and Satan. As we become a more significant threat to the evil one, he will send out flaming arrows against us (see Ephesians 6:16). Praying for God to bind the power of the evil one shouldn't just be in crisis but should be a constant feature in our prayer lest we become harassed and afflicted by Satan.

Pray as children coming to a generous Father. Like the prodigal son in the famous parable (see Luke 15:11-32), we have all rebelled, creating a broken relationship with God. We were born again when we came to our senses, repented of our sins, and put our faith in Jesus. When we walked toward our heavenly Father in faith, He lovingly embraced us as His children (John 1:12). As members of God's family through the Spirit, we should boldly come to the Father and cry "Abba!" for our needs (Romans 8:15, 16). Jesus taught that the Father will shower good gifts on His children as we pray, including His Holy

Spirit (Luke 11:11-13). One critical request we should pray regularly is to be transformed through the Holy Spirit into Christ's likeness to bear fruit.

Pray regularly, not just in times of crisis. We must grow away from praying only in times of difficulty. We are encouraged to be people who pray at all times (see Ephesians 6:18; 1 Thessalonians 5:17). Prayer is an essential spiritual discipline necessary for serving and glorifying God.

Pray with persistence. Jesus told a parable about an unrelenting widow to emphasize the importance of persistence in prayer. The widow sought a judge for justice against an adversary. Though corrupt and ungodly, the judge finally gave the widow justice just so she would stop bothering him. Jesus summarized:

> "Listen to what the unjust judge says. And will not God bring about justice for his chosen ones, who cry out to him day and night? Will he keep putting them off? I tell you, he will see that they get justice, and quickly" (Luke 18:6-8, NIV).

Pray for enemies and those who hurt you. Our prayers shouldn't just be for fellow believers, friends, and family. Jesus commanded His followers to pray for enemies and those who have persecuted, hurt, oppressed, or hated His followers (see Matthew 5:43-48). We are to love, bless, do good, and pray for those who hate, curse, and mistreat us (Luke 6:27-29).

This isn't easy. People may do atrocious things that make it difficult to pray for them. A husband may abandon his wife after years of marriage, destroying the family and leaving her in financial ruin. A criminal may murder a loved one or commit some other heinous crime against us personally or against someone we know. We can pray for such persons only through the Holy Spirit. The Holy Spirit enabled Stephen to pray for his murderers as he was being stoned to death (see Acts 7:60). The Lord Jesus prayed for those crucifying Him as he died (Luke 23:34).

We must love and pray for enemies because Jesus commands it. The benefit is not just to those you are praying for but also for yourself. When I've harbored resentment and bitterness toward someone who has offended me, I've been astounded that the most significant breakthrough came when I began to pray for them. As Jesus pointed out, even evil people love those who love them. We only emulate our Savior and heavenly Father when we love the unrighteous as well as the righteous (see Matthew 5:43-48).

There is a stepwise process to praying for those who have hurt us. First, we must pray that the Holy Spirit will help us love them. Second, as the Holy Spirit changes our heart toward such people, we should continue praying for their salvation through repentance of sin and faith in Jesus. The third step is to pray that the Holy Spirit will bind their hearts from doing evil and grow them in the likeness of Jesus so they do not harm anyone else. We should never pray for bad things or death to happen to someone (see Proverbs 24:17, 18). We are called to love them, give them mercy as God has given us mercy, and do good to them (Luke 6:36).

Prayer requests must be aligned with Scripture truths reflecting God's will. God has expressed His will in Scripture. If we are to pray in God's will, we can't pray for things contrary to scriptural truth and commandments. For example, praying for something bad to happen to someone who has offended or hurt us reveals we have not followed the commandment to love and bless them (see Matthew 6:14, 15; Luke 6:27-30).

Pray privately and pray corporately. Before teaching the disciples to pray, Jesus taught the importance of personal private prayer behind a closed door and cautioned against being like the hypocrites who loved praying publicly for all to see (see Matthew 6:5-8). Jesus didn't condemn this practice because He was against corporate prayer but because of the wrong motives of the hypocrites. In support of corporate prayer, He said, "My house shall be called a house of prayer" (Matthew 21:13). He taught that if two of His followers agreed on something they asked, it would be done by the Father (Matthew 18:19, 20). Every Christ-follower is to pray privately and corporately.

Align prayers with kingdom purposes. The noblest purpose, every person's highest calling, is to glorify their Creator God and fellowship with Him forever. God is glorified and His kingdom of followers built up when we pray with the correct motives. This is the alignment of prayer with kingdom purposes. Every Christ-follower should pray for the following:

- that God will grow us in holiness and give us courage and strength to accomplish the assignments He has given us;
- that we will become the answer for what we are praying;
- for peace and unity within the body of followers of God (see Ephesians 4:3);
- that in all of this, God will be glorified (John 14:13).

FOR WHOM AND WHAT SHOULD WE PRAY?

Beyond the elements of prayer we've already discussed and the needs or concerns of our own lives and families, there are certain people and issues for which all Christ-followers are called to pray. The following are included, but this is not an exhaustive list. Pray for:

- God's workers for the harvest (see Matthew 9:38), including saints to be sent to preach the gospel (Romans 10:13-15), which will result in the building up of the church (Ephesians 4:11-16);
- provision and protection for all the saints (see Ephesians 6:18);
- the church to be built up to spiritual maturity (see Romans 1:8-11; Ephesians 1:15-23, 3:14-21; Philippians 1:9-11; Colossians 1:9-12);
- pastors and elders in your church: that they will fulfill God's calling on their lives as they lead your church;

- people in your sphere of influence, and that you will be faithful to share the gospel and disciple others (see 1 Corinthians 16:9);
- God's will to be done in your life (see Colossians 4:12), and that you will be a vessel for the Holy Spirit, fleeing from youthful lusts and pursuing righteousness, faith, love, and peace (2 Timothy 2:21, 22).

WHEN SHOULD WE PRAY?

Along with personal prayer and Bible study time, we should begin expanding times when we pray throughout the day as we continue to grow in spiritual maturity. Once again, the following is not an exhaustive list, but a good place to start. Pray:

- while you are driving;
- for brothers and sisters in your small group as you meet;
- for your pastor(s) as they preach;
- when you are out evangelizing as a team for your fellow Christ-followers as they present the gospel, and for the people hearing the gospel;
- in real time whenever you encounter something not in line with God's holiness;
- at the onset of any contentious interaction, whether concerning someone at work, on the road while driving, in the grocery store, or encountering others while shopping.

CHAPTER ELEVEN APPLICATION

DISCUSSION QUESTIONS

- Why is it important for prayer requests to be aligned with God's will? Discuss.
- How does a Christ-follower align his or her prayers with God's will?
- For whom and what should we pray?

SELF-EVALUATION

- Do you sense God's presence in your prayers?
- Are there areas you need to improve in prayer? How do you plan to do so?
- Ask God to grow your ability to pray Spirit-led prayers and to have God's heart so you can pray for things that are on His heart.
- Read Watchman Nee's book *Let Us Pray.*[2] This is an excellent additional resource on prayer.

MEMORY VERSE

With all prayer and petition pray at all times in the Spirit, and with this in view, be on the alert with all perseverance and petition for all the saints (Ephesians 6:18).

PART THREE

Growing By Sanctification to Christ's Likeness to Produce Good Fruit

CHAPTER TWELVE

OVERCOMING SIN

"A notable heresy has come into being throughout our evangelical Christian circles—the widely accepted concept that we humans can choose to accept Christ only because we need Him as Savior, and we have the right to postpone our obedience to Him as Lord as long as we want to!"[1]

—A.W. Tozer

We live in a world in rampant rebellion against God's commandments. But things were no different two thousand years ago. Stephen was an early church Christ-follower who demonstrated great wonders and wisdom from the Holy Spirit. Because of this he was brought before the religious leaders in a mock trial based on false charges. His defense was an eloquent summary of how God fulfilled His covenantal promise to Abraham by delivering the Israelites from enslavement in Egypt to the Promised Land (see Acts 7:2-53). Stephen compared Israelite rebellion against God during the exodus, and later in Israel, to the religious leaders' rejection of the Messiah.

> "Our fathers were unwilling to be obedient to him [Moses], but repudiated him and in their hearts turned back to Egypt ... You men who are stiff-necked and uncircumcised in heart and ears are always resisting the Holy Spirit; you are doing just as your fathers did. Which one of the prophets did your fathers not persecute? They killed those who had previously announced the coming of the Righteous One, whose betrayers and murderers you have now become" (Acts 7:39, 51, 52).

Infuriated, the religious leaders took Stephen out of the city and stoned him to death (see Acts 7:54-60). Sadly, many churches today accept people with lifestyles of willful, continuing sin. We are all sinners, but continued willful sin is antithetical to the doctrine of sanctification. While Christ-followers are to love all people, Jesus didn't die on the cross so the church could condone sin and wickedness. Jesus died for forgiveness of sins and reconciliation with God so that those who have repented of their sin and placed their faith in Jesus Christ will be transformed to increase in holiness.

God gave His commandments to the Israelites through Moses. The people were instructed to listen to these commandments and do them all the days of their lives so it would go well with them in their new land (see Deuteronomy 6:17, 18). The prophet Samuel made clear that obedience to God's commandments was more important than offering sacrifices (1 Samuel 15:22).

But humanity, in their own abilities, could not keep God's commandments. Out of His mercy and grace, God provided His only Son, Jesus, to pay the penalty for our disobedience. Moreover, He provided the Holy Spirit so that those who place their faith in Jesus would have the power to overcome sin and grow in obedience. This power through the indwelling of the Holy Spirit was proclaimed by God through His prophet Ezekiel.

> "I will give you a new heart and put a new spirit within you; and I will remove the heart of stone from your flesh and give you a heart of flesh. I will put My Spirit within you and cause

> you to walk in My statutes, and you will be careful to observe My ordinances" (Ezekiel 36:26, 27).

It is God's will for every Christ-follower to grow in holiness through obedience to His commandments. God has not called us to continue floundering in the impurity of sin, but to be sanctified.

> For this is the will of God, your sanctification … For God has not called us for the purpose of impurity, but in sanctification (1 Thessalonians 4:3, 7).

Every Christ-follower has a duty to discipline himself or herself in obedience to God's righteous authority and the imperatives outlined in the Bible. This is growing in the likeness of Jesus Christ. In contrast, too many churches are propagating the misunderstanding that we can accept Jesus as Savior and continue in willful disobedience. A.W. Tozer addresses this false gospel of "cheap grace."

> The truth is that salvation apart from obedience is unknown in the sacred Scriptures.[1]

The apostle Peter's letter to the dispersed Christ-followers in Pontus, Galatia, Cappadocia, Asia, and Bithynia substantiates Tozer's words.

> Peter, an apostle of Jesus Christ, to God's elect, exiles scattered throughout the provinces of Pontus, Galatia, Cappadocia, Asia and Bithynia, who have been chosen according to the foreknowledge of God the Father, through the sanctifying work of the Spirit, to be obedient to Jesus Christ and sprinkled with His blood (1 Peter 1:1, 2, NIV).

Obedience is the submission of "self" to God's righteous authority. Distilled, sin is self exerting its own thoughts, motives, and actions above God's righteous authority. The word "sin" is relational between each person and his Creator to whom he is accountable. For this reason, King David said:

> Against You, You only, I have sinned and done what is evil in Your sight (Psalm 51:4).

"Self" doesn't like this accountability to an almighty God. It is a constant reminder that self is not the preeminent authority in our lives. So it should be no surprise that the word sin has largely disappeared from secular vocabulary. "Sin" is now mainly a church word, and even in that setting it is being abandoned.

Does this mean society has stopped sinning? Not at all. Moral relativism has led to replacing the word "sin" with "poor choices" or "mistakes" to ease consciences of any accountability to God. As the world buries the word "sin," it is rebelling against our Creator's righteous authority and replacing it with the notion that each person—i.e., self—can define his or her own personal truth.

An analogy would be if society deleted the word "cancer." Even if the word was never used again, the devastating disease would still exist. Doing away with the word "sin" doesn't nullify it or eliminate God's righteous coming wrath and judgment. Too many do not realize this is their fate if they disregard the mercy and grace God offers in Jesus Christ. In fact, Scripture tells us that God is holding off His final judgment so we might come to faith and trust in His Son (see 2 Peter 3:7-9).

Sin doesn't just destroy our relationship with God in the next life. It separates us now from God the Father, Son, and Holy Spirit (see Isaiah 59:2). It squelches the power of the Holy Spirit and inactivates our prayers (Psalm 66:18; Isaiah 59:2; Jeremiah 11:10, 11). Sin's impact on humanity is devastating. It destroys relationships with spouses, parents, children, coworkers, employers, neighbors, even strangers passing by on the avenues of life. It causes premature death from disease, murder, and war. It corrupts the human heart to immorality, impurity, sensuality, idolatry, sorcery, enmities, strife, jealousy, outbursts of anger, disputes, dissensions, factions, envying (covetousness), drunkenness, carousing, and the like (Galatians 5:19-21). Add to this deceit, hatred, unforgiveness, bitterness, divisiveness, rebellion, lying, and lawlessness.

Sin deceives us and entangles us by its dominance over our will (see Psalm 32:2; Jeremiah 9:5; John 8:34; Acts 8:23; Romans 6:14, 17, 7:11). It causes evil desires and hardens our heart so there is an even greater propensity to sin (Hebrews 3:13-19). It shortens our lifespan (Proverbs 3:1, 2). It abolishes the peace of the Holy Spirit (Galatians 5:22). When King David sinned, he became despondent and depressed with guilt and separation from God (Psalm 51:1-14). Sin weakens body, soul, and spirit. David exclaimed:

> There is no soundness in my flesh because of Your indignation; There is no health in my bones because of my sin (Psalm 38:3).

MANDATE FOR HOLINESS

The apostle Paul proclaimed, "It was for freedom that Christ set us free" (Galatians 5:1). In context, he was rebuking legalism (i.e., striving for salvation through works). Some have misinterpreted Paul's exhortation to mean that Christ-followers become exempt from a duty to refrain from sin. This is dead wrong! The freedom Paul references is freedom from bondage to sin and from the penalty for transgressing the law. Jesus proclaimed:

> "Everyone who commits sin is the slave of sin … so if the Son makes you free, you will be free indeed" (John 8:34, 36).

We are now under grace (see Romans 6:14), but this in no way absolves the Christ-follower from obedience to God's commandments. Jesus said He didn't come to abolish the law and prophets but to fulfill them (Matthew 5:17). Keeping God's commandments shows our love for the Father and Son (John 14:15; 1 John 5:3). Our faith saves us, not good works. But we are saved to do good works (Ephesians 2:8-10), and the Holy Spirit can't produce a harvest of good works in a Christ-follower who indulges in sin. The apostle Paul describes the sanctified Christ-follower in this way.

> Everyone who names the name of the Lord is to abstain from wickedness. Now in a large house there are not only gold and silver vessels, but also vessels of wood and of earthenware, and some to honor and some to dishonor. Therefore, if anyone cleanses himself from these things, he will be a vessel for honor, sanctified, useful to the Master, prepared for every good work (2 Timothy 2:19-21).

As mentioned earlier, without sanctification by the Holy Spirit "no one will see the Lord" (Hebrews 12:14). Sanctification means growing more like Jesus Christ. This in turn means growing in holiness.

> Therefore, prepare your minds for action, keep sober in spirit, fix your hope completely on the grace to be brought to you at the revelation of Jesus Christ. As obedient children, do not be conformed to the former lusts which were yours in your ignorance, but like the Holy One who called you, be holy yourselves also in all your behavior; because it is written, "You shall be holy, for I am holy" (1 Peter 1:13-16).

Someone earnestly following Jesus cannot trifle with sin. Nineteenth-century minister Charles Spurgeon framed unconquered sin in this way.

> If I had a dear brother who had been murdered, what would you think of me if I valued the knife which had been crimsoned with his blood?—if I made a friend of the murderer, and daily consorted with the assassin who drove the dagger into my brother's heart? Surely I, too, must be an accomplice in the crime! Sin murdered Christ; will you be a friend to it? Sin pierced the heart of the Incarnate God; can you love it?[2]

As Christ-followers, our motive for obedience is our love for the Father and Son because of who they are and what they have done for us (see Ephesians 1:7). This leads to a lifelong heart attitude and obedient actions of doing for others what they have done for us.

> Be kind to one another, tender-hearted, forgiving each other, just as God in Christ also has forgiven you (Ephesians 4:32).

OVERCOMING SIN THROUGH A RIGHT RELATIONSHIP WITH GOD

In considering obedience, caution must be given about what it is *not*—i.e., it is not legalism. Moralizing is directing human behavior toward conformity to a standard of right and wrong. Certainly, these standards are described in God's Word. Some have tried and failed to earn their salvation by striving on their own effort to follow this moral code. This is legalism, and it doesn't work. In our sinful, corrupt state, we can never attain righteousness on our own. The Pharisees exemplified this dead-end approach.

American preacher and seminary professor and president Haddon Robinson[3] can tell you what righteousness is. He grew up in one of Harlem's roughest areas. At age eleven, he and a cousin began attending church because they wanted to play on the church's youth basketball team.[4] The Sunday school teacher was a faithful woman who introduced Haddon to the concept of God's final judgment (see Matthew 25:31-46). Years later, Haddon delivered his sermon "Surprise!!" on this passage at the Kyle Lake Center for Effective Preaching at the Baylor Truett Theological Seminary (September 22, 2009).[4] Haddon defined righteousness not as a list of dos and don'ts but as a right relationship—a true relationship with God and the people He cares about. Here was his takeaway message: increasing obedience comes in those who have had a saving encounter with Jesus Christ and are changed by union with Him to increasingly become like Him and bear His fruit of righteousness.

Seventeenth-century Puritan minister John Owen (1616-1683) wrote that every Christ-follower must put sin to death in his or her life, but they must do it God's way—through transformation by the Holy Spirit. Owen emphasized that this happens in three ways.[5]

- The Holy Spirit causes the believer to abound in the fruit of the Spirit, which counters the works of the flesh (see Galatians 5:17).
- The Holy Spirit is "the fire which burns up the very root of lust."
- The Holy Spirit gives believers communion with Jesus Christ and fellowship in His sufferings (see Philippians 3:10).

Owen quickly points out that the believer can't just sit back, relax, and wait while the Holy Spirit does this. The Christ-follower must do his or her part. He frames it this way:

> He doth not to work our mortification in us as not to keep it still an act of our obedience.[5]

CHAPTER TWELVE APPLICATION

DISCUSSION QUESTIONS

- What is the impact of sin on humankind? On our relationship to God? Discuss.
- Discuss the Christ-follower's call to obedience to God's commandments. Why is this not legalism?
- What is the freedom from the law the apostle Paul refers to in Galatians 5:1?
- What does John Owen mean that overcoming sin is an act of obedience?

- Why is obedience in overcoming sin important for doing good works?

SELF-EVALUATION

- Watch Haddon Robinson's sermon "Surprise!!"[4] What is our source of righteousness (i.e., obedience)?
- Is there willful, continuing sin in your life you are having difficulty overcoming? How will you do so?
- Are you growing in prayer? In particular, are you praying for God to show you sin in your life and give you the power to overcome it?

MEMORY VERSES

> For this reason it says, "Awake, sleeper, and arise from the dead, and Christ will shine on you." Therefore be careful how you walk, not as unwise men but as wise, making the most of your time, because the days are evil. So then do not be foolish, but understand what the will of the Lord is (Ephesians 5:14-17).

CHAPTER THIRTEEN

COOPERATING WITH THE SPIRIT TO OVERCOME SIN

"Do not grieve the Holy Spirit of God, by whom you were sealed for the day of redemption."
EPHESIANS 4:30

Christ-followers must be vigilant in overcoming sin throughout their lives. It should be our business from our first breath after redemption by faith until our last breath on earth. Failure in a Christ-follower to overcome sin puts the very soul in danger. The author of Hebrews warned:

> Take care, brethren, that there not be in any one of you an evil, unbelieving heart that falls away from the living God ... For we have become partakers of Christ, if we hold fast the beginning of our assurance firm until the end (Hebrews 3:12, 14).

And what was the process that led to falling away? Hardening of the heart because of the deceitfulness of sin (see Hebrews 3:13). The writer continues:

> If we go on sinning willfully after receiving the knowledge of the truth, there no longer remains a sacrifice for sins, but a terrifying expectation of judgment and the fury of a fire which will consume the adversaries (Hebrews 10:26, 27).

To be diligent in overcoming sin is to avoid the calamity of shrinking "back to destruction," instead having "faith to the preserving of the soul" (Hebrews 10:39). It is our duty to "cleanse ourselves from all defilement of flesh and spirit, perfecting holiness in the fear of God" (2 Corinthians 7:1). The apostle Paul understood this, writing:

> But I discipline my body and make it my slave, so that, after I have preached to others, I myself will not be disqualified (1 Corinthians 9:27).

It is tragic when a hidden, willful sin is discovered in someone who outwardly appears to be a strong person of faith, particularly pastors and church leaders. There are only two possibilities for this. Either the person never had authentic faith in Jesus that bestows salvation, or they weren't vigilant in continuing to overcome sin throughout their lives. One can only wonder if their accomplishments in ministry led them to think they were no longer vulnerable to lusts of the flesh. This is a lifetime battle for the heart of every Christ-follower.

> Watch over your heart with all diligence, for from it flow the springs of life (Proverbs 4:23).

As we've already discussed, we can't clean up the sin in our lives and become more obedient on our own; we can only do this through cooperation with the Holy Spirit. In the remainder of this chapter, we will examine a number of principles helpful to this process. Some we've already covered in a different context, so we will touch on those only briefly.

Accept Jesus Christ in faith and trust. Our corrupt Adamic nature opposes the Holy Spirit (see Galatians 5:17) and leads to a lifetime of sin. So we must first receive Jesus by faith in order to receive the Holy

Spirit. No one can kill sin apart from a union with Jesus through the Holy Spirit (Ephesians 1:13). The apostle Paul describes what happens when we are born again.

> Knowing this, that our old self was crucified with Him, in order that our body of sin might be done away with, so that we would no longer be slaves to sin; for he who has died is freed from sin (Romans 6:6, 7).

Confess the sin to God, asking for forgiveness. When we discover we have sinned, it is vital to confess that specific sin to God and ask for forgiveness without delay. If we are sincere, He will forgive us (see 1 John 1:9).

Keep in step with the Holy Spirit. A schoolteacher asked her young students how they would help their mother during the upcoming Thanksgiving holiday. One student's response triggered hearty laughter from the teacher: "I stay out of the way."

The child's response has some bearing for the Christ-follower. It is the Holy Spirit who cuts the old sin nature from us, replacing it with Christ's nature (see Colossians 2:11-13). He guides us in all truth (John 16:13). He prays on our behalf for things we don't even yet know we need (see Romans 8:26, 27). He gives us the power to overcome sin (Ezekiel 11:19, 20).

What we bring to the process is a sincere desire to become more holy by obedience. This means walking by the Spirit (see Galatians 5:25) and conforming our lives so we avail ourselves of His power. Persisting in sin extinguishes the power of the Holy Spirit (Ephesians 4:30; 1 Thessalonians 5:19). As the Holy Spirit reveals sin to us, we must promptly ask the Holy Spirit to help us and then put the sin to death.

Immerse yourself in God's Word. We've discussed the importance of this in depth. Sin is noncompliance with God's laws and commandments (see Romans 7:7-24). As we systematically immerse ourselves in Scripture, the Holy Spirit brings conviction of sins we must address

(John 16:8; 2 Timothy 3:16). This is the mind change discussed earlier. We agree with God that it is His law, confess that we are guilty and without excuse, ask for forgiveness, then obey by changing our lives according to the truth the Holy Spirit reveals to us as we study Scripture.

Invoke the power of prayer to overcome sin. Scripture tells us that if we ask anything according to God's will, He will answer us (see 1 John 5:14). It is certainly in His will for Christ-followers to kill sin in their lives. After his profound sin, King David prayed:

> Create in me a clean heart, O God, and renew a steadfast spirit within me. Do not cast me away from Your presence and do not take your Holy Spirit from me. Restore to me the joy of Your salvation and sustain me with a willing spirit (Psalm 51:10-12).

Seek accountability and corporate prayer with other Christ-followers. God has given us other believers to encourage, build up, confess our sins with, and pray for each other (see 1 Thessalonians 5:11; James 5:16). We are to be accountable to each other (Ephesians 5:21; Colossians 3:16).

Develop a plan to kill the sin. When a sports team prepares for a game, the entire team studies its upcoming opponent. When a medical error occurs in a healthcare facility, there is a root cause analysis investigation. What were the factors that led to the medical mistake? What steps must be taken to ensure this doesn't happen again? Similarly, we must diligently pursue a root cause analysis of sins we have difficulty overcoming. A significant part of this is identifying and removing temptations that lead to the sin. Our eyes may see an image that leads us into sexual immorality in thought or action. Alcohol lowers our defense. Anger can lead to impulsive decisions. Some friends and acquaintances can lead us to sin, so it may be necessary to break contact with such people (see 2 Thessalonians 3:6). Careful analysis of sin's circumstances is a vital strategy for killing the sin.

Sometimes one sin compounds another with disastrous consequences. King David's adultery with Bathsheba and subsequent murder of her husband Uriah involved multiple factors (see 2 Samuel chapter 11). Instead of being on the battlefield with his army, David was lounging on his palace terrace. Rather than looking away when he saw a woman bathing, David let his eyes inflame the insidious lust of the flesh, resulting in an adulterous relationship. Instead of confessing his sin when he learned Bathsheba was pregnant, David tried to cover it up by having Uriah killed in battle and taking Bathsheba as his wife. Only when he was rebuked by the prophet Nathan did David repent and confess his sins (2 Samuel 12:1-15).

When it comes to sin, there are three basic sources of temptation—our flesh, the world, and Satan (see Ephesians 2:2, 3). As we will see, there are three basic means for dealing with temptation—flee, faith, and fight.

SOURCES OF TEMPTATION

Our flesh: No matter how spiritually mature we think we are, we are hardwired to corrupted flesh that will tempt us to sin until our last breath (see Galatians 5:19-21; James 1:14). Our flesh is an ever-present "enemy within" able to unleash sin in those who are not diligent by appealing to lusts (Ephesians 2:3). The apostle Paul addressed this in his epistle to the Roman church.

> For sin, taking an opportunity through the commandment, deceived me and through it killed me (Romans 7:11).

The world: There are two places toward which we can orient our mind—God and His kingdom or the world. The world is any system that replaces God's authority and glory. It is opposed to the life Christ-followers should live. We are tempted by the world when we value fame, fortune, success, self-worth, or pleasure over worship and obedience to God. Friendship or conformity with the world is "hostility toward God" (James 4:4; see also Romans 12:2; James 1:27). When we accept Jesus and follow Him, our allegiance changes to a kingdom view rather than the world's perspective. Seeking the world is not an option for the Christ-follower, as we see in the following Scriptures.

> As for me, may I never boast about anything except the cross of our Lord Jesus Christ. Because of that cross, my interest in this world has been crucified, and the world's interest in me has also died (Galatians 6:14, NLT).

> Do not love the world nor the things in the world. If anyone loves the world, the love of the Father is not in Him (1 John 2:15).

Satan: The evil one is the third basic source of temptation to sin. Satan wars against our spirit, that part of us which has fellowship with God.

> For our struggle is not against flesh and blood, but against the rulers, against the powers, against the world forces of this darkness, against the spiritual forces of wickedness in the heavenly places (Ephesians 6:12).

Satan is a deceiver who wants our soul for himself to engage in his rebellion against God (see Revelation 12:9). He was unsuccessful in tempting Jesus but can successfully tempt us. In his book *The Screwtape Letters*, C.S. Lewis portrays the myriad of strategies the evil one and his minions may employ to derail Christ-followers.[1]

METHODS FOR DEALING WITH TEMPTATION

Fleeing: At times Christ-followers are called to literally remove ourselves from the scene of temptation (i.e., avoidance). If the circumstances cause continued temptation, they should be avoided completely. The apostle Paul instructed his young disciple Timothy:

> Flee from youthful lusts and pursue righteousness, faith, love and peace (2 Timothy 2:22).

The eyes are often the portal for temptation. One Christ-follower discovered a pornographic magazine in a seat pocket while on a commercial flight. Though he knew the danger, he still perused the magazine and became severely addicted to pornography. Our eyes may find a work colleague attractive, and we don't immediately look away. Many marriages end in divorce because someone didn't control their eyes.

Temptation can also come through our ears. Years ago I listened to secular music while driving to and from work. I liked one popular song at the time because of the musical score. One evening the Holy Spirit seemed to stir my heart, and I actually listened to the words of the song. When I did, I realized the lyrics were about lust leading to immorality. I fled, abandoning the song and musical group.

There are constant temptations all around us, so we must be vigilant. Escaping is a strategy for protection when temptation comes.

Faith: You may find a particular sin extremely difficult to overcome. To kill sin throughout our lifetime, we must have steadfast, persevering, enduring faith (see Hebrews 10:36). We also need to hold on to the assurance that God Himself is faithful and will provide what we need to overcome sin if we are steadfast, persevere, and endure in faith.

> God is faithful, who will not allow you to be tempted beyond what you are able, but with the temptation will provide the way of escape also, so that you will be able to endure it (1 Corinthians 10:13).

Fight: But it isn't enough to run away or even to passively endure temptation. As we've discussed, Satan uses temptation as an integral part of his warfare against God's children. We must actively fight temptation just as we actively battle the spiritual forces of the evil one (see Ephesians 6:12). It is precisely for this battle that we are instructed to put on God's full armor (Ephesians 6:11). We've already discussed this briefly, but let's examine each element of the armor God has provided us in our fight against Satan.

ARMOR OF GOD

We've already mentioned the two sides of resisting temptation that include both actively fighting against Satan's schemes and steadfastly standing our ground against his attacks. So it shouldn't escape our notice that the full armor of God includes both defensive gear and offensive weapons (see Ephesians 6:13-18).

Shield of faith: The shield of faith defends against the evil one's flaming arrows (Ephesians 6:16). Faith assures us that God wants only good for us and that to follow Him is the much better path.

Helmet of salvation: The helmet of salvation protects our minds and wills. Years ago when I faced a temptation, I believe the Holy Spirit stirred in me the conviction and calling to overcome the temptation as a follower of Jesus. To the Christ-follower, the helmet means keeping our minds persuaded that we are called to something far greater than giving in to temptation.

Breastplate of righteousness: As discussed, righteousness comes as the Holy Spirit transforms us more and more into the likeness of Christ. The more Christ's righteous character pervades our mind and heart, the easier it is to resist Satan's attacks and schemes.

Belt of truth/sword of the Spirit: In the full armor of God, the sword of the Spirit is God's Word. It is an offensive weapon by which we fight Satan and take the gospel of peace to the lost (Ephesians 6:15), snatching those who receive it from Satan's power. Jesus quoted Scripture to rebuke the devil's temptations (see Matthew 4:1-11). But as we've already seen, saturating our minds and hearts with the truth of God's Word is also a protective belt that keeps us from falling prey to Satan's lies and deceit.

When God's children sense Satan's presence, the power of the Holy Spirit enables us to rebuke and banish the evil one by invoking the name of Jesus and quoting the Bible back to Satan, just as Jesus did. We can overcome Satan and his minions because "greater is He [God's Spirit] who is in you than he who is in the world" (1 John 4:4). If we resist the evil one, he will flee (see James 4:7). But this necessitates being alert.

> Your adversary, the devil, prowls around like a roaring lion, seeking someone to devour. But resist him, firm in your faith, knowing that the same experiences of suffering are being accomplished by your brethren who are in the world (1 Peter 5:8, 9).

Prayer: Our other offensive spiritual weapon is prayer, which is so vital for dealing with temptation. It is part of the prayer Jesus taught the disciples:

> "And do not lead us into temptation but deliver us from evil" (Matthew 6:13).

Jesus also exhorted the disciples in the Garden of Gethsemane on the eve of His crucifixion:

> "Pray that you may not enter into temptation" (Luke 22:40).

THE BLESSINGS OF OBEDIENCE

The richest of blessings can be found in obedience because the Father, Son, and Holy Spirit make their home in the Christ-follower as we are faithful to God's commandments (see John 14:23). Scripture expresses how blessed is the one who fears the LORD and walks in His ways (Psalm 128:1; James 1:25). Jesus said, "If you know these things [God's commandments], you are blessed if you do them" (John 13:17).

Obedience brings peace and joy (see Psalm 19:8; Proverbs 3:1, 2; Isaiah 48:18, 19). Obedience allows us to enter into the rest God has created for each of His children (Hebrews 4:1-11). In contrast, God states, unequivocally, "There is no peace for the wicked" (Isaiah 48:22).

CHAPTER THIRTEEN APPLICATION

DISCUSSION QUESTIONS

- What are the means God gives us to overcome sin in our lives?
- Name the three sources of temptation leading to sin; discuss.
- How can the Christ-follower be successful in dealing with temptation? Discuss.
- Can a Christ-follower continue to indulge in willful sin?

SELF-EVALUATION

- Are you relying on God's Word, prayer, the Holy Spirit, and accountability to other Christ-followers to overcome sin in your life?
- When the Holy Spirit reveals sin in your life, are you, through obedience, mortifying it and growing in holiness?
- Do you have a spiritual mentor in your life with whom you regularly meet and discuss your struggles with sin and the progress you are making in overcoming it?

MEMORY VERSE

> For if you are living according to the flesh, you must die; but if by the Spirit you are putting to death the deeds of the body, you will live (Romans 8:13).

CHAPTER FOURTEEN

OVERCOMING PRIDE AND PUTTING ON HUMILITY

"At every stage of our Christian development, and in every sphere of our Christian discipleship, pride is our greatest enemy and humility our greatest friend."[1]

JOHN STOTT

Every day in numerous hospitals, crises arise where the severity of a patient's lung disease prevents adequate oxygen absorption for the needs of the body. If the patient wishes full indicated medical therapy, their treating physician will consult a specialist to perform a procedure called intubation—i.e., the insertion of a breathing tube known as an endotracheal tube[2] through the mouth into the windpipe, also known as the trachea. This allows for the delivery of higher concentrations of oxygen and mechanical ventilation if needed.

While the procedure of intubation usually goes smoothly, on occasion it does not. One of the ever-present hazards is insertion of the endotracheal tube into the esophagus instead of the trachea. There are many contributing factors for this in critically ill patients, including difficulty positioning and other conditions making it more difficult to directly visualize the larynx through which the tube is passed. It is not at all difficult for the tube to bounce off the larynx and go into the esophagus. When this unintended event occurs, the patient is placed at high risk for complications. Keep in mind, these are critically ill patients with severe medical problems that necessitated insertion of the tube. They have little or no reserve for further drop in the oxygen saturation[3] or increase in carbon dioxide levels. Despite imposition of progressive safeguards to minimize the occurrence of esophageal intubation, this continues to be a significant risk in the intensive care units of our country.[4]

When esophageal intubation does occur, it is crucial that it be promptly recognized so the tube can be removed and an inflation bag and face mask can be used to breathe the patient with oxygen to get their oxygen saturations back to a safe range. Unfortunately, this is where human factors can contribute to the problem. The problem is threefold. First, there needs to be prompt recognition of the complication. This is related to the medical team's training and following up-to-date guidelines for intubation and confirmation of correct placement of the breathing tube (i.e., that it is in the trachea). Second, the medical team must be paying attention to detail and not distracted. It is the third factor, however, that is more difficult to address.

In the course of my medical training and professional practice, I have observed this third factor interfere in the delivery of medical care. It is the refusal by a medical provider to admit that their procedure, treatment, or diagnosis was incorrect. In the case of intubation, it manifests itself as reluctance—or refusal by the provider—to admit that the tube they inserted is in the esophagus rather than the trachea, and reluctance to remove the tube. This occurs even when they are staring at falling oxygen saturations after tube insertion and other members of the team correctly recognize the problem and are urging them to remove the tube. What is this underlying human behavioral characteristic? It is pride.

Pride is a serious issue. It leads to mismanagement of patients. It led to the "unsinkable" Titanic plunging to the bottom of the icy Atlantic Ocean with tremendous loss of life. It has led to countless wars. Pride doesn't just harm people and relationships with other people. It destroys our relationship with God. The psalmist portrays pride this way.

> For the wicked boasts of his heart's desire, and the greedy man curses and spurns the LORD. The wicked, in the haughtiness of his countenance, does not seek Him. All his thoughts are, "There is no God" (Psalm 10:3, 4).

Pride arises out of a severe addiction found in every human. An addiction to self. Among any toddler's first words is "mine!" As the child's mind grows to adulthood, their self-pronouns expand from "mine" to include "I," "me," "my," and "myself." These pronouns are used extensively by every person. Unless the Holy Spirit regenerates our hearts, these pronouns will always dominate our relationships, not just with others but with God. A.W. Tozer portrays "self-will" as one of the "veils that obscures God's face."[5]

Pride is a root sin that gives birth to countless other sins. Satan represents the epitome of pride, wanting to become greater than God (see Isaiah 14:12-15). It was Satan who infected Adam and Eve with pride. Satan tempted them with a lie as to why God didn't want them eating fruit from the forbidden tree.

> "God knows that in the day you eat from it your eyes will be opened, and you will be like God, knowing good and evil" (Genesis 3:5).

Through pride, Adam and Eve were disobedient and rebelled against God, bringing about the downfall of all humanity. Andrew Murray frames it this way.

> Even so it was, when the Serpent breathed the poison of his pride, the desire to be as God, into the hearts of our first

> parents, that they too fell from their high estate into all the wretchedness in which man is now sunk. In heaven and earth, pride, self-exaltation, is the gate and the birth, and the curse, of hell.[6]

The prophet Habakkuk similarly proclaimed:

> Behold, as for the proud one, his soul is not right within him (Habakkuk 2:4).

So what exactly is *pride*? Pride is a claim of one's dignity or position based on such things as heritage, accomplishments, possessions, status, or associations. Usually linked with pride is *arrogance*, a feeling of superiority above others because of these things.

You can see the problem here. Pride defines our value based on factors apart from God. It denies that we have the things we do only because God gave them to us. We incorrectly attribute what we've acquired or accomplished to some particular attribute, ability, or status we have. We become deceived, thinking we deserve them. Moreover, we begin to think that things which impress the world impress God. Scripture, however, tells us this mindset is from the world.

> For all that is in the world, the lust of the flesh and the lust of the eyes and the boastful pride of life, is not from the Father, but is from the world (1 John 2:16).

In contrast, *humility* is lowliness of mind, not thinking highly of oneself. It is self-effacement. It is a willingness to listen to other people and be led by other people. It is a willingness to submit. Humility considers all others and their interests equal to or greater than yourself. It is being a servant to God and others. Murray defines humility with the following attributes:[6]

- acknowledging the truth of our position as the creature, and yielding to God His rightful place;

- acknowledging that self has nothing good in it except as an empty vessel which God must fill;
- displacement of self by the enthronement of God, i.e., where God is all, self is nothing.

King David described the essence of humility as follows.

> The sacrifices of God are a broken spirit; a broken and a contrite heart, O God, You will not despise (Psalm 51:17).

Humility is a heart that has been broken and emptied of self. What humility is not is wallowing in unworthiness and crawling with our face to the ground. It isn't being submissive in every circumstance. Nor is it being namby-pamby, weak, and indecisive. Murray also addressed this.

> Men sometimes speak as if humility and meekness would rob us of what is noble and bold and manlike. Oh, that all would believe that this is the nobility of the kingdom of heaven, that this is the royal spirit that the King of heaven displayed, that this is Godlike, to humble oneself, to become the servant of all.[6]

Misunderstanding humility could lead us to avoid sharing the gospel or discipling others out of fear of offending. If humility is incorrectly grasped, it could make us reticent to speak against sin. Jesus is our perfect example of humility. He never sinned, yet He manifested righteous indignation in casting out the moneychangers from the temple (see Matthew 21:12, 13).

The sin of pride didn't end with Satan or Adam and Eve. Throughout Scripture we see a pandemic of pride. When the prophet Samuel didn't arrive expeditiously to offer sacrifices to God before a battle with the Philistines, pride led King Saul to offer the sacrifices in Samuel's place. This sin resulted in God taking the kingdom away from Saul and giving it to David (see 1 Samuel 13:8-14). Pride led Saul to attempt to kill David so he couldn't succeed him on the throne (1 Samuel chapters

19-24). Whenever someone in the Bible went astray in their relationship with God, there was a root of pride, including King Solomon, King Amaziah, King Asa, and King Hezekiah. Pride was the undoing of most of the kings of Judah and Israel.

Pride is an abomination to God, and He will punish the prideful. Throughout Scripture, He exhorts us to overcome pride and put on humility.

> Pride and arrogance and the evil way and the perverted mouth, I hate (Proverbs 8:13).
>
> Pride goes before destruction, and a haughty spirit before stumbling. It is better to be humble in spirit with the lowly than to divide the spoil with the proud (Proverbs 16:18, 19).
>
> Haughty eyes and a proud heart, the lamp of the wicked, is sin (Proverbs 21:4).
>
> The proud look of man will be abased and the loftiness of man will be humbled, and the LORD alone will be exalted in that day (Isaiah 2:11).
>
> "The arrogance of your heart has deceived you, you who live in the clefts of the rock, in the loftiness of your dwelling place, who say in your heart, 'who will bring me down to earth?' Though you build high like the eagle, though you set your nest among the stars, from there I will bring you down," declares the LORD (Obadiah 1:3, 4).
>
> He has told you, O man, what is good; and what does the LORD require of you but to do justice, to love kindness, and to walk humbly with your God? (Micah 6:8)
>
> All of you, clothe yourselves with humility toward one another, for God is opposed to the proud, but gives grace to the humble. Therefore humble yourselves under the mighty hand

of God, that He may exalt you at the proper time (1 Peter 5:5, 6).

CHAPTER FOURTEEN APPLICATION

DISCUSSION QUESTIONS

- What is pride? Discuss.
- What is humility? What is *not* humility?
- Why is pride such a devastating sin?

SELF-EVALUATION

- Do you agree it is important to overcome pride and grow in humility? Read on.

MEMORY VERSES

Therefore I, the prisoner of the Lord, implore you to walk in a manner worthy of the calling with which you have been called, with all humility and gentleness, with patience, showing tolerance for one another in love, being diligent to preserve the unity of the Spirit in the bond of peace (Ephesians 4:1-3).

CHAPTER FIFTEEN

CAUSES AND CONSEQUENCES OF PRIDE

God is opposed to the proud, but gives grace to the humble.
JAMES 4:6

All pride stems from taking our eyes away from God and looking only at ourselves and others. There are many causes of pride, including those outlined in the figure below. Let's look at these individually.

CAUSES OF PRIDE

Amnesia: Forgetting what God has done for us leads to a prideful heart. The prophet Moses warned the Israelites that when they had been blessed with food, shelter, and prosperity to not become prideful, forgetting that all their blessings were from the Lord: "You may say in your heart, 'My power and the strength of my hand made me this wealth'" (Deuteronomy 8:17).

Shame: Many people struggle with guilt, inadequacy, unworthiness, and self-hate. They become prideful as a counter-defense for these feelings. Because of their feelings of inadequacy, they strive to avoid being caught in a mistake and are often reluctant to acknowledge an error or apologize.

Wisdom: True wisdom comes from God and begins with the fear of God. In contrast, the world's definition of wisdom is to use knowledge to make "good" decisions. This in turn means making judgments and decisions according to a relativistic definition of "good." As humans become wise in their own eyes (see Isaiah 5:21; Romans 1:22; 1 Corinthians 1:20), they incorrectly presume their level of knowledge has reached that of the Creator. Such self-exaltation leads them to believe they have no need for God.

God has given humanity the gift of intelligence above all other creatures. Over time we have increased our understanding of how He created things. Scientists continue to discover new subatomic particles, including quarks, anti-quarks, bosons, and the like.[1]

But the reality is that new discoveries such as these only lead to more questions by scientists. For example, since Watson and Crick described the central role of deoxyribonucleic acids (DNA) in cell programming in 1962, molecular biologists have characterized the nucleic acid sequence codes that instruct the cell to synthesize complicated proteins. It is known that the complete genetic code for all proteins in the body is present in the DNA in the nucleus of every cell. Transcription factors in the nucleus regulate the differential expression of genes that guides the cell to differentiate into specialized cells, such as skin, blood vessel muscle, heart muscle, or brain. But the way in which they do this is poorly understood. From the unaided eye to primitive telescopes to the Hubble Telescope to the James Webb Space Telescope, humans have increasingly described the universe. Peering into the depths of space with greater resolution only leads to more questions.

Mind you, we can't create atoms, living cells, planets, or stars. We can only describe God's creation. At our best, we can reverse-engineer. We build artificial devices to support patients with failed hearts, lungs, or kidneys. These are only stopgap measures to the transplantation of natural organs created by God. But transplanted organs are often rejected by the patient's body, and medicines to prevent rejection often cause complications that decrease survival. It is terrific that these technologies have been developed. But humanity has yet to come close to designing anything that resembles the wonder of a natural human organ that God creates in us, such as a heart, lung, liver, or kidney.

As this progression in knowledge has occurred, too many have replaced the Creator's wisdom with the creature's intellect. As humanity has learned more about how the Creator made things, they have decided they don't need the Creator, attempting instead to surpass God's glory with human knowledge and technology. This is pride and arrogance. The apostle Paul described this:

> Professing to be wise, they became fools, and exchanged the glory of the incorruptible God for an image in the form of corruptible man … for they exchanged the truth of God for a lie, and worshiped and served the creature rather than the Creator (Romans 1:22-25).

Strength and Self-Sufficiency: Many become prideful with the acquisition of things like power, position, possessions, or even piety. When man receives acclaim from others, he thinks he has accomplished these things in his own strength. He forgets that everything, including the intellect and skills leading to accomplishments, are gifts from God. The Bible lists many examples of this.

> "Let not a wise man boast of his wisdom, and let not the mighty man boast of his might, let not a rich man boast of his riches; but let him who boasts boast of this, that he under-

> stands and knows Me, that I am the LORD who exercises lovingkindness, justice and righteousness on earth; for I delight in these things," declares the LORD (Jeremiah 9:23, 24).

> For who regards you as superior? What do you have that you did not receive? And if you did receive it, why do you boast as if you had not received it? (1 Corinthians 4:7)

Self-sufficiency is a mindset that "self" is all someone needs for everything. Such persons do not need God, and they do not need others. The sad words of the British poet William Ernest Henley (1849-1903) describe such hearts.

> Beyond this place of wrath and tears looms but the Horror of the shade,
>
> And yet the menace of the years finds and shall find me unafraid.
>
> It matters not how straight the gate, how charged with punishments the scroll,
>
> I am the master of my fate, I am the captain of my soul.[2]

Elitism: The love of self wants to elevate self above other people. This form of pride originates when we take our eyes off God and begin looking at other people. This leads to classifying people arbitrarily into different groups. Naturally, one's own group is superior to other groups. When based on ethnicity, this is racism, which includes antisemitism. When based on gender or age, it is sexism or age discrimination.

The anecdote is told of a man who moved to and lived the remainder of his life in a particular state in the USA. At his funeral, a person native to the state gave his eulogy, saying, "You know, he was almost one of us." This is elitism based on heritage. Intellectual elitism divides people into classes by perceived intellect and educational pedigree.

Churches are not exempt from the pride of elitism. Church people often classify others based on perceived holiness, spiritual maturity, good works, training, or the more spectacular spiritual gifts. This leads to favoritism, inner circles, and closed groups, all because of unwillingness to associate with those they view as spiritually inferior. Conversely, people who don't view themselves as spiritually mature sometimes dismiss other church members as "hypocrites." This is another form of elitism.

Jealousy and the dislike of being surpassed by others: Years ago I was rafting down a river with another man to flyfish. I didn't know him well, but he'd been cordial in past encounters. Within two hundred feet of starting our float, I caught a huge brown trout. As our fishing guide navigated the boat downriver, I continued to catch large trout, both browns and rainbows. My companion was catching nothing. I wasn't celebrating or taunting him, but his anger and contempt increased with every fish I caught. I've experienced his plight—one person catching, another not—in fishing with others. It is one of the mysteries of fly fishing. But rather than celebrating with me and basking in the beauty of our surroundings, this man only wanted my success, and his caustic remarks made the morning unpleasant. Pride was manifesting as jealousy (see 1 Corinthians 13:4).

Fear: Inherent in fear is a lack of trust in God, which also leads to pride. Some fear if they are humble or show a potential weakness such as forgiving someone, they will invite further offenses or others will take advantage of them. Fear of inadequacy, guilt, and unworthiness can also lead to striving for inappropriate standards of perfection with strong criticism of others who don't meet these standards.

CONSEQUENCES OF PRIDE

It was pride that caused Satan to be cast out of Heaven, and it is pride that leads many to eternal damnation. Pride even leads some within the church to reject repentance and surrendering to God in order to follow Jesus. Instead they choose to live their lives on their own terms. Such people have fruitless lives. If someone is truly good soil, as we saw in the Parable of the Sower (see Matthew 13:1-23; Luke 8:5-15), they will allow the seed of the gospel to put down a taproot of humility, not pride. Only then can they bear good fruit.

The calling of a Christ-follower is clear. To become like Christ we must put to death pride and put on humility through the power of the Holy Spirit, as the apostle Paul wrote to the Colossian church.

> So, as those who have been chosen of God, holy and beloved, put on a heart of compassion, kindness, humility, gentleness and patience (Colossians 3:12).

Pride is a downstream disorder from an upstream broken relationship with God and Jesus Christ. If not overcome, it is an insurmountable obstacle to maturation into the likeness of Jesus Christ. Sadly, humility is neither emphasized nor modeled well in the organized church today. The unregenerated heart seeks favor and blessing from others, stepping on people to attain this goal. It views others as either in the way or someone who can be used to get a leg up to exalt self. Having eyes only on people, the unregenerated heart schemes pridefully to portray self in the best possible light to others.

We cannot get to humility by our own power through obedience to the law. The Pharisees were skilled in displaying obedience to the law on the outside, but inwardly they were not transformed. Andrew Murray wrote:

> The law may break the heart with fear; it is only grace that works that sweet humility which becomes a joy to the soul as its second nature.[3]

We must take our eyes off people and look upward to God. When we only look horizontally at other people, we scheme and devise ways to deceive ourselves that we are somehow better than they are. The apostle Peter denied Jesus three times just before His crucifixion. The apostle John describes the beautiful restoration and commissioning of Peter by the risen Christ (see John 21:15-17). After restoration to fellowship, what did Peter immediately do? He looked at John and compared what the Lord had commissioned John to do to the calling Jesus had just given him. He had taken his eyes off Jesus and was looking at other disciples.

Jesus responded to Peter, "If I want him to remain until I come, what is that to you? You follow Me!" (John 21:22) True humility is obtained by continuing to look up to God. Only when we do this can we realize how we measure up and understand we are not even a detectable ripple on the Richter scale.

THE SUPREME REPRESENTATION OF HUMILITY

Losing humility was the most significant injury to the human heart in the fall from grace. If our relationship with God is to be restored, the heart must overcome pride and arrogance and regain humility. God does not expect us to do it on our own. Murray pointed out:

> And so Jesus came to bring humility back to earth, to make us partakers of it, and by it, to save us. .... Meekness and lowliness of heart are supposed to be the distinguishing feature[s] of the disciple as they were of the Master.[3]

Jesus Christ is the supreme representation of humility. To those who receive Him, He gives the power to be reconciled to God through the forgiveness of sin, to put pride to death, and to become humble through union with the Holy Spirit. The secret to deliverance from pride is twofold. First, study Jesus' humility. Second, have our hearts transformed by His Spirit so we can live out His humility.

When we look up and behold Jesus Christ on the cross, we see tears of blood mixed with love for us streaming down. Jesus, the Prince of Peace, has reconciled us to His Father at a great price. He is our most outstanding example of humility. He modeled it for us when He walked on earth. We are to have the mind of Jesus, who was with God as His Son, yet took the form of a humble servant and submitted

Himself in obedience, even to death on a cross, so that men and women might be reconciled to God (see Philippians 2:5-9).

Jesus said much about this. He said that He came not on His own initiative but to speak the things His Father taught Him and to do His Father's will (see John 6:38, 8:28). He made it clear He did not come to seek His own glory from humanity (see John 5:41, 8:50). He was lowly, gentle, humble, and modeled being a servant to all (see John 13:14, 15). His purpose was to demonstrate perfect obedience to His Father's will even in death on the cross (see Luke 22:42). His whole life was a "life yielded to God."[3]

Are our hearts transformed? Do they live out the humility of Jesus? Humility is a gift of grace from God through union with His Son by means of His Spirit. As the Holy Spirit transforms us in spiritual maturation, Christ's humility can become our humility. Humility is a fruit of the Holy Spirit. Humility is the language of Jesus' precious blood shed for us. Given the price Jesus paid to redeem us, how dare we wallow in pride?

The old "self" is the origin of pride. Through the blood of Jesus, the former "self" was crucified with Jesus to do away the "body of sin" enslaved to sin (Romans 6:6). Once self is deposed, we become able to submit to God, serve Him, and do likewise to others (see Ephesians 5:21; Philippians 2:3-5; James 4:6). Pride must die for a Christ-follower to put on the humility of Jesus Christ.

When we become secure in our love of Christ, we can love others and lay down our lives the way He calls us to. As we learn to speak the language of Christ's love, we no longer look at others and try to devise some way to place ourselves above them. We understand that, compared to God, no one is righteous, not one (see Romans 3:10). We become aware that we need mercy and grace for our sins just as much as anyone else. We realize that all our efforts are filthy rags before a righteous God (Isaiah 64:6, NIV). We recognize that we have absolutely nothing apart from God's mercy and the grace He bestows on us. Unless we successfully put pride to death and put on Christ's humility, we will not grow to spiritual maturity. Humility is the first fruit of becoming like Jesus. In humility, self is emptied from the heart so the Holy Spirit can grow us in His likeness. We are then able to overcome sin, forgive unconditionally, and grow in affliction. In humility, the Holy Spirit empowers us to serve in love (agape) by giving, discipling, evangelizing, and "one-anothering." Andrew Murray wrote:

> Humility toward men will be the only sufficient proof that our humility before God is real. … In the creature, humility is the one thing needed to allow God's holiness to dwell in him and shine through him.[3]

Through humility, God blesses us, as Scripture makes clear.

> "For everyone who exalts himself will be humbled, and he who humbles himself will be exalted" (Luke 14:11).

> Humble yourselves in the presence of the Lord, and He will exalt you (James 4:10).

Murray adds this:

> The deepest humility is the secret of the truest happiness, of a joy that nothing can destroy.[3]

CHAPTER FIFTEEN APPLICATION

DISCUSSION QUESTIONS

- Name eight causes of pride. Discuss.
- What is the source for humility? Can true humility be obtained in any other way?
- Why does Murray state humility is so important in sanctification?

- What does Murray state is evidence that a Christ-follower's humility toward God is genuine?
- Read Murray's book *Humility: The Beauty of Holiness.*[3]
- Consider Murray's plea, "Oh for the humility of Jesus in myself and all around me!" Is that your cry?

SELF-EVALUATION

- To overcome pride, you must first admit you have it. Can you identify in yourself any of the eight signs of pride outlined?

MEMORY VERSE

"For everyone who exalts himself will be humbled, and he who humbles himself will be exalted" (Luke 14:11).

CHAPTER SIXTEEN

RECOGNIZING AND OVERCOMING PRIDE

"The distinguishing feature of counterfeit holiness is its lack of humility."[1]
Andrew Murray

To grow spiritually, every Christ-follower must overcome pride. This will be a vigil throughout the Christ-follower's life since the deceit of pride and our vulnerability to it are not dead until we are. It is an affliction of the human condition. Our deceitful hearts are extremely skilled at disguising pride. It is usually more evident to others. As Andrew Murray wrote in the epigraph atop this chapter, pride is the enemy of growth in holiness. The first hurdle is to recognize pride in our lives. Once we recognize a form of pride, we must strive to allow the Holy Spirit to remove it. While the Holy Spirit empowers this, it takes discipline on our part.

Following are some specific indicators of pride and how to overcome each. Strong emphasis is placed on internalizing Scripture to overcome these facets of pride. Memorizing Scripture is an exceptional way of having it take effect in your heart.

We think we are better than others. In "first world" countries such as the United States, many people become upset by the loss of life of Americans from tragedies, natural disasters, Covid-19, mass shootings, homelessness, starvation, and the like. But when such losses occur in other parts of the world, they demonstrate little or no concern. This is pride, in essence caring more about people who are like us than those in different cultures. It considers oneself better than people of other ethnic groups, biological sex, education level, social strata, or spiritual status.

To overcome: Pray that the Holy Spirit will enable you to value all others above yourself. Memorize the Scripture passage below.

> Do nothing from selfishness or empty conceit, but with humility of mind regard one another as more important than yourselves; do not merely look out for your own personal interests, but also for the interests of others. Have this attitude in yourselves which was also in Christ Jesus (Philippians 2:3-5).

We show favoritism and partiality. Pride can lead to a greater willingness to meet, associate with, or show preference for some people compared to others. In churches, this may be an "inner circle" of "more spiritually mature" people, or people with "greater social standing." Nothing is more harmful to discipleship within a church than when people are unwilling to meet with others who need to grow in their faith because they think they are spiritually superior to them. This is the pride of partiality, and it is sin (see James 2:1-9).

To overcome: Seek out people who aren't the "elite" in your church, neighborhood, or sphere of influence. Invite them for coffee, dinner, or to be included in your small group. Pray that the Holy Spirit will enable you to value them and their companionship more than "esteemed" people. Memorize the passage below.

> Be of the same mind toward one another; do not be haughty in mind, but associate with the lowly. Do not be wise in your own estimation (Romans 12:16).

We ignore attempts from others to communicate. This is not about messages from marketers and advertisers. Nor is it about someone who has hurt you in which responding might invite additional injury. This references people who reach out to encourage you, invite you for coffee, be in a small group, have issues they need to discuss, or simply have a desire to talk with you. It could be a neighbor reaching out to get to know you, request help, or borrow something. The way of the world is to "cancel" or marginalize people. This is condescending and should not be the way of Christ-followers. Ignoring an attempt to communicate when people reach out to us is not a sign of a servant's heart.

To overcome: Pray the Holy Spirit empowers you with a servant's heart to respond thoughtfully and respectfully to every communication within your sphere of influence. You may not be able to accommodate every request, but out of humility and tolerance, in love (agape), you need to at least respond (the only exceptions being those noted above). Memorize this Scripture.

> Walk in a manner worthy of the calling with which you have been called, with all humility and gentleness, with patience, showing tolerance for one another in love [agape], being diligent to preserve the unity of the Spirit in the bond of peace (Ephesians 4:1-3).

We display jealousy. Are you troubled because a colleague received an award, recognition, or promotion? Maybe you think you deserved it more than they did. Are you unhappy that your small group leader asked someone else to read a Bible verse or pray, and not you? Similarly, an associate pastor may be unhappy the search committee didn't choose him to replace the outgoing lead pastor, so he undercuts and opposes the new pastor. Jealousy is sin of an unregenerated heart (see Galatians 5:19-21). Often, this is a lack of trust that God will look after you. Love (agape) is not jealous (1 Corinthians 13:4).

To overcome: Pray that the Holy Spirit will enable you to grow in your trust to the point you can afford to replace jealousy with love (agape) for all people. When your heart is headed toward jealousy, confess it and ask for forgiveness. In certain circumstances, you may need to go to the person, confess your jealousy, and ask for forgiveness. Memorize the Scripture passages below.

> Trust in the LORD with all your heart and do not lean on your own understanding. In all your ways acknowledge Him, and He will make your paths straight (Proverbs 3:5, 6).

> Love [agape] is patient, love [agape] is kind and is not jealous; love [agape] does not brag and is not arrogant (1 Corinthians 13:4).

We have difficulty receiving criticism, advice, or teaching while simultaneously criticizing others. Some people are very willing to give teaching or criticism but can't receive either. They are too proud to admit to learning something from others. This is often seen in people who believe they have attained knowledge above everyone else (see 1 Corinthians 8:1). In some, this leads to constant criticism of others. Remember Jesus' teaching that we need to get the log out of our own eye before criticizing the speck in the eye of another (Matthew 7:1-5). Check your motives before you are critical of others.

To overcome: Remember this when you receive advice or criticism, especially from a fellow Christ-follower: "Faithful are the wounds of a friend, but deceitful are the kisses of an enemy" (Proverbs 27:6). Pray the Holy Spirit will enable these verses in your heart and that you will value agape above knowledge in your interactions with and comments about others. Memorize the Scriptures below.

> Knowledge makes arrogant, but love [agape] edifies (1 Corinthians 8:1).

> Everyone must be quick to hear, slow to speak and slow to anger (James 1:19).

We have to be right, always, or insist on our own view. Church people involved in "God's work" are frequently intolerant of the viewpoints of others (see Romans 12:16). They fall out over secondary doctrines not unambiguously stated in Scripture such as pre-election versus free will or mundane issues like carpet color, style of worship music, conspiracy theories, vaccinations, and more. While there are essential doctrinal issues on which we may have to, in love, disagree and perhaps even separate (see Appendix 3), this isn't the case for most church disunity today. It is largely due to pride, as Scripture states: "Where there is strife, there is pride" (Proverbs 13:10, NIV).

To overcome: Pray that the Holy Spirit will guide you to see where you can, in love, accept another person's view while having wisdom to know where a Christ-follower must not compromise. Reread the above memory passages: Romans 12:16 and Ephesians 4:1-3. Read Francis Chan's book *Until Unity* (David C. Cook, 2021), or, at minimum, chapters eight and nine. Memorize this Scripture.

> Who among you is wise and understanding? Let him show by his good behavior his deeds in the gentleness of wisdom (James 3:13).

We have difficulty admitting sin, mistakes, or wrongdoing. A prideful heart that puts itself above God and others will have difficulty admitting sinful actions, repenting, and asking for forgiveness. We are commanded to do all three—to God and to others. Scripture warns: "He who conceals his transgressions will not prosper, but he who confesses and forsakes them will find compassion" (Proverbs 28:13).

To overcome: Memorize these Scripture passages.

> Confess your sins to one another, and pray for one another so that you may be healed (James 5:16).
>
> If we confess our sins, He is faithful and righteous to forgive us our sins and to cleanse us from all unrighteousness (1 John 1:9).

We consider ourselves above doing certain tasks considered mundane: If we consider certain tasks too mundane for us, pride lurks in our heart. In humility, we are called to consider all others better than ourselves. There may be reasons for turning down a task. If it is because you feel you are above it, it is likely pride. Jesus washed His disciples' feet to emphasize that following Him is a life of humble servanthood (see John 13:12-14), and we are to model His perfect example of humility.

To overcome: Memorize these Scriptures.

> "If I then, the Lord and the Teacher, washed your feet, you also ought to wash one another's feet" (John 13:14).
>
> Who, although He existed in the form of God, did not regard equality with God a thing to be grasped, but emptied Himself, taking the form of a bond-servant, and being made in the likeness of men (Philippians 2:6, 7).

We are prone to boasting. Pride leads to boasting even in Christ-followers. This can be about accomplishments, attributes, plans, or abilities. Such people want to be the center of attention, dominate group discussions, and are not self-effacing. When someone shares how God is leading them to evangelize and make disciples, it can encourage others in a small group. But one small group member shouldn't dominate to the point that there is inadequate time for others to share their struggles or how God is using them. *Agape* does not boast (see 1 Corinthians 13:4). We must be careful in communicating our plans as even stating our plans to others can be boasting (see James 4:13-17).

To Overcome: Memorize these passages.

> Some boast in chariots and some in horses, but we will boast in the name of the LORD, our God (Psalm 20:7).
>
> "Whoever exalts himself shall be humbled, and whoever humbles himself shall be exalted" (Matthew 23:12).
>
> Instead, you ought to say, "If the Lord wills, we will live and also do this or that" (James 4:15).

We are unwilling to submit to authority. Lawlessness is the way of the world. To discover this, you only have to drive your car at the posted speed limit for a few minutes. Pride leads to resistance over any authority God has placed in our lives for our good. Scripture exhorts Christ-followers to be subject to God (see James 4:7, 8), governing authorities (Romans 13:1-3), church leaders (Hebrews 13:17), and, for children, their parents (Ephesians 6:1).

To overcome: Memorize the following passages.

> Every person is to be in subjection to the governing authorities (Romans 13:1).
>
> Children, obey your parents in the Lord, for this is right (Ephesians 6:1).

> Obey your leaders and submit to them, for they keep watch over your souls as those who will give an account (Hebrews 13:17).

> Submit therefore to God. Resist the devil and he will flee from you (James 4:7).

We jump ahead of others: People jumping ahead of others is evident all around us. Have you ever been traveling at the speed limit on a highway and, as you approach an exit, someone passes you and cuts into your lane with barely enough time to exit ahead of you? In the workplace, people undercut, criticize, and put obstacles in the way of their peers to rise above them in rank. This also happens in churches where people sometimes try to climb over others to attain "status." There is a worldly saying: "It doesn't matter what route you take as long as you get there." How Christ-followers are to "get there" is not like the world but through modeling the humility, gentleness, and meekness of Jesus.

To overcome: If you find yourself impatient with someone, pride is likely lurking in your heart, telling you that person is in the way of your goal. Jumping in front of someone is clearly a sign of pride. In every compartment of our lives, we are always to put others first. Review Matthew 23:12 above, and memorize this passage as well.

> "So the last shall be first, and the first last" (Matthew 20:16).

We are obsessed about appearances. Andrew Murray wrote that "death to self has no surer death-mark than a humility which makes itself of no reputation, which empties out itself, and takes the form of a servant."[1] It is pride when we are obsessed with appearances valued by the world such reputation, attire, vehicles, choice of schools, friends, social clubs, churches, and the like.

To overcome: Memorize these Scriptures.

> "Do not be worried about your life, as to what you will eat or what you will drink; nor for your body, as to what you will put on. Is not life more than food, and the body more than clothing?" (Matthew 6:25)

> For all that is in the world, the lust of the flesh and the lust of the eyes and the boastful pride of life, is not from the Father, but is from the world (1 John 2:16).

We are proud of our holiness (religiosity). Pride is a master of disguise, and even spiritual activities can lead to pride when we begin thinking such activities make us better than others, or we do them out of a motive to look better to others. Jesus used the parable of the Pharisee and tax collector to emphasize the heart attitude we are to avoid: "God, I thank you that I am not like other people" (Luke 18:11). It was the heart of the tax collector Jesus commended: "God, be merciful to me, the sinner!" (Luke 18:13). Even being proud of our humility is a sin. Benjamin Franklin (1706-1790) framed it in this way.

> There is, perhaps, no one of our natural passions so hard to subdue as pride. Disguise it, struggle with it, stifle it, mortify it as much as one pleases, it is still alive, and will every now and then peep out and show itself; you will see it, perhaps, often in this history. For, even if I could conceive that I had completely overcome it, I should probably be proud of my humility.[2]

To overcome: Your prayer time should be largely alone and your tithing discreet (see Matthew 6:2-6). Pray that the Holy Spirit will give you the correct motive when you pray or do other things with people.

During a Bible study I was involved in, the leader invited several to pray. I was about to pray when the Holy Spirit convinced me I was doing it out of pride. I refrained from praying that evening. Memorize this Scripture.

> "Beware of practicing your righteousness before men to be noticed by them; otherwise you have no reward with your Father who is in heaven" (Matthew 6:1).

SEEKING HUMILIATION

Humiliation is the path by which we grow into Christ's likeness since, if we are following His will for our life in this world, we will lose face with many. We will be humiliated. The prophet Isaiah prophesied the coming Messiah and His obedience to God.

> I did not cover My face from humiliation and spitting. For the Lord God helps Me, therefore I am not disgraced (Isaiah 50:6, 7).

How far this is from many present churchgoers who strive to maintain their reputation in the world at the expense of obedience in being identified as Christ-followers and evangelizing others. The humble person is meek, not caring about praise from the world. A.W. Tozer wrote:

> The meek man cares not at all who is greater than he, for he has long ago decided that the esteem of the world is not worth the effort.[3]

CHAPTER SIXTEEN APPLICATION

DISCUSSION QUESTIONS

- What behaviors are symptoms of pride? Which do you observe in others around you? Which do you identify in yourself?

- Do you view any person who annoys you or gets under your skin as a means of God's grace to grow in humility from the Holy Spirit?

SELF-EVALUATION

- How do you plan to overcome the areas of pride you have discovered in your life?
- Ask your spouse, someone discipling you, your pastors, and/or other Christ-followers if they see evidence of Christ's humility in you, or whether they see pride.
- As you discover pride, repent and ask God to forgive you. Pray for the Holy Spirit to transform you to overcome pride and develop humility.
- There may be some people you have hurt or taken advantage of from pride. Go to them, apologize, and ask for forgiveness. If you need to make amends, do so.

MEMORY VERSES

> Do nothing from selfishness or empty conceit, but with humility of mind regard one another as more important than yourselves; do not merely look out for your own personal interests, but also for the interests of others. Have this attitude in yourselves which was also in Christ Jesus (Philippians 2:3-5).

CHAPTER SEVENTEEN

CAUSES AND CONSEQUENCES OF UNFORGIVENESS

"Our obedience is charged with the power to forgive and bless and serve others because we have been captured by God's own pardon and acceptance of us by free grace."[1]

JACK MILLER

Unforgiveness is the way of the world, but it is also sin. It is rebellion against God. Many people professing to be Christ-followers struggle with forgiveness. It becomes a cancer that eats at the soul of those who harbor it. It hinders spiritual growth to maturity. The unforgiving person allows the offenses of others to restrict them spiritually, and this in turn brings out additional sins of a corrupted heart in the unforgiving person—bitterness, anger, and hatred (see Galatians 5:20; Hebrews 12:15, KJV). Because we have been forgiven by God, people who follow Jesus Christ are to forgive unconditionally and without limit (Matthew 18:21, 22; Luke 17:3, 4; Ephesians 4:32; Colossians 3:12, 13). Christ-followers are not only called to forgive hurtful offenses in their daily lives but even inexcusable injuries and suffering. Someone may say, "But you don't know what this person did to me!" That may be the case, but there is no provision in Scripture for withholding forgiveness based on the severity of the offense.

Louie Zamperini was an Olympic athlete imprisoned and tortured in Japanese prisoner-of-war camps in World War II.[2] He returned to the U.S. a broken man plagued by anger, bitterness, and unforgiveness. Louie turned to alcohol but could find no relief. In 1949 his wife convinced him to go with her to a Billy Graham Crusade. It was through that evangelistic outreach that Louie accepted Jesus Christ and was able to overcome his problems with alcohol and unforgiveness for the prison guards who had so severely mistreated him. He spent the rest of his life in a ministry to others using his example of forgiveness.

Pastor Anthony Thompson experienced the worst kind of offense when his wife Myra was murdered in 2015 at a Bible study at Emanuel African Methodist Episcopal Church in Charleston, South Carolina, with eight other people. The murders were determined to be racially motivated. Yet Pastor Thompson forgave his wife's murderer.[3]

Louie Zamperini and Pastor Thompson are two examples of Holy Spirit-mediated forgiveness of the inexcusable. Indeed, they were/are sons of their Father in Heaven, as Jesus once stated.

> "You have heard that it was said, 'You shall love your neighbor and hate your enemy.' But I say to you, love your enemies and pray for those who persecute you, so that you may be sons of your Father who is in heaven … For if you love those who love you, what reward do you have? Do not even the tax collectors do the same?" (Matthew 5:43-46)

In the history of humankind, unforgiveness has continued to be a perpetual spiritual blight. It ends relationships and causes disharmony, distrust, generational feuds, murders, and recurrent wars. Unforgiveness and its sidekick bitterness arrest spiritual maturation. That is why dealing with unforgiveness and bitterness is essential for spiritual growth.

Unforgiveness is antisocial, the opposite of what God intends. We avoid the person who has offended us, which naturally also impairs relationships with the offender's friends and acquaintances. We want the person who offended us to be miserable and isolated but discover that we have instead foisted isolation and misery on ourselves.

An unforgiving spirit also cuts the unforgiving person off from God (see Isaiah 59:2; Matthew 6:14, 15; Mark 11:25, 26; Ephesians 4:30-32). Don't be deceived. Unforgiveness is a dangerous spiritual poison, and the spiritual consequences include blocked prayers, attenuating the fruit of the Spirit (Galatians 5:22, 23), and a return to the fruit of the flesh, such as anger, strife, enmity, rivalries, dissension, and division (Galatians 5:19-21).

FORBEARANCE VERSUS FORGIVENESS

God calls us to forbearance, and this allows us to walk in a manner worthy of our calling (see Ephesians 4:1-3). I was reminded of this recently picking up laundry at my cleaners. A staff member asked for my telephone number so she could locate my shirts. As I was giving her the number, her coworker interrupted me mid-sentence to ask her a question. I paused until her question was answered. In the past, I would have taken offense at the interruption. Why? Pride.

Pride is the enemy of forbearance because pride leads to being easily offended. Go back and review the manifestations of pride. If they have not been overcome, they act like hair triggers for taking offense rather than rendering forbearance. When self is preeminent, there are many offenses taken and much to forgive.

Every negative interaction with other people can go one of two ways. We can either take offense to or overlook a potential grievance. Forbearance does not take offense. This is humility of mind, and it regards others as more important than ourselves (see Philippians 2:3, 4). When there is forbearance, there is nothing to forgive. The event is shed like water off a duck's back. Such forbearance is a sign of the humility of the spiritually mature Christ-follower under the sway of the Holy Spirit.

I once observed a great example of such forbearance by Dr. Frank Sutton. I was present when another Christ-follower said something to him to which I would have been offended. I followed up with Frank, and he taught me forbearance through his response.

> I did hear [his] comments, but I am way past being offended in any matter or way. All my personal offenses were hung on the cross, and He [Jesus] also took away my right to "be offended" by anyone who walks in/by the flesh.[4]

I know of no better description of the forbearance to which every Christ-follower is called (see Colossians 3:12, 13). We will always encounter offenses, some resulting in injury to far more than our pride, impacting our lives, jobs, reputations, finances, physical well-being, or someone we care deeply about. These are not so easily repelled by forbearance and are more likely to result in anger, resentment, malice, desire for vengeance, and loss of hope. But as we mature spiritually, we will increase in forbearance, leaving fewer offenses to forgive.

WHAT FORGIVENESS IS AND IS NOT

When someone hurts another person, forgiveness is a process in the heart and mind of the aggrieved person which leads to healing. Forgiveness frees the injured person of resentment, bitterness, anger, and hatred for a person who has wounded them. If this is not done, the weight of the wrongful actions of another person can be carried for a lifetime. Forgiveness throws off the weight of the offenses. It prevents the wrongful actions of another from being a continuous lifelong affliction and source of continuing sin in the life of the injured person.

There is much misunderstanding about forgiveness.

- Forgiveness does not condone the offender's actions or infer those actions were right or deserved.

- Forgiveness does not require reconciliation and reinstitution of the relationship. It is not uncommon for an offender to inflict additional injury and suffering when relationships are resumed. If the offense involves physical violence or a threat of physical violence, the offended should not continue the relationship in any form. Resumption of a relationship depends on the nature and severity of the offense, the offender's remorse, and the willingness of the offended person to be reconciled.
- Forgiveness is not abandonment of civil justice. Full justice should be sought by civil authorities for offenses such as extortion, fraud, theft, sexual abuse including rape, other types of assault, and murder.
- Forgiveness by a Christ-follower is not a judicial pardon by God. When God forgives, it is a judicial act. Forgiveness by Christ-followers is not. Even when justice cannot be obtained through the legal system, God ultimately will apply justice (see Romans 12:19-21). In the end, it is He who will hold every person accountable for their actions.

CAUSES FOR UNFORGIVENESS

There are many reasons we struggle with unforgiveness. The following are prime examples, if not exhaustive ones.

Desire for fairness and justice: We want to right the wrong and make the person who has offended or harmed us and/or others pay. This confuses forgiveness and justice, assuming wrongly that unforgiveness is a form of justice. The follower of Jesus Christ is called to forgive with no strings attached. God will render justice through His appointed civil authorities and at His final judgment. This doesn't mean we should abstain from notifying civil authorities of egregious offenses, filing charges, or testifying. But the Christ-follower should not withhold forgiveness because of a desire for justice.

Lack of trust: Sometimes we don't forgive because we don't trust God's ability to protect us. This is often an underlying motive for unwillingness to forgive offenses that threaten reputation (vocationally or socially), position, prosperity, power, or something else precious to us. When a colleague at work unfairly criticizes us to others, we are more prone to be unforgiving if we don't trust that God will look after our vocation. A lack of trust can also lead to the mistaken belief that harsh unforgiveness for the offender will protect from future offenses. It is a mindset that declares, "I am not going to be a doormat for your attacks."

This is wrong-headed and likely from the voice of the evil one. Scripture is replete with instructions to trust God (see Proverbs 3:5) and not worldly power (Psalm 20:7). If we genuinely believe God has created us for specific assignments, that we are in the palm of His hand, and nothing can happen to us outside of His plan for us, we can forgive others (see Psalm 56:11, 118:6; Hebrews 13:6).

Pride: If we are honest, many of us have become indifferent about our own sins. We need to remember what wretches we are. In arrogance, we think we deserve to be forgiven by God. As this line of sinful thought progresses, we begin thinking, "You know, I am a pretty good person." So when someone offends us, we take umbrage out of sinful spiritual pride. "How dare they do that to me?"

Unrepentant offender: Someone may say that a Christ-follower is to forgive only when the offender is repentant, basing the viewpoint on this Luke passage.

> "If your brother sins, rebuke him; and if he repents, forgive him. And if he sins against you seven times a day, and returns to you seven times, saying, 'I repent,' forgive him" (Luke 17:3, 4).

There are numerous Scriptures in which the commandment for forgiveness is unconditional (see Matthew 6:14, 15, 18:21, 22, 35; Mark 11:25, 26; Luke 6:37; Ephesians 4:32; Colossians 3:13). Only the

Luke passage ties forgiveness to repentance by the offender. This is the single passage which does this. To use the passage in Luke to link forgiveness to repentance is to not interpret it in the context of other Scripture.

Jesus told a parable about a king considering what to do with a debtor who couldn't pay a debt of ten thousand talents (see Matthew 18:23-35). In today's economy this would be astronomical since a talent was what a laborer might earn in fifteen years. The standard penalty was to seize all assets and sell the debtor and his entire family into slavery to cover the debt. Falling to his knees, the debtor pleaded for mercy. The king showed mercy and forgave the debt. But as soon as he was forgiven, the debtor went out and seized a colleague who owed him a relatively small amount, one hundred denarii—or what a laborer would earn in about three months. When the colleague begged for mercy, the first debtor had the second thrown in prison until he could pay. When the king learned of the first debtor's action, he told that man he should have shown the same mercy the king had rendered to him. Because he didn't, the king reinstated the first debtor's original penalty for nonpayment of his debt. Jesus ends this parable with a sobering admonition.

> "My heavenly Father will also do the same to you, if each of you does not forgive his brother from your heart" (Matthew 18:35).

The one action identified for Christ-followers in the Lord's prayer is to forgive our debtors (see Matthew 6:12). After teaching the disciples this prayer, Jesus warned them.

> "For if you forgive others for their transgressions, your heavenly Father will also forgive you. But if you do not forgive others, then your Father will not forgive your transgressions" (Matthew 6:14, 15).

Someone might argue that strong consideration of these warnings is a "Jesus and" gospel: i.e., legalism. It is not. Consider unforgiveness a sin of the flesh just like other sins of the flesh. As we grow in the likeness of Christ, we begin to overcome sin and manifest mature fruit of holiness. The danger of unforgiveness is similar to continuing in any other willful sin. We are saved by faith, but the faith that saves will bring about an increasingly holy life by a progressive defeat of sin. One of those sins is unforgiveness.

Every Christ-follower is called to unconditional forgiveness. It frees us from bondage to injuries from the offenses of others and allows us to love unconditionally. To require repentance before forgiveness gets into the danger of judging others and continuing in willful sin.

Additional insight into the mandate for unconditional forgiveness can be found in teachings by Rev. Joel Kim, president of Westminster Seminary California, and Pastor John Piper, founder and teacher of desiringGod.org and chancellor of Bethlehem College & Seminary.[5, 6]

CHAPTER SEVENTEEN APPLICATION

DISCUSSION QUESTIONS

- Is forgiveness for others optional? Discuss.
- What are the consequences of unforgiveness?
- What is the difference between forgiveness and forbearance?
- What are the causes of unforgiveness?
- Is a Christ-follower only to forgive when the offender repents?
- Does forgiveness require condoning the offender's action? Does it require restoration of the relationship?

SELF-EVALUATION

- Is there anyone in your life (present or past) against whom you harbor unforgiveness or bitterness? How do you plan to move toward forgiving them?

MEMORY VERSES

> Then Peter came and said to Him, "Lord, how often shall my brother sin against me and I forgive him? Up to seven times?" Jesus said to him, "I do not say to you, up to seven times, but up to seventy times seven" (Matthew 18:21, 22).

CHAPTER EIGHTEEN

FORGIVENESS IS NOT OPTIONAL!

So, as those who have been chosen of God, holy and beloved, put on a heart of compassion, kindness, humility, gentleness and patience; bearing with one another, and forgiving each other, whoever has a complaint against anyone; just as the Lord forgave you, so also should you.

Colossians 3:12, 13

As covered in the previous chapter, Jesus was clear that forgiveness is not optional for Christ-followers (see Matthew 6:14, 15; 18:35). We have been forgiven an outstanding debt. In turn, God commands that we "let go" of the small offenses of others and forgive them. When asked what was the greatest commandment in the law, Jesus responded:

> "You shall love [*agape*] the Lord your God with all your heart, and with all your soul, and with all your mind. This is the great and foremost commandment. The second is like it, you shall love [agape] your neighbor as yourself. On these two

commandments depend the whole Law and the Prophets" (Matthew 22:36-40).

The apostle John also emphasizes that we may say and even believe we are in the light, but if we hate our brother or sister, we are still blinded and walking in darkness (see 1 John 2:9). As with every other element of sanctification, we can't forgive on our own power. God has administered mercy and grace by forgiving us, and He has given us the means to do likewise through the Holy Spirit. That said, while the Holy Spirit empowers forgiveness in a Christ-follower, God still makes it an act of obedience, so we must discipline ourselves to forgive.

True unconditional forgiveness as commanded in Scripture can only occur in people who have taken up their cross to follow Jesus. It is a sacrificial love (agape) where, through the Holy Spirit, a Christ-follower surrenders his or her desire to get even or be angry and displays *agape* for the offender (see Ephesians 1:13, 14). Four different steps are essential in forgiveness, and these can be represented by the mnemonic R-E-E-A-L. These do not necessarily occur sequentially as the Holy Spirit works in the Christ-follower consoling us, empowering us to forgive, and healing the hurt.

R = Remind: A starting point in forgiveness is reminding ourselves that God calls us to forgive and submitting to that call. Through the Holy Spirit and Scripture, we must both admit and submit to three things. First, as Christ-followers, we must forgive out of obedience. Second, the person who has offended us is an "image-bearer" of God and, like us, loved by God. Third, if the person hasn't yet accepted Christ, they are created with the potential to become a Christ-follower. This isn't to say God loves or approves of the offender's sinful actions. But God loves sinners. He loved us as sinners, and He calls us to love sinners even when they sin grievously against us.

E = Enjoin and Entrust: When someone offends against us, we **enjoin** the Father in prayer: the sooner after the offense, the better.

A sincere prayer might be, "O God, I can't forgive this person on my own. Please help me to trust You. Please give me Your power through the Holy Spirit to completely forgive them."

When we pray this, we are truly praying in God's will. We should also pray that we will be faithful in our response to the offense, that the offender would come to know the love of Jesus, and that God would bind them from committing further offenses. While we should pray for justice, we must pray with the right motive—not to get even but rather for the offender's good.

We should also **entrust** them to God, both for their salvation and for justice for their actions (see Matthew 12:36; Romans 14:12).

The first book of the Bible profiles how Joseph forgave his brothers after they treated him viciously and sold him into slavery (see Genesis chapters 37, 39-50). Because of his brothers' jealousy, Joseph was abducted to a foreign land and estranged from his father Jacob. But God used his brothers' sinful motives to save Jacob and his descendants, the recipients of God's promise to Abraham, from famine. When he was reunited with his brothers, Joseph forgave them, telling them that what they intended for evil God used for good (see Genesis 50:20, 21).

A = *Agape*: As the Holy Spirit works, He enables us to view the offender as God's image-bearer (see Genesis 1:26) and surrender our right to get even (Romans 12:19). The Holy Spirit subdues and removes resentment, anger, bitterness, hatred, envy, malice, or desire for vengeance. These feelings are replaced by empathy, compassion, and *agape*, or sacrificial love, which hopes the best for the offender and even desires to bless them. We stop dwelling on the offense (1 Peter 3:9) and instead want the other person to come to faith in Jesus if they have not done so.

If the offenders are Christ-followers, we are to follow Christ's own instructions for dealing with an offense by another believer (see Matthew 18:15-17). This doesn't mean a face-to-face meeting with them alone if severe emotional or physical trauma is involved. Communication may be in the accompaniment of another brother or sister in Christ or through written communication depending on the circumstances. There are situations where it is prudent there be no further contact, which Christ's instructions also address (Matthew 18:17).

Forgiveness has been described as a "self-help" process. It is not. The only way anyone can forgive another person who has grievously wounded them is through the power of the Holy Spirit. This is the Spirit of the One, Jesus Christ, who said, "Father, forgive them" as He died from suffocation and unspeakable pain on the cross (see Luke 23:34). Jesus was true to His own exhortation.

> "But I say to you who hear, love your enemies, do good to those who hate you, bless those who curse you, pray for those who mistreat you" (Luke 6:27, 28).

L = Let it go: In my youth, a common expression swirling around stated, "Don't get mad, get even!" Such a sentiment is not of God or His Son. In obedience to Scripture and through the Holy Spirit, Christ-followers give up our right to vengeance or retribution and instead trust God. Rather than getting even, we are to render mercy and grace, withholding what the offender deserves and giving them instead what they don't deserve: a blessing (see Luke 6:27, 28). This should sound familiar as it is what God did regarding our offenses against Him. We must hold on to this promise.

> Do not say, "I will repay evil"; Wait for the LORD, and He will save you (Proverbs 20:22).

The corrupt human heart tends to emulate animal behavior by licking past wounds. Once we've forgiven someone, we need to avoid this behavior. As we are to be careful to turn our eyes away from things that cause us to stumble, we need to be careful to turn our hearts away from previous offenses we have forgiven (see Psalm 119:37; Proverbs 4:23). Otherwise, our hearts can fan embers into recurring flames of unforgiveness.

A PROCESS THAT TAKES TIME

It is unrealistic to believe that biblical forgiveness occurs instantly after every offense. Louie Zamperini had to first come to faith in Jesus Christ before he could forgive. Even in Christ-followers, unconditional forgiveness often takes time.

In true forgiveness, we are commanded by God to replace anger, bitterness, hatred, malice, and resentment toward the offender with love (agape) for the person (see Ephesians 4:31, 32). The human heart is deceitful and wicked (Jeremiah 17:9, NKJV), and our hearts can deceive us about unforgiveness. One grave danger of early cancer, while it is still curable, is its subtility. Unforgiveness and bitterness are like that.

How might you recognize when you still haven't forgiven? Watch your tongue, your heart, and your feet. If there are expressions of anger or frustration to others about someone who has offended you, beware. Here are some examples.

"I hate the guy!"

"I forgive her, but I am going to avoid her in the future."

Look out if you greet or talk to someone who has offended you differently than you would greet or talk to others. You have likely not forgiven them. If you blame them for how things have turned out in your life, you have likely not forgiven them.

My own feet are a dead giveaway for unforgiveness. Years ago I found myself walking in a certain direction simply to avoid greeting a particular person in the hallway. The Holy Spirit convicted me that I had not forgiven this man for something he had done. On reconsideration, I prayed for the person, which was the beginning of my forgiveness for him.

One ultimate way to test your forgiveness is to seek out the person and tell them you forgive them. Not all situations allow this. It depends on the nature and severity of the offense. But meeting with the offender face-to-face is an excellent way to evaluate if your forgiveness is genuine.

FORGIVENESS DOESN'T REQUIRE FORGETTING

This doesn't mean we should forgive our brothers and sisters in Christ or other people only when they come to us and apologize. Christ-followers are to forgive unconditionally. This is where forbearance in the face of offense, loving those who hurt us, praying for those who persecute us, and doing good to those who despitefully use us comes into play. While repentance makes possible a restoration of unity and harmony, forgiveness is at the very least as much for the person hurt as for the offender, preventing the offense from inducing unholy thoughts and actions. When the offender is unrepentant, forgiveness is more for the person hurt by the offense and as a display of the aroma of Jesus Christ to the offender and the world.

Forgiveness doesn't mean erasing from our memories egregious offenses against us. Scripture tells us that when God forgives our iniquities, He remembers them no more (see Jeremiah 31:34; Hebrews 8:12). What exactly that means in context of God's omniscience we will never understand this side of Heaven. What we do know is that when He forgives us, God "blots out" our repented transgressions from the judicial ledger of sin that separates every fallen human being from God (Isaiah 43:25), seeing in their place Christ's imputed righteousness (Romans 4:1-8; 2 Corinthians 5:21; Philippians 3:9).

Some have used this to suggest true forgiveness has not occurred until the offended person has "forgotten" the transgression. I do not think this is the correct view. I believe there are countless examples of Spirit-led forgiveness where a person has the memory of the offense for the rest of their life. But while they may retain that memory, through forgiveness they've discarded bondage to the offense and the sins of the flesh it triggered.

FORGIVING ONESELF

Sometimes people have more difficulty forgiving themselves for something. The evil one likes to whisper in our ears, "You are not worthy of God's love"; or, "How can you be reconciled to God when you did something like that?"; or, "How can God use you when you have sinned so greatly?"

A bit of caution and balance is needed here because we can feel discomfort from the Holy Spirit when we get outside the rails of God's will for our lives. That discomfort guides us to repent, confess, and refrain from the sin. Conversely, the Holy Spirit will never tell us God doesn't love us or won't forgive us if we confess the sin and turn from it even if we've done something extremely boneheaded or fallen repeatedly into the same sin. When we are spiritually down from something we've done, we need to ask God to forgive us. Then we should go to the person we've hurt and ask the same thing. We should make restitution to the best of our ability. We must pray for the Holy Spirit's power to refrain from doing the thing again.

Remember that God uses broken, sinful people. Think of those He's used in remarkable ways. King David, referred to as a man after God's own heart (see Acts 13:22), not only committed adultery but intentionally murdered Bathsheba's husband. Abraham misrepresented his wife as his sister not once but twice (Genesis 12:10-20, 20:1-18). God forgave these and many, many other people in Scripture. It is His character to forgive if we confess our sins and are repentant (1 John 1:9). So don't get down on yourself when you sin. Repent, ask forgiveness, and ask for power to do better next time. We have to forgive ourselves as we do others.

We should also graciously accept forgiveness from others. Sometimes we have difficulty receiving forgiveness from someone we've offended—or who believes we've offended them. Why is this? It hurts our pride. It implies we've done something wrong. Just as we thankfully accept mercy and grace from God when He forgives us, we need to accept it with evident appreciation when others forgive our offenses against them.

President Abraham Lincoln closed his second inaugural address with these words: "With malice toward none, with charity for all, with firmness in the right as God gives us to see the right, let us strive on to finish the work we are in .... "[1] This great man would be dead in six weeks from an assassin's bullet. He was rallying the nation toward hearts unencumbered from unforgiveness and bitterness.

Most of us will never be tortured in a prison camp or have the love of our life murdered as experienced by Louie Zamperini and Anthony Thompson, respectively. Their ability to forgive demonstrates how the Holy Spirit enables forgiveness that we can't achieve on our own. But we shouldn't be deceived that the call for forgiveness pertains only to such extreme offenses. In the course of our lives, there will be lesser offenses that can stall our spiritual growth if we harbor unforgiveness and bitterness. A colleague takes credit for an idea that is our intellectual property. A spouse is unfaithful. A "friend" is saying untrue things about our child behind our back.

God has given us the means of grace for unconditional forgiveness—the Holy Spirit. Forgiveness sets the Christ-follower free and on a Spirit-directed path to grow in the likeness of Jesus.

Last, forgiveness counters the way of the world. A sign in front of one Baptist Church reads: "Forgive your enemies—it messes with their heads."

CHAPTER EIGHTEEN APPLICATION

DISCUSSION QUESTIONS

- Describe the R-E-E-A-L steps in forgiving someone.
- How can someone recognize in their actions that they haven't forgiven another?
- Unless there are mitigating circumstances (such as a severe offense), how might one test their forgiveness?
- Does a persistent memory of an offense mean you have not forgiven? Discuss.

SELF-EVALUATION

- Pray that the Holy Spirit will show you where there is unforgiveness in your life and give you the power to forgive.
- Has the Holy Spirit shown you people you have not yet forgiven? What steps will you take to do so?

MEMORY VERSES

> So, as those who have been chosen of God, holy and beloved, put on a heart of compassion, kindness, humility, gentleness and patience; bearing with one another, and forgiving each other, whoever has a complaint against anyone; just as the Lord forgave you, so also should you (Colossians 3:12, 13)

CHAPTER NINETEEN

GROWING IN AFFLICTION

"The Refiner's Fire is simply an instrument by which God accomplishes His purposes in our lives."[1]

—A.W. Tozer

When the apostle Paul was afflicted with a "thorn in the flesh," he asked God three times to remove it. God answered, "My grace is sufficient for you, for power is perfected in weakness" (2 Corinthians 12:9). Paul's response to God's answer illuminates the attitude Christ-followers should exhibit in affliction.

> Most gladly, therefore, I will rather boast about my weaknesses, so that the power of Christ may dwell in me. Therefore, I am well content with weaknesses, with insults, with distresses, with persecutions, with difficulties, for Christ's sake; for when I am weak, then I am strong (2 Corinthians 12:9, 10).

Andrew Murray wrote that every Christ-follower goes through two stages in the acquisition of humility. The first stage is to avoid it. It isn't what "self" wants. We enter the second stage when we come to the mindset of the apostle Paul. This stage is an understanding that

God works through circumstances of affliction to grow us in humility and have our weaknesses glorify His strength. For us, like the apostle Paul, humbling through affliction arrests a resurgence of the heart to "self-exalt." Murray wrote:

> The school in which Jesus taught Paul is our school, too. He watches over us with a jealous, loving care lest we exalt ourselves.[2]

Horatio Spafford was a Chicago attorney who, in 1873, sent his wife and four young daughters ahead of him on a transatlantic steamship voyage for a vacation in Europe. The ship sank en route, killing two-thirds of the passengers and crew. Spafford received a telegram from his wife Anna: "Saved alone. What shall I do?"[3]

Spafford immediately embarked to be with his wife. As the ship passed near the spot where his daughters had died, he penned the words to the great hymn, "It Is Well with My Soul."

Pain, suffering, trials, and affliction are subjects most of us would rather not talk about. But they are a very real part of the human condition. I don't have all the answers as to why they occur, but God's Word provides insight. The scourge of suffering and affliction in humankind began with its rebellion against God (see Genesis chapter 3). It will continue until the return of Jesus as the conquering King when He will create a new Heaven and a new earth without suffering and affliction.

> Then I [apostle John] saw a new heaven and a new earth … And I heard a loud voice from the throne, saying, "Look! God's dwelling place is now among the people, and He will dwell with them. They will be His people, and God Himself will be with them and be their God. He will wipe every tear from their eyes. There will be no more death or mourning or crying or pain, for the old order of things has passed away" (Revelation 21:1, 3-4, NIV).

We live in a world between these two milestones—the fall of humanity and the return of Jesus as King. Distilled to their root cause, hardship, trials, suffering, and death are all due to sin. Every person is guilty. And because humanity has fallen, evil in human hearts is also responsible for much pain and suffering.

Illnesses, disease, and death are at the top of the list as causes for affliction and suffering. This becomes increasingly clear as we age. Starting at age sixty, the number of prescription medications generally equals or exceeds the number of decades of life. High blood pressure, heart attacks, cancer, asthma, Alzheimer's Disease, and the like are examples. Illness and disease can occur from genetic disorders or be unrelated to genetic background. There is no reliable estimate of the total number of diseases afflicting humankind in the twenty-first century, but it's safe to say it is a large number.

Suffering occurs from natural disasters such as hurricanes, tornados, flooding, drought, famine, forest fires, volcanic eruptions, earthquakes, and the tsunamis they spawn. There are also biological disasters. Smallpox was prevalent at the time of the Revolutionary War. The last century saw the influenza pandemic of 1918-1919 and the poliomyelitis epidemic. And, in this century, there was the Sars-CoV-2 pandemic.

Sadly, evil in human hearts adds significantly to the suffering in this world. This may be through actions of single individuals but is far more prevalent on a societal and international level. Wars initiated by evil hearts have been responsible for massive deaths throughout history. The Nazi regime murdered six million innocent Jews during the Holocaust solely because of their ethnicity. The Atlantic slave trade of Africans incurred a death toll likely exceeding the Holocaust.

The state can be responsible for suffering by not adequately securing borders, thereby contributing to illicit drug use or human trafficking. The impoverished suffer as a result of poor education, lack of training in vocational skills, oppression, and racism. There is also suffering and affliction exclusive to Christ-followers—oppression and persecution for their faith in God and serving Him. Jesus said:

> "If the world hates you, you know that it has hated Me before it hated you" (John 15:18).

The apostle Paul warned that everyone living a godly life in Jesus Christ will be persecuted (see 2 Timothy 3:12). Scripture is certainly filled with examples of God's people who experienced trials and suffering because of their faith in and obedience to God. Shadrach, Meshach, and Abednego were Jewish exiles in Babylon when they refused to worship the golden image King Nebuchadnezzar had created and were thrown into the fiery furnace (Daniel chapter 3). Their companion Daniel was placed in a lion's den for continuing to pray to the one true God, Yahweh (Daniel 6:13-24). The apostle Paul was given thirty-nine lashes five times, beaten three times, stoned, and deprived of food, water, and protection from the cold (see 2 Corinthians 11:24-28). In the above examples, God rescued His followers from their trials. Other trials resulted in death, such as the first early church martyr, Stephen (Acts chapter 7), and ultimately the apostle Paul (2 Timothy 4:6-8).

These servants of God were willing to pay a very steep price—they gave their very lives (see Revelation 12:11). In contrast, how often do we compromise our relationship with God in our jobs or participate in things counter to His principles just because of fear of what others might think? Nominal Christians want God to relieve them of trials while at the same time providing His abundant blessings. This is one of the great fallacies of the prosperity gospel.

That said, not all persecution Christ-followers undergo is because of serving Him. Being shunned or otherwise treated in a way we don't like because of sinful attitudes or actions toward others is not blessed. Insensitive, thoughtless, unloving statements can provoke undesirable responses. This isn't being persecuted because of Christ but sheerly because of sinful attitudes and behavior. Persecution is blessed when it occurs because of the believer's identity in Christ and actions taken in obedience to Him (see Matthew 5:10).

SPECIFIC SIN AS A CAUSE FOR AFFLICTION

As we've already discussed, specific sin in someone isn't always the cause of affliction, but it can be. Conversely, obedience to God's Word is one important way to avoid some affliction, hardship, and death. Hananiah was a false prophet who died for his rebellion against God in opposing Jeremiah (see Jeremiah 28:16, 17). Ananias and Sapphira died for their deceit (Acts 5:1-10). When Jesus healed the invalid of thirty-eight years, He admonished the man: "Do not sin anymore, so that nothing worse happens to you" (John 5:14).

Scripture exhorts us to treat our bodies with reverence as temples for the Holy Spirit (see 1 Corinthians 3:16, 17). We have been bought at a high price and are to glorify God in our bodies (1 Corinthians 6:19, 20). This encourages us not to indulge in strong alcoholic beverages (Proverbs 20:1; Isaiah 5:11) or other things hazardous to our health. For example, many people who smoke develop emphysema or lung cancer. Partaking in excessive alcohol consumption or illicit substances results in significant disease and premature death. Rather than be drunk with wine, we are urged to be filled with the Holy Spirit (Ephesians 5:18).

That said, we must use extreme caution in assuming sin in someone's life is responsible for their pain, suffering, and affliction. We've already discussed Jesus' admonition that when horrific things happen to people, it isn't necessarily because those people committed greater sin than others (see Luke 13:1-5). Another example is the man Jesus identified as born blind not because of sin but to glorify God (John 9:1-3).

Dr. D.A. Carson, professor emeritus at Trinity Evangelical Divinity School and cofounder of the Gospel Coalition, notes that we all live in the "effluent of the fall."[4] That effluent includes disease, natural disasters, accidents, and corrupt hearts prone to evil. Bad things happen to people simply because we all live in a fallen world. Accordingly, it's unconscionable to tell someone undergoing suffering and affliction that their sufferings are because of unconfessed sin or because they have inadequate faith required for healing.

SUFFERING AND AFFLICTION IN THE UNSAVED VERSUS CHRIST-FOLLOWERS

Pain and suffering are common in all humankind, for both the righteous and the wicked (see Ecclesiastes 9:2). Pain and suffering remind us of our frailty and the inevitability of death. The purpose of affliction and trials in the unsaved can be to draw them into a relationship with a mighty God. We see this when God spoke to Israel through the prophet Amos about how He had afflicted them "yet you have not returned to Me" (Amos 4:10).

In Christ-followers, God uses pain, affliction, and suffering in an additional way—to humble us so we will grow to maturity. One surprise of early space exploration was the adverse effect of weightlessness on the human body. In the absence of gravity, human muscles become weak, the spine's normal curvature is lost, the vertebrae in the spine lose calcium, and back pain ensues.[5] Thus, the physical activities we do against gravity on earth such as climbing stairs, bicycling, running, and even sitting in a chair are necessary for the health of our heart, blood vessels, muscles, and spine.

Suffering and affliction work in this way for our spiritual growth. They are unpleasant, but if we let them, they grow and strengthen our faith, endurance, and character. As Christ-followers, we are told not to be surprised when we encounter trials (see Hebrews 12:6; 1 Peter 4:12). On the contrary, Scripture makes clear we experience difficulties so we may grow in holiness.

> He [God] disciplines us for our good, so that we may share His holiness (Hebrews 12:10).

None of this says that sorrow, anguish, and grief are pleasant or that we should seek them out. But to save us, God did not spare His own Son from physical death and suffering on the cross. Why would He withhold trials and suffering from us when that very discipline will spiritually mature us to become more like His Son?

THE FURNACE OF AFFLICTION TO TEST AND PURIFY

God's purpose for saving us is so we may become like His Son Jesus. Every Christ-follower must therefore be purified by removing the world and our flesh nature from every compartment of our lives. Through the "furnace of affliction" (Isaiah 48:10) God burns off the things that contaminate our righteousness and impede our spiritual growth. The prophet Malachi refers to this as the "refiner's fire" where "He will purify the sons of Levi and refine them like gold and silver, so that they may present to the LORD offerings in righteousness" (Malachi 3:2, 3). The furnace of affliction leaves behind no vestige of worldliness, no component of retaining control, no embers for self-exaltation, nothing counter to the nature and character of God.

God's purpose is not to make our lives more relaxing and pleasant on earth, as the prosperity gospel advocates. A.W. Tozer asserts that God uses His refiner's fire for His purposes for each of us.[1] Trials and afflictions reveal flaws in our hearts that we must overcome.

The greatest battle to be fought and won is the battle over the transformation of our hearts by the Holy Spirit. When I drive out of my friendly middle class neighborhood, it's easy to wave fondly at my neighbors with great peace and love in my heart. But my true nature is revealed when one of those neighbors sends me an aggressive email or note. My true heart is revealed when a tailgater pulls within ten feet of my back bumper while I'm driving at speed limit. Trials and hardships test the genuineness of our faith and push us to grow in spiritual maturity.

The diagnosis of asthma in some patients is difficult because the results of their pulmonary function (breathing) tests are normal. We doctors often order a bronchial provocation test to detect asthma in these patients. This is done by having the patient inhale tiny concentrations of an irritant called methacholine. In concentrations used, methacholine has little effect on healthy patients who don't have asthma. After challenging their airways through inhalation of methacholine, their breathing tests do not significantly change. But asthmatic patients have overreactive bronchial passages which react to the methacholine, provoking a significant fall in airflow.

Similarly, trials and hardships are the irritants in a spiritual provocative test of our hearts (see James 1:2-4). They expose what is hidden in our hearts, including what A.W. Tozer calls "veils that obscure God's face."[1] What are these veils? Tozer identifies pride and stubbornness, self-will, religious ambition, claims of ownership, fear, money, friendships, and social position.[1] Such veils influence our relationship with God and transformation to Christ's likeness. Tozer comments:

> God only wants His children to grow and develop into full-fledged Christians. Sometimes in order to accomplish this, God must send us through severe and harsh trials and temptations. But the destination is Christian perfection in the person of the Lord Jesus Christ.[1]

Hardships and trials test our faith, provide proof of it, grow us in holiness, and result in "praise and glory and honor at the revelation of Jesus" (1 Peter 1:7; see also Hebrews 12:10). In the fire, self-dependence is burned off, expunging any notions for boasting and self-glory so that all glory is reflected to God (Psalm 115:1; 1 Peter 4:11). Through each trial we see God's love, power, and care, and these in turn grow our trust that He will provide for us even in our weaknesses (2 Corinthians 4:7-18, 12:8-10). In the crucible of affliction, we develop endurance, character, and hope to persevere in the struggles and battles of this world (Habakkuk 3:17-19, Romans 5:3-5).

Instead of being discouraged, we should be encouraged by the presence of the trials and tribulations, because God loves those He chastens as a loving father disciplines his children.

> For those whom the Lord loves He disciplines, and He scourges every son whom He receives (Hebrews 12:6).

> Consider it all joy, my brethren, when you encounter various trials, knowing that the testing of your faith produces endurance. And let endurance have its perfect result, so that you may be perfect and complete, lacking in nothing (James 1:2-4).

We should be far more concerned when there is no evidence of God's discipline in our lives, as that is a sign we may be illegitimate and don't belong to Him.

> Endure hardship as discipline; God is treating you as his children. For what children are not disciplined by their father? If you are not disciplined—and everyone undergoes discipline—then you are not legitimate, not true sons and daughters at all (Hebrews 12:7, 8, NIV).

It is through the furnace of affliction that we produce the good fruit of righteousness (see Hebrews 12:11). Only by attachment to Jesus, the True Vine, can we produce good fruit in the harshest conditions (John 15:1-8). Hardships, trials, and afflictions drive us to a closer attachment with the vine who is Jesus. This is why the apostle Paul says:

> But we have this treasure in earthen vessels, so that the surpassing greatness of the power will be of God and not from ourselves; we are afflicted in every way, but not crushed; perplexed, but not despairing; persecuted, but not forsaken; struck down, but not destroyed; always carrying about in the body the dying of Jesus, so that the life of Jesus may also be manifested in our body. For we who live are constantly being delivered over to death for Jesus' sake, so that the life of Jesus also may be manifested in our mortal flesh (2 Corinthians 4:7-11).

CHAPTER NINETEEN APPLICATION

DISCUSSION QUESTIONS

- What are the causes of sufferings and afflictions in humans?
- When someone is suffering, is sin always the cause? Discuss.
- What is the purpose of suffering and affliction in the unsaved?
- What form of suffering and affliction is unique in Christ-followers?
- What is the purpose of trials and afflictions in Christ-followers?
- In regard to suffering and affliction, when should a Christ-follower be concerned?

SELF-EVALUATION

- Read Hebrews 12:1-14, then strive to apply it to your life.
- Begin learning how to respond to the small trials for spiritual growth. These prepare you for bigger trials and afflictions when they come.
- Read *The Crucified Life* by A.W. Tozer.[1]

MEMORY VERSE

All discipline for the moment seems not to be joyful, but sorrowful; yet to those who have been trained by it, afterwards it yields the peaceful fruit of righteousness (Hebrews 12:11).

CHAPTER TWENTY

CORRECTLY EMBRACING AFFLICTION

"We may have advanced believers, famous teachers, and men of heavenly experiences who have not yet fully learned the lesson of perfect humility, gladly glorying in weakness."[1]
ANDREW MURRAY

Jesus didn't hide from His disciples that He would suffer (see Matthew 16:21, 17:12) or that they would share in His suffering (Matthew 10:38, 39). Everyone who follows Jesus has been granted to share in His sufferings so they may share in His glory (Romans 8:17; Philippians 1:29). To suffer persecution for our faith in Jesus is blessed.

> "Blessed are those who have been persecuted for the sake of righteousness, for theirs is the kingdom of heaven" (Matthew 5:10).

Can you handle suffering and affliction that comes your way? How we respond to pain, suffering, and affliction depends on us. All of us will have trials, but not all will grow from them. Many people don't recognize that trials and afflictions are discipline from God for their good. Even when they do, some become bitter and angry and fail. In them, the trial does the opposite of what God intends. It drives them away from God rather than bringing a closer relationship with Him. We should embrace our trials and afflictions as loving discipline from the Father and allow them to achieve God's purpose to grow us to the likeness of Jesus. A.W. Tozer cautions:

> How many times have we missed the fragrance of God's presence because we resist the furnace and the tribulation and the suffering before us?[2]

The apostle Paul said that for the sake of Jesus, he had contentment in his hardships, trials, and persecutions (see 2 Corinthians 12:10). We are to rejoice and not lose heart when we encounter difficulties (Romans 5:3; 2 Corinthians 4:16; James 1:2; 1 Peter 4:13). Nothing can bring our spiritual faith into the light more than trials, affliction, and suffering. What a contrast to the prosperity gospel with its error of belief in the availability of "health, wealth," and other "name it and claim it" blessings for all people with the "right type of faith." There are a few principles we need to understand if we are to correctly embrace trials and afflictions as Jesus did.

We don't choose our trials. God disciplines us through an obstacle course of afflictions and hardships designed individually for each person's specific benefit (see Hebrews 12:10). We don't get to choose which trials and afflictions will enter our lives. If we were able to choose, we would either say, "No thanks, I'll pass," or "I'll take the mild one, please." Instead, we are exhorted to run with endurance the specific obstacle course God has laid out for each of us, which we can only do by keeping our focus on Jesus, who ran the race before us.

> Lay aside every encumbrance and the sin which so easily entangles us, and let us run with endurance the race that is set before us, fixing our eyes on Jesus, the author and perfecter of faith, who for the joy set before Him endured the cross,

> despising the shame, and has sat down at the right hand of the throne of God (Hebrews 12:1, 2).

God's consolation will carry us through suffering and affliction. God promises never to give us more than we can bear (see 1 Corinthians 10:13). We are to bring all things in prayer to Him, and He promises us that His peace "will guard your hearts and your minds in Christ Jesus" (Philippians 4:6, 7). This includes our pain, suffering, and afflictions. Amid trials and tribulations, God is our source of comfort and reassurance, as the psalmist exclaims:

> God is our refuge and strength, a very present help in trouble. Therefore we will not fear, though the earth should change and though the mountains slip into the heart of the sea (Psalm 46:1, 2).

This is why Paul can assert that he has learned "to be content in whatever circumstances I am" (Philippians 4:11). God has given us His Word to comfort us in affliction, as the psalmist also declares:

> This is my comfort in my affliction, that Your word has revived me … O may Your lovingkindness comfort me, according to Your word to Your servant (Psalm 119:50, 76).

We learn from trials and afflictions. To benefit, every Christ-follower must believe that pain, affliction, and hardship are from a loving God to grow them to Christlikeness and spiritual maturity (see Hebrews 12:6). Only then can we respond correctly. It is difficult to come to a proper theology in the midst of affliction and hardship. How much better to have a firm foundation on suffering before we are in it!

Small group fellowship is important during affliction. God also provides comfort and help in times of trouble through His body, i.e., other Christ-followers. For this to happen, Christ-followers must be willing to live in true Christian community with other Christ-followers. As with Jesus and His twelve disciples, a group of ten to fifteen brothers and sisters in Jesus Christ is an effective size to grow to deeply love and trust each other (see Acts 2:42). Such small groups provide comfort and support when their members encounter an affliction or trial. They pray and care for each other and stand in the gap for the afflicted, as did the friends of the paralyzed man who lowered him through the roof to be healed by Jesus (see Luke 5:17-26).

Some Christ-followers may believe their support in affliction should come from the leaders in the church. But that is not their job. Church leaders, including pastors, are to train up the church's laity to comfort and support each other.

> And He [God] gave some as apostles, some as prophets, some as evangelists, some as pastors and teachers, for the equipping of the saints for the work of service, to the building up of the body of Christ (Ephesians 4:11, 12).

After the trial, move on. When a medical student or resident physician became sad or depressed about an unfortunate outcome in one of our patients, I would tell them, "Learn from it and move on." It was vital for that young person not to keep dwelling on the event, as that would affect their care of subsequent patients.

The same can be said for every trial God puts in our path for discipline. Embraced correctly, the affliction molds our spiritual growth to maturity. We need to learn from our trials, but then we must move on. Pastor D.L. Moody noted:

> Some people go back into the past and rake up all the troubles they ever had, and then they look into the future and anticipate that they will have still more trouble, and they go reeling and staggering all through life.[3]

God uses trials and afflictions to grow the necessary roots for bearing fruit. Watchman Nee, Chinese Bible teacher and church leader during the Mao regime,[4] was imprisoned for his faith in 1952 and kept isolated from family and friends until he died twenty years later, still in prison. Nee is among those credited with launching the house church movement in communist China. He authored books still read widely today for spiritual growth, including *The Normal Christian Life,*[5] *Let Us Pray,*[6] and *Sit, Walk, Stand.*[7]

Like a twentieth-century Paul, Watchman Nee became an example of God's provision of strength during suffering and affliction. He modeled endurance, perseverance, character, and hope. He was impervious to brainwashing, although the communists tried. And like Paul, there was undoubtedly no guard who escaped his love and evangelism (see Philippians 1:13).

Oppression of faith in Jesus and His church had the opposite effect of what Mao and his communist successors intended. The numbers of Christ-followers throughout China skyrocketed. The prophet Isaiah declared that because Sennacherib persecuted Judah, "the house of Judah will again take root downward and bear fruit upward" (Isaiah 37:31). South African missionary Johan Gous puts it like this: "Hammering a Christian into the ground only causes stronger roots."[8]

There is no substitute for hardship, trials, and persecution in the growth to spiritual maturity. Like the absence of gravity on the human body, there is a danger in prosperity. We become soft and complacent in our faith and trust in God. When affliction and hardship do come, many fall from their faith because of inadequate roots. This is what the parable of the sower describes as seed "sown on the rocky places" (see Matthew 13:6, 20). God never promises a problem-free journey through life. Go back and look at Genesis chapter 3. What He promises us is that He will be with us (Deuteronomy 31:6; Joshua 1:5; Hebrews 13:5, 6). This is what we need!

Moses' life was not trouble-free. After leading the Israelites from Egypt to the wilderness, the Israelites sinned greatly by building a golden calf to worship while Moses was on the mountaintop (see Exodus chapter 32). When he talked with God about resuming the journey toward the Promised Land, Moses could have pleaded for no more problems. But that wasn't what Moses asked for. He sought God's presence.

> "If Your presence does not go with us, do not lead us up from here" (Exodus 33:15).

RECURRING QUESTIONS DURING TRIALS AND AFFLICTION

Two questions are commonly asked regarding pain and suffering: "Why me, Lord?" and "How can a loving God allow pain and suffering?" The story of Old Testament patriarch Job is helpful in answering these questions. God described Job as a "blameless and upright man, fearing God and turning away from evil" (Job 1:8). But Satan insisted Job only followed God because of the great blessings he'd received.

In demonstration, God withdrew His blessings from Job. After Job had lost all his wealth, health, and even his ten children, Job's wife admonished Job to curse God. He refused, upholding God's characterization of him as a righteous man. But Job did become frustrated over the perceived injustice of God's actions.

> "I [Job] cry out to You for help, but You do not answer me; I stand up, and You turn Your attention against me. You have become cruel to me; with the might of Your hand You persecute me" (Job 30:20, 21)

Job did this because he was looking at himself and his affliction. When God rebuked him, Job instead looked up and realized how infinitesimally small he was compared to God. God said to Job:

> "Who is this that darkens counsel by words without knowledge? Now gird up your loins like a man, and I will ask you, and you instruct Me!" (Job 38:2, 3)

After God gives Job a glimpse of His mighty power (see Job chapters 38-41), Job confesses:

"I have heard of You by the hearing of the ear; but now my eye sees You; therefore I retract, and I repent in dust and ashes" (Job 42:5, 6).

CHAPTER TWENTY APPLICATION

DISCUSSION QUESTIONS

- What are two recurrent questions when someone encounters a severe trial? How do you answer these questions?
- Why is it important to move on after going through a trial?
- What is the role of biblical community with other brothers and sisters in Christ in suffering and affliction?
- When should the Christ-follower engage in biblical community?

SELF-EVALUATION

- Do you seek to use suffering and affliction that occur for your spiritual growth?
- At the beginning of every trial, do you pray for God to show you what He is trying to teach you and for the Holy Spirit to help you grow from the affliction to glorify Him?
- Are you in genuine Christian fellowship through a small group with fellow Christ-followers? Has the group formed loving, trusting relationships with each other to support one another through trials?
- Which best describes your response to hardship and affliction? Trust that God is using trials for your spiritual growth? Just trying to get through the trial? Resentment toward God and/or others for allowing trials?

- Read D.A. Carson's *How Long O Lord?*[9] This is an excellent resource on pain and suffering.

MEMORY VERSES

Therefore we do not lose heart, but though our outer man is decaying, yet our inner man is being renewed day by day. For momentary, light affliction is producing for us an eternal weight of glory far beyond all comparison (2 Corinthians 4:16, 17).

CHAPTER TWENTY-ONE

GROWING THROUGH GIVING

"I urge you, brothers and sisters, in view of God's mercy, to offer your bodies as a living sacrifice, holy and pleasing to God— this is your true and proper worship."
ROMANS 12:1, NIV

Did you know giving is a form of worship? Every time we give, we are moving from "self" toward generosity so long as the motive isn't to bring glory to ourselves (see Matthew 6:1-4). To give means to "hand over, bestow, entrust, present, or deliver something" to another. There are many forms of giving. Giving can be intangible, such as giving love, glory, praise and thanksgiving, mercy, grace, forgiveness, or humility. It can also be tangible such as providing for others money, food, clothing, shelter, a Bible, or the gospel message.

The greatest example of giving is God's free gift of love to humankind in providing for our redemption through Jesus Christ's death on the cross, rescuing those who receive Him from the domain of darkness to the kingdom of Jesus Christ (see Colossians 1:13). The mercy, grace, and love of the Father and His Son are our ultimate examples of giving (Jeremiah 31:3; John 3:16; Ephesians 2:8, 9). Because of what the Father and Son have given us, we in turn are not to be shy, tentative, reluctant givers—but cheerful, exuberant givers.

GIVING TO GOD

The story is told of a mission church meeting in Scotland in the early nineteenth century during which the church took an offering.[1] When the offering plate came to a young lad who had nothing to give, he asked that the plate be placed on the floor. Then he stepped into the plate. This youth became the great missionary and Bible translator Dr. Robert Moffat, who served in Africa from 1817 until 1870. If only all of our hearts could become like this man's!

This is what is needed to serve God—to give Him ourselves. He wants all of each of us. This is our proper response to the gospel—denying ourselves and giving ourselves to God and His image-bearers. This is what is meant to be a servant of Jesus Christ: to follow Him. Repeatedly, the apostle Paul refers to himself as a servant of Jesus Christ (see Romans 1:1; Titus 1:1). The Greek word for servant describes someone who belongs to another, is owned by them, and is totally and fully submitted to them.

There are many ways in which every Christ-follower is to give to God. The greatest calling for a Christ-follower is to first give love, honor, glory, and worship to God the Father and His Son Jesus Christ. We do this in numerous ways.

- Having love for God with all of our heart, soul, and mind (Deuteronomy 6:5; Matthew 22:37).
- Giving God the glory due His name in fear, worship, exaltation, thanksgiving, and praise (Psalm 29:2, 34:3, 57:5, 71:8, 95:2, 100:4, 107:32; Revelation 14:7).
- Giving complete obedience by walking in all God's ways (Deuteronomy 5:33).

- Doing everything in Jesus' name and giving thanksgiving to the Father through Him (Colossians 3:17).
- Following and serving Jesus Christ (John 12:26).
- Loving God's Word, meditating on it, and giving it absolute authority over our lives (Psalm 40:8, 119:97).
- Giving the gospel message to others (Colossians 1:28; 1 Peter 3:15).
- Loving God's righteousness, truth, justice, and purity while hating iniquity (Philippians 4:8).

God created us to have a relationship with Him. He wants us to love Him for Himself, not for the things He gives us. Jesus said:

> "Behold, I stand at the door and knock; if anyone hears My voice and opens the door, I will come in to him and will dine with him, and he with Me" (Revelation 3:20).

Jesus wasn't referring to earthly food here but Himself as the source of spiritual food (see John 6:27) and living water (John 4:14), leading to eternal life. We are to fellowship with Him. We have been given the sacred privilege of a relationship with the Father, Son, and Holy Spirit. We honor God when we seek Him as our reward and nothing else. Salvation is a relationship with God not to be defiled by motives for material blessings. A.W. Tozer wrote:

> We must repudiate this great, modern wave of seeking God for His benefits. The Sovereign God wants to be loved for Himself and honored for Himself, but that is only part of what He wants. The other part is that He wants us to know that when we have Him, we have everything—we have all the rest.[2]

DIRECTING GLORY AND HONOR TO GOD

God does not give His glory to another (see Isaiah 48:11). When the world bestows praise and glory on us, it usurps the glory due to

God. The following Scriptures make clear that we were created for God's glory and, in whatever we do, say, or give, only God should receive the glory.

> Everyone who is called by My name, and whom I have created for My glory, whom I have formed, even whom I have made (Isaiah 43:7).

> For from Him and through Him and to Him are all things. To Him be the glory forever. Amen (Romans 11:36).

> "Let your light shine before men in such a way that they may see your good works, and glorify your Father who is in heaven" (Matthew 5:16).

Since as humans we struggle with pride, it is easy to glory in human praise. Over my career as a healthcare provider, a patient or family member would occasionally express thankfulness and praise to me for improving their health problem. While I appreciated the gesture, I endeavored to communicate to my patients that their medical improvement or healing was from God, not me. Jesus is the Great Physician, not me or any other healthcare worker. We were/are just His agents. This redirected them to give their praise and glory to whom it truly belongs: God.

Somewhere in the middle of my medical mission trips to South America, the Holy Spirit convicted me that we were not correctly reflecting glory to God. Our mission team was focused mainly on delivering health care. It seemed we weren't consistently communicating to the patients that we were there on behalf of God and that their benefit from the clinical encounter was from Him. I changed how I approached each patient in the clinic, requesting the Spanish interpreter tell the patient, "I am seeing you on behalf of el Señor Jesucristo [the Lord Jesus Christ]. He loves you, and so do I."

I was astounded to see the warm smile that appeared on every patient's face when they heard this. After dealing with the medical issue,

I asked each patient through the interpreter if I could pray that "el Señor Jesucristo" would heal them. They all agreed. To me, this is taking care to reflect to God the glory that is His.

Scripture gives examples of men who redirected glory from themselves to God when someone tried to praise them. Joseph was imprisoned in Egypt after his brothers sold him into bondage (see Genesis chapters 39-41). When Joseph accurately interpreted dreams by Pharaoh's cupbearer and chief baker, Pharaoh called on Joseph to interpret his own puzzling dream. Joseph quickly deflected any glory from himself to God.

> "It is not in me; God will give Pharaoh a favorable answer" (Genesis 41:16).

After Jesus healed ten lepers, he pointed out that only one had given Him praise and glory (see Luke 17:18). An angel struck King Herod with a deadly affliction "because he did not give God the glory" (Acts 12:23). It is a dangerous thing to divert glory away from God. The prophet Jeremiah pleads:

> Give glory to the LORD your God, before He brings darkness and before your feet stumble (Jeremiah 13:16).

We stop glorifying God by giving Him praise and thanksgiving when we forget what God has done for us. Moses warned the Israelites not to forget how God had delivered them out of bondage from Egypt and led them through the wilderness (see Deuteronomy 6:12, 8:2). They demonstrated ingratitude toward their Deliverer by complaining about the provision of water and food (Exodus 15:23, 24, 16:3, 17:3). Ungrateful hearts are an offense to God, as the apostle Paul points out.

> For even though they knew God, they did not honor Him as God or give thanks, but they became futile in their speculations, and their foolish heart was darkened (Romans 1:21).

Like every succeeding generation since Adam and Eve, many people today scoff at God with ingratitude, ridicule, mocking, and rebellion. To enter God's presence, we must have thankful hearts. We need to remember God's goodness and blessings in our lives. And if we ever doubt that God has led us out of bondage as He did the Israelites, we need to remember that God has freed us from even greater bondage, i.e., the bondage of sin, which devastates the present life and the life to come.

The founders of the United States understood the importance of giving thanksgiving to God. The nation's first president, George Washington, proclaimed a National Day of Thanksgiving in 1789. On December 26, 1941, just three weeks after the Japanese bombed Pearl Harbor, drawing the United States into World War II, President Franklin Delano Roosevelt signed a proclamation making every fourth Thursday in November a national holiday of thanksgiving. These proclamations for a day of thanksgiving occurred when our land was in perilous situations, and the outcomes were uncertain. Sadly, in our current time of relative peace and prosperity, Thanksgiving Day has become, for many, a secular holiday involving a good meal with family and friends capped by a football game.

Remembering with thankful hearts can be enhanced by where we direct our eyes and ears. We need to look up more. When we encounter God's presence with His love, splendor, and beauty, we are reminded of the greatness of the blessings He gives us.

HONORING GOD THROUGH GIVING TO HIS IMAGE-BEARERS

One of the most significant ways we honor and glorify the Father and the Son is to love sacrificially those whom they love. Every living human being, whether in the uterus or after birth, was created by the Father, Son, and Holy Spirit in their image (see Genesis 1:26).

Everything we give to God's image-bearers is also given to God. Remember Jesus' teaching.

> "To the extent that you did it to one of these brothers of Mine, even the least of them, you did it to Me" (Matthew 25:40).

We honor God when we honor and care for our fathers and mothers (see Exodus 20:12); the aged (Leviticus 19:32); orphans and widows (James 1:27); the oppressed treated unjustly (Isaiah 58:6); the hungry, homeless, and inadequately clothed (Isaiah 58:7); our spouses through fidelity to our marriages (Hebrews 13:4); and our brothers and sisters in Christ (Romans 12:10). Jesus emphasized that the second greatest commandment is to love your neighbor as yourself (Matthew 22:39) and that love for each other would identify His disciples (John 13:35).

All righteous giving is Spirit-led and motivated by love. We live in a hurting world where most people are in love with themselves and in which love for others is scarce. Love is the greatest gift we can give to people around us.

> If I give all my possessions to feed the poor, and if I surrender my body to be burned, but do not have love, it profits me nothing (1 Corinthians 13:3).

The love we are to have for others is not just an inner, warm, fuzzy feeling. It must be evident in our actions, as the apostle John points out.

> Little children, let us not love [agape] with word or with tongue, but in deed and truth (1 John 3:18).

How do we love people in deed and truth? By putting their needs above our needs (see Philippians 2:3, 4). By giving them our treasured resources. This includes our words. One uniqueness God has bestowed on us as His image-bearers is the ability to speak to each other. Our tongues are windows on our hearts and often used as instruments of corrupted flesh. James describes the difficulty of controlling the tongue (James 3:8-10). Christ-followers are commanded to give blessings and grace to other people with our words.

> Let no unwholesome word proceed from your mouth, but only such a word as is good for edification according to the need of the moment, so that it will give grace to those who hear (Ephesians 4:29).

We are faithful to our brothers and sisters in the faith when we encourage and build each other up (see 1 Thessalonians 5:11). As a kingdom of priests (1 Peter 2:9), we are to do likewise to the unsaved world.

Forgiveness is another way we honor God and love His image-bearers in deed and truth. It is a form of being sacrificial by giving up completely any right to anger, bitterness, or personal desire for vengeance. When, by faith in Jesus, our sins were nailed to the cross, we were forgiven a staggering debt and freed from the punishment of eternal death (see Romans 5:9, 10). In turn, He calls on us to give mercy to others even when they do not deserve it, and to forgive them of the much smaller debts they've incurred against us.

We also honor God and love His image-bearers when we give away the wealth with which God has blessed us (see Proverbs 3:9). When a minister encourages tithing or a ministry requests money, some roll their eyes and exclaim, "Here we go!" This is unsurprising since there are indeed past and present charlatans who "fleece the flock" for personal gain. God condemns this (Ezekiel 34:10, 11). But the presence of such fraudsters doesn't free us of God's command to give our wealth to Him and others. We do need to use discernment in where our money and resources go, ensuring they are used for purposes of God's kingdom and do not go into the pockets of scammers.

CHAPTER TWENTY-ONE APPLICATION

DISCUSSION QUESTIONS

- Name all the things Christ-followers are to give to God. What is the greatest thing we give Him? Discuss.
- What are the ways in which a Christ-follower honors God directly and in how we interact with His image-bearers?
- How is forgiving someone a form of giving?
- Discuss the importance of thanksgiving.

SELF-EVALUATION

- Are there compartments in your life you are holding back from God? Is it time for you to step into the offering plate as Robert Moffat did?
- Do you give thanks to God for all He has done and is doing in your life? If not, how do you plan to improve?
- Are there areas in your life where you are being praised and given glory that belongs to God? If so, pray for forgiveness and how you can redirect the glory to God in those situations.

MEMORY VERSE

"For those who honor Me I will honor, and those who despise Me will be lightly esteemed" (1 Samuel 2:30).

CHAPTER TWENTY-TWO

BIBLICAL REASONS FOR GIVING

"If God has given us a gift, it's never only for ourselves. It's always to be offered back to Him, and very often it has repercussions for the life of the world."[1]

—Elisabeth Elliot

Can you handle your prosperity and comfort? To grow spiritually, we must learn to handle these things correctly. The Bible contains many precedents and commandments for giving to others and the work of God's kingdom. Scriptures teach three central reasons for giving our money and possessions away: *Obedience. The plight of those in need.* And, *our own spiritual benefit.* Let's examine each.

OBEDIENCE

Simply put, we are commanded to give our money and possessions. Moreover, obedience to these commandments is also giving our love to Jesus (see John 14:15). In ancient times, God instructed the people to contribute a portion of their crop, or "firstfruits," to God as a tithe.

> "Out of all your gifts you shall present every offering due to the LORD, from all the best of them" (Numbers 18:29).

> "You shall surely tithe all the produce from what you sow, which comes out of the field every year" (Deuteronomy 14:22).

> The sons of Israel and Judah who lived in the cities of Judah also brought in the tithe of oxen and sheep, and the tithe of sacred gifts which were consecrated to the LORD their God, and placed them in heaps (2 Chronicles 31:6).

These tithes supported God's priests so they could perform their duties. The tribe of Levi, which was dedicated to serving God in the temple and as priests, was allotted no land and had no other means of supporting themselves (see Numbers 18:8-24). God rebuked the Israelites for robbing Him by withholding tithes and offerings due Him (Malachi 3:8, 9).

In the first century, contributions from the churches supported the work of the apostles. Like ministers today, it allowed them to fully dedicate their work to the ministry and be freed from tent-making vocations on the side to care for their financial needs. The apostle Paul wrote:

> For the Scripture says, "You shall not muzzle the ox while he is threshing," and "The laborer is worthy of his wages" (1 Timothy 5:18).

In other words, a full-time worker in Christian service should partake of the financial blessings generated by the ministry. If there were no contributions to the ministers of God, there could be no full-time workers in those ministries.

Someone might object that the sacrifices and offerings through the Levitical priesthood were abolished by the Messianic Covenant. I believe the same commandment for giving continues throughout the Bible. Insight into this can be found in the patriarch Abraham. After

Abraham had rescued Lot by defeating the kings who had kidnapped him, Melchizedek, king of Salem, blessed Abraham (see Genesis 14:11-20). In response, Scripture states, Abraham gave him one tenth of everything he had.

Giving a tenth is the biblical definition of the tithe. The author of Hebrews speaks of Melchizedek as representing a different priesthood from the Levitical priesthood: "Made like the Son of God, he remains a priest perpetually" (Hebrews 7:3). Moreover, Jesus Christ is "a priest forever according to the order of Melchizedek" (Hebrews 7:17). Abraham's response after being blessed by King Melchizedek was to give him one tenth. A Christ-follower's response, having been blessed by King Jesus, is to do likewise.

THE PLIGHT OF THOSE IN NEED

A second reason for giving is because of the needs of people around us for food, clothing, and shelter. Randy Alcorn wrote, "Christians are God's delivery people, through whom He does His giving to a needy world."[2]

Even in industrialized, prosperous nations, many remain food-challenged and in need of adequate clothing and shelter. Many people must decide between food on the table, medications, or gasoline to drive to work. Some can't afford healthcare insurance and are one medical crisis from financial devastation. Scripture warns us that if we are deaf to the cries of the poor, God will not answer us (see Proverbs 21:13). James calls out those who ignore someone in need.

> If a brother or sister is without clothing and in need of daily food, and one of you says to them, "Go in peace, be warmed and be filled," and yet you do not give them what is necessary for their body, what use is that? Even so faith, if it has no works, is dead, being by itself (James 2:15-17).

The apostle Paul makes clear what our response as Christ-followers should be in obedience to God's commandments.

> While we have the opportunity, let us do good to all people, and especially to those who are of the household of the faith (Galatians 6:10).

OUR OWN SPIRITUAL BENEFIT

A third reason to give is to avoid the adverse effects of money and possessions on our own spiritual growth. A sadly common secular maxim states: "He who dies with the most toys (or stuff) wins!" Many would decry this notion with their lips, but their actions betray them. Money and possessions are among the thorns that choke out the seed and ruin the good soil, leading to unfruitfulness (see Matthew 13:22; Mark 4:19).

This is a particular problem in affluent countries. As of 2021, North America possessed 32 percent of the world's wealth.[3] This represents a massive wealth-to-population disparity since North America makes up only 4.7 percent of the world's population.[4] Wealth and materialism become a contest in which we compare ourselves to people around us. The houses we live in. The vehicles we drive. The clothes we wear. The schools our children attend. Our recreational activities. And yes, our toys.

Materialism is spiritually devastating. It is fueled by pride. It's one of the many ways we esteem the glory of the world more than the glory of God. It blinds us and deafens us to the needs of impoverished, destitute people around us. What good is our wealth of possessions if we keep them to ourselves? We can't take them with us to the next life.

Jesus taught that we shouldn't hoard the treasures of this life while we are here. They will only depreciate with inflation, be stolen, rust, or go out of fashion. Instead, He challenged His followers to build up treasures in Heaven (see Matthew 6:19, 20; Luke 12:33, 34). He warns, "Where your treasure is, there your heart will be also" (Matthew 6:21).

Dr. Ken Elzinga is a committed follower of Jesus Christ and economics professor at the University of Virginia. Speaking at our church, he suggested to the congregation that if money causes a temptation, the Christ-follower should give it away. The practice of generosity is the antidote for greed and materialism. It's the solution to the phenomenon of "money burning a hole in your pocket." If you give it away, it no longer tempts you.

Dr. Elzinga has discipled many groups of students and peers to grow in Christlikeness. He always includes a session on "Stewardship and Giving," which includes the following valuable guidelines.[5]

- Establish a pattern of proportional giving because this will affect our stewardship over our other assets and resources. Many people benefit from a rule, principle, or benchmark for giving.
- Establish a pattern of generous giving if only to help "give away" some of our selfishness.
- Establish a pattern of thoughtful giving because this will help direct our prayer life. Giving away money is difficult because of: (1) the prospect of fraud; (2) the sheer number of prospective recipients; (3) the question of church vs. non-church allocation of gifts.
- Begin the pattern of giving when you are young. How you handle money may be as important as how you handle your prayer life. Don't prolong getting the principle of giving established in your life (and being of one accord on this subject with a prospective spouse).

Don't think you are where you need to be in giving just because you give. We quibble about what is the tithe and what will fulfill the requirement of the tithe. (Should it be based on after-tax income? Is it tax-deductible?)

Giving must also be for the right motives in obedience to, love for, and thankfulness to God and out of love for people. We must do a heart check for any notion in which we give to get back material blessings. Doing so is buying into the counterfeit prosperity gospel. Jesus was aware of stinginess in worshippers at the temple when he praised a poor widow.

> He [Jesus] saw a poor widow putting in two small copper coins. And He said, "Truly I say to you, this poor widow put in more than all of them; for they all out of their surplus put into the offering; but she out of her poverty put in all that she had to live on" (Luke 21:2-4).

God has blessed many of us financially to such a point that the amount we give has a negligible impact on our standard of living. True generosity is not defined by how much we give but by our hearts. It reflects our faith, trust, and reliance on God for our material needs, joy, and contentment. Randy Alcorn wrote, "Tithing is intended to train people to put God first in their lives."[2]

Why should we give with the right motives until it hurts? Because we are stepping out from the world's mindset and saying the kingdom of God is a reality. My salvation through Jesus is a reality. Both are worthy of my financial support. It is saying I value obeying and serving God more than esteem from people around me because of the stuff I have. It is saying to God, "I love You, I'm giving to show my gratitude and thankfulness for what You've done for me, and I trust You to provide for all my needs."

An expectation that God will bless us with even greater prosperity is most definitely not the motive from which to give. That said, God does want us to be prudent and plan wisely. It's wise to have savings accounts and not be in debt. It's wise to have health insurance. It is appropriate to have retirement plans such as 401Ks and other resources to provide for our needs in later life. We should plan for the long-range needs of our families. But we shouldn't hoard our financial blessings in significant excess of being discerning planners. When we stockpile our money and possessions beyond prudent planning, it is a statement of the heart.

Despite being rescued from Egypt and taken into a Promised Land flowing with milk and honey, Israel was captured and taken into captivity in 722 B.C. This occurred because of the nation's sin against God and refusal to obey His commandments (see 2 Kings 17:7-18). The Israelites served the false gods of other nations and were refractory to warnings God gave them through His prophets. They even murdered many of the prophets.

God condemned the Israelites through the prophet Amos for basking in their blessings and living soft, self-indulgent lives: "Woe to those who are at ease in Zion and to those who feel secure in the mountain of Samaria" (Amos 6:1). What did the Israelites do that brought such condemnation? Amos 6:1-14 tells us.

- They ate meat much more frequently than the average person (v. 4).
- They consumed wine from "sacrificial bowls" and indulged themselves in the "finest of oils" (v. 6).
- They did not grieve over the ruin of Joseph, which meant they were unconcerned about the spiritual decay of Israel (v. 6).
- They were arrogant and relied on their own efforts for safety (v. 8).
- They "turned justice into poison" (v. 12).
- They were themselves spiritually bankrupt, not pursuing the fruit of righteousness (sanctification) in their own lives (v. 12).

Amos announced Israel's impending capture and exile to a foreign nation because of its self-indulgence and lack of concern about its relationship with God, or the people God cared about, the poor and oppressed in their midst. Prosperity corrupts. Randy Alcorn identifies the mindset that leads to this.

> Too often we assume that God has increased our income to increase our standard of living, when his stated purpose is to

> increase our standard of giving (look again at 2 Corinthians 8:14 and 9:11.)[2]

A solution for distancing ourselves from materialism and greed is to begin passing the blessings God has given us on to others. We don't have to look far to find people who need food, clothing, and shelter. If you can't find such persons, you can find organizations in your area to help you get your financial resources to people in need.

Jesus taught us to care for people in need. After preaching to the five thousand, Jesus instructed the disciples to feed the mass of people in front of them (see Matthew 14:16; Mark 6:37; Luke 9:13). We are to do likewise. Your local community, urban outreach, or church food banks are an excellent place to start. God defines true fasting as follows.

> Is it not to divide your bread with the hungry and bring the homeless poor into the house; when you see the naked, to cover him; and not to hide yourself from your own flesh? (Isaiah 58:7)

I know of instances where Christ-followers temporarily take people into their homes to provide shelter. The downside to such a decision is the potential risk of harm. Karren and I have taken relatives and a student into our home but no homeless people to date. Even if you don't take them into your home, there are many organizations you can support that aid people experiencing homelessness with shelter, meals, and clothing. A simple internet search will likely reveal churches and other Christian organizations to which you can contribute financially or as a volunteer.

I've found that going through my closet will reveal clothes I can do without or will never wear again such as shirts, pants, winter coats, gloves, and hats. If you aren't using them, pass them on. There will likely be multiple agencies in your area that will receive clothing and distribute it to those in need.

DISTRIBUTION OF FINANCIAL GIFTS

The question frequently arises regarding who and what are appropriate recipients of financial giving by Christ-followers. While there are general principles, it must be said that Scripture does not directly address this. We have already discussed that Jesus is a priest in the eternal order of Melchizedek and that Abraham established the precedent of giving King Melchizedek one tenth (see Hebrews chapter 7). The institution Jesus identified as pre-eminent was His church.

> "I will build My church; and the gates of Hades will not overpower it" (Matthew 16:18).

In most local churches, the majority of financial support is through financial offerings from the congregants. There are Christ-followers who earnestly believe their contributions to parachurch ministries, missionaries who share the gospel, and organizations that provide food and necessities to people in need are also part of the tithe. Others believe that the first 10 percent (i.e., the tithe) should be directed to the local church. A larger question is the proportion of Christ-followers who set, as a goal, giving at least 10 percent of their income. Scripture is clear on this mandate. It is the starting point.

GIVING OUR TIME

One of our most treasured and protected resources is our time. We guard our time as carefully as money and possessions. But guard it to do what? Time analysis typically reveals we hoard our time to nurture "self." This may be entertainment, exercise, socializing, time with family members, or retreating from the busyness of life for solitude. These are not necessarily bad things, but such devotion becomes misplaced if we spend time on them disproportionally. Church people are often unwilling or believe themselves too busy to spend time with other Christ-followers in small-group settings. One way we show our love is by giving our time to meet with and encourage one another (see Acts 2:42; Hebrews 10:25).

One of the most significant gifts Christ-followers can offer is *ourselves*, which means giving our time. I asked a seasoned pastor why the organized church has so little disciple-making. His quick response was that it is hard and very time-consuming. Jesus retreated at times from the disciples for prayer and solitude. But He also gave His time generously to the disciples and all the people He encountered. He lived with the disciples for three years, traveling from town to town, eating together, co-laboring in ministry. Christ-followers are to live a life of serving others. Their time belongs to others and not just to themselves.

GIVING TO THE SICK

Jesus charged the disciples to "heal the sick, raise the dead, cleanse the lepers, cast out demons. Freely you received, freely give" (Matthew 10:8). When Peter and John walked into the temple one day, a man paralyzed from birth begged them for alms. Peter told him, "I do not possess silver and gold, but what I do have I give to you: In the name of Jesus Christ the Nazarene—walk!" (Acts 3:6). James encouraged Christ-followers to pray over the sick and anoint them with oil because prayer offered in faith would restore them (see James 5:13-15).

As a physician who has practiced medicine for more than five decades, I believe God heals through healthcare professionals, and God also heals miraculously. As discussed earlier, God does not always choose to heal. But even when healing does not occur, we are always to provide comfort. How then should Christ-followers be givers to the sick?

- Foremost, by praying for healing as exhorted by James (see James 5:16). On hospital wards, in my clinics, in small groups, I have frequently seen prayer result in recovery.

- By enhancing participation in conventional health care through encouraging someone to have a symptom checked out by a healthcare professional. This includes directing people to healthcare facilities and specific healthcare professionals or simply enabling them to get a medical evaluation.
- By removing financial barriers when these are an obstacle, whether providing financial resources to pay for medical care or medications or donating to free clinics that provide health care to those unable to afford it.
- By volunteering our services to free clinics, especially those of us in health care such as dentists, nurses, optometrists, physical therapists, physicians, and social workers.
- Lastly, by giving our time to encourage, love, and comfort the sick, including visiting them at home or in the hospital (Matthew 25:36; 1 Thessalonians 5:11).

GIVING TO WHOEVER ASKS

We also honor God by giving to whoever asks. Years ago, I loaned a carpenter's level to a remarkable young graduate student who, with his wife, attended a small group we hosted at home. After he completed his studies and moved away, I realized he'd never returned the level. That bothered me for a while. I liked that level and have yet to find a replacement.

If you are like me, you may struggle with the mindset that your possessions are your "things" which you magnanimously share on occasion so long as they are returned. But we need to change how we view "things." Everything belongs to God. He gives us the ability and skill to learn a vocation, the opportunity to earn a living, and the health to perform the work. We breathe the air and drink the water He provides. We eat the fruit of plants He designed. So how is it we think that our "things" belong to us? God has freely given to us, and we should freely give to others without expecting back. Jesus exhorted us in this.

> "Give to him who asks of you, and do not turn away from him who wants to borrow from you" (Matthew 5:42).

In fact, Jesus went on to say that if someone takes something from us, we shouldn't demand it back (see Luke 6:30). I am learning! You see, there is a final thing each of us must give, as the apostle Paul reminds us, which is an account of our lives to God.

> So then each one of us will give an account of himself to God (Romans 14:12).

> For we must all appear before the judgment seat of Christ, so that each one may be recompensed for his deeds in the body, according to what he has done, whether good or bad (2 Corinthians 5:10).

This will include the extent to which we have kept to ourselves resources we should have given to the church and others—money, food, clothing, grace, mercy, forgiveness, even our time and availability. This isn't to say it is a salvation issue. It may more likely be an issue of rewards in Heaven (see Matthew 6:19, 20, 16:27; Revelation 20:12).

CHAPTER TWENTY-TWO APPLICATION

DISCUSSION QUESTIONS

- What are the three reasons for practicing generosity of our financial assets and possessions?
- Why does God bless Christ-followers financially?

- What is the tithe? Is there a biblical mandate for tithing? Discuss.
- Do you practice generosity with your time?
- How does a Christ-follower practice giving to those who are ill?

SELF-EVALUATION

- How would you characterize your giving to God and people in need? At a level that affects your lifestyle? Regularly to the church, but little to people in need? Never?
- What kind of giving have you identified? Money? Possessions? Time? Love for others?
- If you have identified areas in your life where you need to improve in giving, how do you plan to do so? Set specific steps such as sorting out clothing and shoes you don't need, contributing to local food banks, or donating to organizations in your area that help people experiencing homelessness.
- Helping those in need is not simply throwing financial and material resources at them and ignoring their spiritual and social needs. To do so may not address the problem, and it also may create dependency and loss of dignity. People in need must be loved, discipled, and counseled, for this will preserve their dignity and minimize dependency. Read *When Helping Hurts* by Steve Corbett and Brian Fikkert.[6]

MEMORY VERSE

"Sell your possessions and *give* to charity; make yourselves money belts which do not wear out, an unfailing treasure in heaven, where no thief comes near nor moth destroys. For where your treasure is, there your heart will be also" (Luke 12:33).

CHAPTER TWENTY-THREE

SHARING THE GOSPEL AS YOU GO WHEREVER YOU GO

"Whoever will call on the name of the Lord will be saved. How then will they call on Him in whom they have not believed? How will they believe in Him whom they have not heard?"

ROMANS 10:13, 14

Another form of giving central to worshipping God is giving the good news of the gospel to others. Many Christ-followers talk about evangelism, but too few actually do it despite partaking in the miraculous gift of the gospel. At the 2002 national meeting of a Protestant denom ination, I heard Christian pastor and evangelist D. James Kennedy ob serve that all eager to rush to the microphones and ask questions or make comments should have a requirement of having led at least one person to faith in Christ within the preceding year.

God doesn't save us for our salvation alone but to direct others to Him through the gospel. At the end of a person's life, the final instructions to that person's heirs are what he or she views as most important. Jesus' final exhortations to His disciples after His resurrection, and just prior to ascending to join His Father, were to evangelize and make disciples.

> "Go into all the world and preach the gospel to all creation" (Mark 16:15).

> "All authority has been given to Me [Jesus] in heaven and on earth. Go therefore and make disciples of all the nations, baptizing them in the name of the Father and the Son and the Holy Spirit, teaching them to observe all that I commanded you; and lo, I am with you always, even to the end of the age" (Matthew 28:18-20).

There is a misunderstanding by some about the use of the verb "go." In both passages above, the same Greek word, *poreuthentes*, is used. This is the word Jesus used when He sent the disciples back to John the Baptist to give him an answer to the question of whether Jesus was the expected Messiah (see Matthew 11:2-6). South African missionary and evangelist Johan Gous[1] brought me to a greater understanding of this word. He clarifies "go" to mean "as you go, wherever you are." I believe the intended meaning in the Great Commission is better understood by this phrase. As every Christ-follower is going in their specific sphere of life—to the grocery store, a sports event, to teach, heal, etc.—they are to evangelize. It should be our daily lifestyle. The apostle Paul referred to evangelism as the ministry of reconciling to God those who haven't yet come to faith in Jesus Christ.

> Now all these things are from God, who reconciled us to Himself through Christ and gave us the ministry of reconciliation, namely, that God was in Christ reconciling the world to Himself, not counting their trespasses against them, and He has committed to us the word of reconciliation (2 Corinthians 5:18, 19).

God gives a stark warning through the prophet Ezekiel for people who are complacent in proclaiming God's message to those around them.

> "Now as for you, son of man, I have appointed you a watchman for the house of Israel; so you will hear a message from My mouth and give them warning from Me. When I say to the wicked, 'O wicked man, you will surely die,' and you do not speak to warn the wicked from his way, that wicked man shall die in his iniquity, but his blood I will require from your hand" (Ezekiel 33:7, 8).

The prophet Ezekiel was a "watchman" for Israel. Watchman Nee was a "watchman" for communist China, where he was severely tortured and eventually died in prison. It is now our turn as Christ-followers to be "watchmen" and "watchwomen" to our communities and nations, whether the Americas, Europe, Africa, Asia, or to the ends of the earth.

The ministry of reconciliation (i.e., evangelism) is sowing the seeds of the gospel into the soil of a human heart. Once born again, a Christ-follower is referred to in Scripture as a "saint" (see Romans 1:7; 1 Corinthians 1:2; 2 Corinthians 1:1). The ministry of reconciliation is followed by a ministry to the saints (i.e., discipleship; 2 Corinthians 9:1). This nurtures the gospel seed sown in good soil so it produces good fruit that will last (Matthew 13:1-23). Disciple-making can only occur after a person comes to faith and trust in Jesus Christ through evangelism.

THE RIGHT MOTIVE

The objects of evangelism are those persons who have yet to come to faith in Christ. The right motive for evangelism is *agape*, not wanting anyone to perish. When we are faithful in evangelism, we also show *agape* for the Father and Son and honor them. The greatest gift a Christ-follower can ever give another person is to direct them to

Jesus Christ. Jesus entered Jerusalem prior to His death. This scene followed.

> He saw the city and wept over it, saying, "If you had known in this day, even you, the things which make for peace! But now they have been hidden from your eyes" (Luke 19:41, 42).

HOLY SPIRIT POWER

As with every other aspect of our journey as Christ-followers, we can do nothing on our own. We are privileged to proclaim the gospel of Jesus Christ, but only the Holy Spirit can transform the heart of the hearer to become good soil for the gospel (see Acts 1:8; 1 Corinthians 12:3). In fear, the apostle Peter denied Jesus three times on the night of His arrest just before His crucifixion. After Pentecost, the Holy Spirit emboldened Peter to proclaim the gospel to the same crowds who killed Jesus (Acts 2:14-41, 4:7-12).

Christ-followers don't need slick presentations to share the gospel. They need only to be led by the Holy Spirit. The apostle Paul proclaims this.

> I was with you in weakness and in fear and in much trembling, and my message and my preaching were not in persuasive words of wisdom, but in demonstration of the Spirit and of power, so that your faith would not rest on the wisdom of men, but on the power of God (1 Corinthians 2:3-5).

Evangelism is anointed as Christ-followers are in tune with the Holy Spirit and led by Him. For this to happen, they must be vessels properly prepared for His use by the Spirit (see 2 Timothy 2:21), not squelching the Spirit's presence in their lives (1 Thessalonians 5:19). Every time the gospel message is presented, the hearer should be led to a decision point: i.e., are you ready to place your faith and trust in Jesus? That said, it is a misunderstanding that evangelism means "sealing the deal" on every encounter; i.e., that the recipient accepts Jesus or we've failed. This is not biblical, as the apostle Paul states.

> I planted, Apollos watered, but God was causing the growth. So then neither the one who plants nor the one who waters is anything, but God who causes the growth (1 Corinthians 3:6, 7).

God often provides multiple opportunities for people to receive Him. Some people accept Jesus the first time they hear the gospel, as was the case for hearers of Peter's proclamation at Pentecost (see Acts 2:14-41). In others, it is a process that takes months or years. The apostle Paul is a prime example, having heard the gospel from the martyr Stephen (Acts chapter 7) but only coming to faith in Christ after his Damascus road experience (Acts 9:1-19).

Accepting Christ is the most critical decision of our lives, so when we evangelize, we shouldn't be disappointed if the other person doesn't come to faith at the end of every interaction. We are all on a faith journey, and a Christ-follower's evangelistic interaction may be just one of many gospel intrusions by God into that person's life. Christ-followers are called to present the gospel, then leave the outcome to God.

Such was the case for me. God brought the gospel to me through many people. A faithful mother. Numerous church ministers during my youth. My wife Karren. When a Christ-following physician at the University of Alabama where I was doing my pulmonary residency invited me to an early morning Bible study, God had already reached out to me through numerous people and circumstances. Most importantly, my heart had been changed by the Holy Spirit (see 1 Corinthians 12:3).

I attended that Bible study, and Dr. Frank Sutton and another attending physician befriended me. I witnessed them living out the gospel. I heard the gospel proclaimed loudly and clearly in their words and in their Bible study curriculum, *Design for Discipleship*, by the

Navigators. This time, the seed of the gospel message took root. I have never been the same. Praise God!

Soon after I came to faith in Jesus, I was exuberant to share the gospel with others. As I presented the gospel to one man about salvation through faith in Jesus Christ, he politely but firmly ended the conversation. We never discussed the gospel again. Several years later, after Karren and I had moved to Charlottesville, he called me and informed me that he had accepted Jesus. Since then he has been an incredible servant of God in many capacities. The Holy Spirit guided him to faith through many other Christ-followers after we had last talked about the gospel.

C.S. Lewis was likely the most influential Christian writer of the twentieth century. His journey to faith was not easy. An avowed atheist in earlier life, Lewis came to believe in God in 1929, yet it would take additional time for him to place his faith in Jesus.[2] This occurred on September 28, 1931, as he went with friends to visit the Whipsnade Zoo. He didn't have faith when they started the journey, but by the time they reached the zoo, he believed in Jesus Christ.

EVANGELIZING PEOPLE WE KNOW AND DON'T KNOW

Without question, God places each person in unique spheres of influence to share the gospel with people we know. We should all prioritize evangelizing our children, grandchildren, and even great-grandchildren if God extends our life. Evangelizing people we know is often termed *relational evangelism*. But this shouldn't be our only evangelism. For one, if we share the gospel only with people we know, one question becomes how well we have to know them before sharing. Taken to extreme, this could mean investing years of relationship-building before sharing the first sentence about the gospel. An additional trap is that waiting for a relationship can result in reluctance to share the gospel for fear of adversely affecting the relationship.

Sharing the gospel with people we don't know has been termed *cold evangelism* as in the idiom of doing something "cold turkey." But there is nothing cold about sharing the gospel. A better term is *spontaneous evangelism.* Weary from travel, Jesus was sitting alone at Jacob's well in Samaria when a woman approached to draw water (see John 4:7-26). Jesus initiated a conversation. By the end of that talk, she was running to her village to bring others to meet the Messiah.

One form of spontaneous evangelism I practice is calling up people I don't know well and asking if they'd like to get together over coffee to talk about life's big questions. Does God exist? If so, what does He want from us? In other words, I invite people I barely know for an evangelism session over coffee!

When I'm in line at a coffee shop, I ask the barista if they know for sure they are going to Heaven. If the ensuing conversation makes clear they haven't accepted Jesus, I will briefly share the gospel. As they hand me my coffee, I give them a pocket New Testament[3] and suggest they read the Gospel of John. I've also participated in an evangelism booth at our local county fair where we share the gospel with people who approach the booth.

Jesus frequently shared the message of salvation with people He did not know; therefore, His followers should do likewise. Nor should sharing the gospel depend on the level of response we receive. In *spontaneous evangelism* we may never see the person we are talking with again. But *relational evangelism* is by definition sharing with someone in the Christ-follower's sphere of influence. Writing off another person because they indicate they aren't interested in the gospel message is not displaying *agape.* Continue showing the person unconditional love.

This is where the motives of a Christ-follower become quite evident. Our interest should be in the person, not merely accumulating them as a successful "notch on our belt" in sharing the gospel. Of course, there needs to be a balance. If the Christ-follower is to evangelize effectively, they can't develop in-depth social relationships with every person with whom they've shared the gospel. We must also be careful not to harass, with recurrent gospel conversations, those who've indicated they have no interest. A time does come when a Christ-follower needs to lovingly move on and trust God to use others to bring the gospel to this person.

COMPLACENCY IN EVANGELISM

We've discussed complacency within the church in both disciple-making and prayer. Complacency about sharing the gospel, whether with people we know or don't know, is another widespread problem within the church. Nor is this a new phenomenon. Jesus reminded His disciples that the harvest is plentiful but the workers few (see Matthew 9:37, 38).

Bottom line: we humans are good at wriggling out of things that are difficult or possibly unpleasant. When God called Moses to lead His people out of Egypt, Moses offered objection after objection as to why he wasn't the person for the task (see Exodus 3:11, 4:1, 10, 13). After his last expression of reluctance, God's anger "burned" against Moses (Exodus 4:14). I wonder how often God has been angry with us for our unwillingness to share the gospel with others. Ultimately, God used Moses in a great and mighty way, but Moses had to overcome his reluctance, likely motivated by fear and lack of trust in God. The same is true for us.

CHAPTER TWENTY-THREE APPLICATION

DISCUSSION QUESTIONS

- Discuss Bible verses exhorting Jesus' followers to share the gospel and make disciples.
- How does the phrase "as you go" help in understanding the Great Commission? Discuss.
- What is the admonition God gave the prophet Ezekiel regarding not warning people of the coming wrath when they do not reconcile with God?
- What is the difference between evangelism and making disciples? Discuss.
- Why is the Holy Spirit required in evangelism?
- Has a Christ-follower failed in evangelism if the person doesn't accept Christ at the time of the gospel presentation?
- Are Christ-followers called to share the gospel only with people they know?

SELF-EVALUATION

- Which best describes your evangelism of others in the past twelve months? Have you shared the gospel with multiple people each month? At least one to two people in the past year? You've shared your faith in Jesus but not in the past year? You're trained in evangelism, but just don't do it? You've never shared the gospel with anyone?

MEMORY VERSE

And they overcame him [the accuser] because of the blood of the Lamb and because of the word of their testimony, and they did not love their life even when faced with death (Revelations 12:11).

CHAPTER TWENTY-FOUR

DEFENSES OFFERED FOR NOT EVANGELIZING

"The Christian ideal has not been tried and found wanting. It has been found difficult; and left untried."[1]
—G.K. Chesterton

Let's look at some common defenses for an unwillingness to share the gospel. These are not legitimate excuses. The underlying cause for most of them is the first.

"I'm afraid of what people will think or do." Too many Christ-followers are concerned about repercussions if they share the gospel. In *Honest Evangelism*,[2] Rico Tice describes his heart attitude that led to him not sharing the gospel with his unsaved grandmother in the last weeks of her life. He selfishly valued the esteem of his family more than his grandmother's eternal destiny. Sharing the gospel will undoubtedly cause some people to think less of us. This may break relationships, affecting occupations, business interactions, social interactions, and more. Even worse, some may be imprisoned or martyred for sharing their faith. Jesus told His disciples:

> "You will be hated by all because of My name, but it is the one who has endured to the end who will be saved" (Matthew 10:22).

In 2000, I participated in a mission trip to central India. We were told of a Christian missionary who'd been murdered in the area by the radical Hindu paramilitary organization Rashtriya Swayamsevak Sangh (RSS). I will never forget sitting in a worship service packed with people while the preacher, Pastor John Hall, exclaimed, "There is something more powerful than the RSS, and His name is Jesus Christ!" Instinctively, I shrank in my seat for less visibility, acutely aware of the danger that RSS members might have covertly infiltrated the audience.

Jesus was killed two millennia ago for proclaiming He was the Messiah. Today, people are still being killed globally for their faith in Jesus. In the industrialized west, threat of actual physical harm for proclaiming the gospel remains low. A greater issue for most of us is a desire to protect our image, employment, or relationships. Sadly, there are even Christ-followers who value these things more than honoring our Lord and showing our love for Him and others by sharing the gospel.

As Christ-followers, we need to understand that the road to follow Jesus is not an easy, prosperous existence lived as we desire. It is a call to do the difficult thing, the hard thing. One of those difficult things is rejecting esteem from friends, family, or the world and valuing only the esteem of God the Father and Son. It is about loving the Father and Son above ourselves and being obedient to their commandments. It is about loving others above ourselves to the point of accepting the consequences of evangelism so they can escape eternal punishment. Jesus warned about the danger of denying Him to others.

> "Everyone who confesses Me before men, I will also confess him before My Father who is in Heaven. But whoever denies

> Me before men, I will also deny him before My Father who is in heaven" (Matthew 10:32, 33).

We must not shrink back from evangelizing. Jesus spoke of the apostle Paul after Paul's encounter on the Damascus road: "I will show him how much he must suffer for My name's sake" (Acts 9:16). And indeed Paul did suffer greatly for the gospel of Christ, but he did not shrink back. He affirmed he was not ashamed of the gospel, for it is God's power to all for salvation (see Romans 1:16). The critical point here is that God's kingdom is advanced, and the evil one is overcome through evangelism.

> And they overcame him [the evil one] because of the blood of the Lamb and because of the word of their testimony, and they did not love their life even when faced with death (Revelation 12:11).

In other words, being willing to testify to the gospel of salvation through Christ's sacrifice on the cross even at the cost of their own lives. In the same way, the road for a Christ-follower today is not an easy one. On the contrary, following Jesus will result in suffering and persecution along with loss of esteem by the world. Yet in the midst of tribulation, we have our Lord's promise.

> "These things I [Jesus] have spoken to you, so that in Me you may have peace. In the world you have tribulation, but take courage; I have overcome the world" (John 16:33).

Until the Christ-follower gets his or her heart in the right place, there will be abundant other excuses for wriggling out of evangelism, many of which are discussed below.

"We live in a 'Christian' nation and most people are already Christians." Some think evangelism is something done by missionaries to people groups considered still unreached by the gospel such as majority Hindu, Buddhist, Muslim, and atheist nations, or remote animistic tribes. This is a lie from the evil one. Increasingly, once

Christianized nations such as Europe and the Americas are turning their backs on God and actively rebelling against His commandments. God's commandments are decried as "wrong" while practices that are sin and abominations to Him are called "right" (see Isaiah 5:20; 1 Corinthians 6:9, 10; 2 Timothy 3:2-5). In the post-Christian industrialized west, biblical illiteracy is soaring while church attendance continues to decline. Evangelism is needed in nations that still consider themselves culturally "Christian" as much as in places where the gospel has not yet been shared.

"God has already predestined those who will be saved, so there is no need to evangelize." Some mistakenly believe that the following words of the apostle Paul preclude evangelism because those prechosen will be saved, and those who aren't can't come to faith.

> He [God] chose us in Him before the foundation of the world, that we would be holy and blameless before Him. In love He predestined us to adoption as sons through Jesus Christ to Himself, according to the kind intention of His will (Ephesians 1:4, 5).

The alleged contradiction of the commandment to evangelize and the doctrine of pre-election can be resolved by the following viewpoint: it is God's will that there are elect who will be saved (Ephesians 1:4, 5). God has also ordained the means to His will; i.e., by His followers sharing the good news of the gospel with them so they would come to faith (see Romans 10:14).

In other words, as in previously discussed scriptural mysteries that may seem contradictory to our human minds but not to God, Scripture supports both predestination and the mandate for evangelism. A Christ-follower cannot know whom God has prechosen. Regardless of where we may fall in understanding and reconciling pre-election and evangelism, our calling to evangelize others with the gospel is unambiguous.

"The Great Commission was for the original disciples." Jesus did indeed use the twelve disciples to launch His church (see Acts 1:24-26, 5:41-42). But the dramatic growth of the first-century church went far beyond evangelism carried out by the twelve. This was a grassroots movement where new converts shared the good news with others, who in turn shared it with others, and so on. Just a sample of New Testament saints we see evangelizing include Paul and Barnabas (Acts 11:22-26), Timothy (Philippians 2:22), Priscilla, Aquila, and Apollos (Acts 18:24-28), Epaphras (Colossians 1:7), Andronicus and Junias (Romans 16:7), and many, many more. This includes Mark and Luke, who weren't of the original twelve but, between them, wrote two of the Gospels and the book of Acts.

Jesus' Great Commission in Matthew 28:18-20 is to all Christ-followers always "even to the end of the age" (Matthew 28:20), not just the original twelve disciples during the first years of the church.

"Evangelism is not in my gift set." Another misunderstanding is that evangelism is a specific spiritual gift assigned to certain people, so if we don't have that gift, we aren't called to evangelize. A common passage cited to support this is one we've seen already.

> And He gave some as apostles, and some as prophets, and some as evangelists, and some as pastors and teachers, for the equipping of the saints for the work of service, to the building up of the body of Christ (Ephesians 4:11, 12).

But this passage also makes clear these are offices of church leadership Jesus appoints to train the laity. Evangelists are to teach the saints to do evangelism, not be the only people sharing the gospel. Pastors and teachers equip the saints to do discipleship, not be the only ones discipling others. Nowhere in Scripture is the exhortation to fulfill the Great Commission through evangelism and disciple-making restricted to those with a special gift. For every follower of Jesus, fulfilling the Great Commission is an act of obedience.

"I'm not spiritually mature or holy enough." Another cause for reluctance to evangelize is believing we lack sufficient spiritual maturity or knowledge of Scripture to share the gospel. But growing to Christlikeness includes boldly claiming the work of Jesus on the cross to reconcile all who will hear. Sharing the gospel with others is a sacred calling for every Christ-follower that also contributes to our spiritual growth.

Christ-followers must recognize that we know more than we may think we know. Every authentic Christ-follower was born again by hearing the gospel. It's not that complicated. We don't need to be salespersons by vocation. We just need to tell our own personal story of coming to faith and point the glory to God, as the apostle Paul wrote.

> For Christ did not send me to baptize, but to preach the gospel, not in cleverness of speech, so that the cross of Christ would not be made void (1 Corinthians 1:17).

That said, an evangelism training course can be helpful in building confidence. For many, evangelizing in tandem with a more experienced Christ-follower also helps allay anxiety when sharing the gospel. Early in my Christian walk, I was part of a "spontaneous evangelism" team that knocked on doors and shared the gospel with strangers. This was very helpful in overcoming my hesitation about sharing the gospel.

Just keep in mind that reading, talking about, and training for evangelism doesn't fulfill the Great Commission. It only helps prepare you for the assignment. Nor is there an exception in Scripture that evangelism is for "when you have become spiritually mature" or "those without sin." Getting out there and actually sharing the gospel is a calling of all who follow and love God. There is great spiritual joy that rewards those who give witness of the gospel to others.

"I witness by my life, not words." I was encouraging a small group to share the gospel when a man spoke up to claim evangelism is simply how we live our lives in front of others. He supported this with a quote sometimes attributed to St. Francis of Assisi: “Preach the gospel at all times, and use words only when necessary.” In fact, the source of this quote remains unknown.[3] But it is deceptive precisely because it contains an element of truth.

Yes, people are often watching Christ-followers for consistency in how our lives measure up to our proclaimed belief in Jesus Christ. But we are deceived if we believe we are fulfilling the Great Commission solely by living good lives in front of unbelievers. Nor are displaying crosses, fish symbols, Christian axioms, or Bible verses on clothing, bumper stickers, or license plate inscriptions sufficient for evangelism. In fact, such displays may even profane the gospel when those displaying them exhibit actions inconsistent with Jesus’ life and commandments.

At this same meeting, the same man introduced a second misconception: that Christ-followers should only share the gospel if someone asks them. He supported this assertion by citing the apostle Peter.

> Sanctify Christ as Lord in your hearts, always being ready to make a defense to everyone who asks you to give an account for the hope that is in you, yet with gentleness and reverence (1 Peter 3:15).

There is, again, an element of truth in the idea that every Christ-follower should be prepared to share the gospel if someone asks. But Peter wasn’t saying here that you should *only* give an account of the gospel if you are asked. After all, Peter himself did so boldly and publicly (see Acts chapters 2, 3). To suggest evangelism should be done only when people ask is a great disservice to the Great Commission—and to the immortal souls of others. If someone is asleep at night and doesn’t realize their house is on fire, do you wait for them to ask, or do you bang on the door and tell them?

The onus is on Christ-followers who know the peril to take the initiative in pointing out to unsaved persons that they are sinners and in enmity with God. We take action with words to tell others how to be saved from God's wrath by repenting of sin and accepting Christ's free gift of salvation through faith alone. Evangelism is through sharing a gospel of words, not just how we live our lives. This is why Paul wrote to the Roman church that salvation comes from confessing and believing, which in turn comes from hearing, and hearing comes from preaching (see Romans 10:8-17).

Imagine what the first-century church would have looked like if the apostles had adopted such a false notion of evangelism. We find no evidence in Scripture that the disciples witnessed just by how they lived their lives or only when someone asked. On the contrary, the book of Acts is filled with bold, proactive verbal evangelism. In consequence, the gospel spread like wildfire. Moreover, how would false doctrines and behavior issues in the early church have been addressed if the apostles only lived their faith versus actually speaking it? Evangelism and discipleship both involve using words to proclaim the gospel and teach God's Word.

> We proclaim Him [Jesus Christ], admonishing every man and teaching every man with all wisdom, so that we may present every man complete in Christ (Colossians 1:28).

We must consistently demonstrate the power of the gospel by how we live, but that alone is insufficient. We must share the gospel with others with our words. It is not "either/or" but "both/and." Sharing the gospel with others is by words, not just how we live among them.

"It is improper to foist my spiritual beliefs on other people." The Constitution of the United States and many other democratic nations include a provision that prevents the "state" from imposing a specific religion on citizens. This came about initially as a reaction to oppression suffered due to the imposition, at government level, of a particular religion, not to mention the countless wars fought for centuries between proponents of different branches of the same religions—Catholics versus Protestants, Church of England versus Puritans, Sunni Islam versus Shiite Islam. But in recent decades, freedom of religion and tolerance of other people's spiritual beliefs have been increasingly subverted to an incorrect assertion that people shouldn't share their spiritual beliefs at all.

Spiritual proselytizing is defined as converting someone from another religion to their own. Early in my career at the University of Virginia, a colleague accused me of proselytizing because I'd told him I prayed with some patients. The truth is that a relationship with God should be a high priority in all conversations if we truly love people and want them to escape God's wrath. One morning over coffee, a brother in Christ and I were discussing sharing the gospel with the unsaved. Suddenly, his eyes filled with tears. He was overwhelmed by what awaits those who haven't been reconciled to God through Jesus.

That should be the heart that all of us have. The most important conversation we will ever have with another human being is about faith in Jesus for forgiveness of sins and reconciliation with God. It is out of love for people that we share the gospel, as Paul reminded the new believers in Thessalonica.

> Having so fond an affection for you, we were well-pleased to impart to you not only the gospel of God but also our own lives, because you had become very dear to us (1 Thessalonians 2:8).

That said, it is essential to be considerate and enter into spiritual discussions only if the other person is willing. I always ask permission before discussing faith matters with another person. If the person says "no," I graciously accept their response and respect their wishes.

"In my vocation, it would be inappropriate." There are certain vocational circumstances or professional relationships where a Christ-follower should take care in sharing their faith. Even if you ask permission, the other person may not feel free to decline due to concern their response may jeopardize their professional status. As a professor of medicine, I was cautious in sharing my faith with medical students or physicians-in-training where they might feel declining an offer to discuss spiritual matters could jeopardize their grade or evaluation. The same situation existed when I was division chief for faculty and staff regarding those over whom I had direct supervision and rendered periodic performance evaluations.

Some strongly oppose healthcare workers ever having a spiritual discussion with their patients. I view patients differently. Illnesses of the body also affect the mind and spirit. Born again healthcare workers bring not only our God-given intellect and medical judgment but the hope of the gospel and fruit of the Spirit that provides peace and endurance amidst suffering. They also bring prayer, an additional valuable means God has given to stand in the gap for patients and to provide comfort and healing.

Through my five decades as a physician, I have prayed with countless patients. Out of respect for the patient's autonomy, my practice has always been to ask permission before discussing spiritual things or praying with someone. I can count on one hand the times a patient turned down an offer of prayer. When they allowed me to do so, the effects of prayer were astounding.

Any time we offer prayer or a discussion of spiritual matters, it should be done with gentleness and respect (see 1 Peter 3:15). We need to be sensitive to circumstances where a person might feel they are in a bind. Forcing our spiritual beliefs on someone when they don't want to hear them is not respectful. When we do ask permission, most people are willing to have the conversation or allow the Christ-follower to pray for them.

"My church doesn't emphasize evangelism or have an active evangelism program." Today more than ever, God's Word is available in a myriad of translations on paper and electronically. Yet even in churches, a high percentage of people are scripturally illiterate. Many believe they will hear all they need to know from the pulpit. If your pastor doesn't emphasize scriptural mandates for spiritual growth to maturity and evangelism, are you free from God's commandments? No!

In the eighteenth year of King Josiah's reign over Judah, he sent a man named Shaphan to the high priest Hilkiah with instructions to proceed with repairs to the temple (see 2 Kings chapters 22, 23). During this interaction, Hilkiah told Shaphan he had found the book of God's law, which the priests had lost over previous ungodly generations. Taking the book to the king, Shaphan read it aloud. When King Josiah heard how much Judah had strayed from obedience to God's law, he tore his robe and repented, leading the entire nation to do so. Yet God still punished Judah because of their ignorance of God's law.

God has made His Word available to each of us. We must examine the Scriptures to see what they say and apply them to our lives. Don't think for a moment God won't hold you accountable because your pastor doesn't faithfully present the mandate for evangelism in the Bible from the pulpit. Losing God's law didn't free Judah from its commandments. If your church doesn't emphasize God's commandments for evangelism, discipleship, and growth to spiritual maturity, you are still personally responsible to obey them.

"I just don't have enough time." People become time-poor in many ways. Electronic devices are one enemy that eats up people's discretionary time. Most institutional churches have many good programs, but that doesn't mean the Christ-follower must participate in all of them. When we say we don't have time for evangelism, we are saying that all the activities in which we've invested our discretionary time have greater priority than evangelism. One day, God will ask us to account for how we've used this precious commodity He gives us (see 2 Corinthians 5:10). We must be good stewards, using our time wisely for God's kingdom and the harvest.

CHAPTER TWENTY-FOUR APPLICATION

DISCUSSION QUESTIONS

- What is the most common reason for reluctance in sharing the gospel with others? Why is this?
- Why is evangelism not obviated by Scripture describing pre-election (see Ephesians 1:4)?
- Is evangelism just for church pastors and leaders or also for lay people who follow Jesus? Does the commandment in the Great Commission apply to you? Discuss Ephesians 4:11-16.
- Discuss the misconception in the saying, "Preach the gospel at all times, and use words only when necessary." What is the proper way to present the gospel?
- What is the fallacy in the defense, "It is improper to foist my spiritual beliefs on other people"?

SELF-EVALUATION

- Read Rico Tice's powerful book on evangelism in the twenty-first century, *Honest Evangelism.*[2]
- Are you where you need to be in the practice of evangelism? If not, which of the defenses outlined are responsible? If your reservation is not addressed by this chapter, you should discuss your concern with a mature Christ-follower or one of the pastors in your church.

MEMORY VERSES

And He said to them, "Go into all the world and preach the gospel to all creation. He who has believed and has been baptized shall be saved; but he who has disbelieved shall be condemned" (Mark 16:15, 16).

CHAPTER TWENTY-FIVE

ADDRESSING OBJECTIONS TO THE GOSPEL

"Some were being persuaded by the things spoken, but others would not believe."
ACTS 28:24

When we present the gospel, we will typically encounter a spectrum of objections. I will list some below. Those given are, again, not an exhaustive list but cover the most common objections I've come across. Let's look at each individually along with a biblical response to the specific objection that you can offer the person.

"It's unfair!" Some reject the gospel because they claim it is unfair. The unfairness charge is usually an excuse. The real issue is the person's unwillingness to submit their life to Jesus. Others object to spiritual condemnation of those who have never heard of Jesus. People often think of closed nations without religious freedom or tribal groups still out of contact with the modern world. But surprising numbers in developed nations with full access to Christian literature, TV, radio, social media, and institutional churches have never heard the gospel.

This should motivate us to evangelize! But even if someone has never heard of Jesus, Scripture states they've been given evidence of God's existence.

> For since the creation of the world His invisible attributes, His eternal power and divine nature, have been clearly seen, being understood through what has been made, so that they are without excuse (Romans 1:20).

A colleague once told me, "I can't believe in a God who would condemn someone to hell because of the family, and religion, they were born into."

It's true people generally adopt the religious beliefs of their family and community. Someone born in a Hindu family will likely be Hindu; in a Muslim family, all things being equal, a Muslim. But it's important to keep in mind Jesus' own words.

> "I am the way, and the truth, and the life; no one comes to the Father but through Me" (John 14:6).

This didn't originate from arbitrary human minds. Jesus said it! Faith in Jesus is clearly based on the authenticity of Jesus. God stated, "I, even I, am the LORD, and there is no savior besides Me" (Isaiah 43:11). The apostle Peter proclaimed:

> "There is salvation in no one else; for there is no other name under heaven that has been given among men by which we must be saved" (Acts 4:12).

One response to this objection is to ask the person stating it about their plan for dealing with their sin. Most will acknowledge they've committed sins that have violated God's commandments. It is then appropriate to query what means other religions provide for the forgiveness of sins. Did Mohamed die for sin? Did Buddha? Do the Hindus have a method for forgiveness? No! Out of love, God sent His Son to reconcile us to Him through Christ's death on the cross. If Jesus doesn't redeem us, we will suffer the penalty for our sins—spiritual death. There is a verse for anyone who is obstinate about unfairness.

> There is a way which seems right to a man, but its end is the way of death (Proverbs 14:12).

"I'm just going to be as good as I can." This deception is the top response when I ask someone in the U.S. why God should let them into Heaven. If they're as good as they can be, they hope, a good moral life will get them into Heaven. There's just one problem, which we've already discussed. God does not vacate the death penalty for sin based on good works (see Romans 3:20; Galatians 2:16; Ephesians 2:9; Titus 3:5). More so, breaking one of God's laws makes us guilty of all of them no matter how much other good we've accomplished.

> For whoever keeps the whole law and yet stumbles in one point, he has become guilty of all (James 2:10).

If their answer to how they plan to deal with their sin remains the good things they've done and strive to do, ask how that works when they get a speeding ticket. He or she needs to understand a point we discussed earlier. The penalty for their sin can be on only one of two persons—on themselves or on Jesus. If they haven't placed their faith and trust in Jesus, when they die their sin will still be on them, and they will undergo spiritual death. Never forget: at all times, try to gently persuade, but never argue.

"I have never sinned." While most people will acknowledge they are sinners, for those who deny they've ever broken God's law, a series of noncombative questions will quickly reveal to the person that they are sinners. Have they ever told a lie? Been unkind? Stolen something? Coveted someone's possessions, talents, or position in life? Committed adultery or even lust?

Once they've admitted to having broken any one of God's laws, you can proceed with presentation of the gospel. It's important to lead with Scriptures that show all have sinned and the consequences of that sin (see Romans 3:12, 23; 6:23). If they still don't acknowledge being a sinner, reveal to them what the Bible says about those who won't admit to sin.

> If we say that we have no sin, we are deceiving ourselves and the truth is not in us (1 John 1:8).

"The Bible is full of inconsistencies and errors." On occasion when sharing the gospel, a person will immediately raise the objection that the Bible is just a collection of old writings rife with errors and contradictions, implying that only the naïve and gullible would believe anything from such a book. This is a clever strategy since, if your gospel presentation is based solely on Scripture, such a claim can presume to stop it abruptly. This person has become a judge presiding over the discussion, and in their mind the Bible can't be entered into evidence.

These allegations are, again, typically a smoke screen. The real issue is the person doesn't want to surrender their will to God or themselves to the lordship of Jesus. But they should be given the benefit of the doubt that their concern is sincere. Ask in a respectful way what they believe is an error or inconsistency in the Bible. If they can't cite something, ask permission to continue, but change your presentation to your personal experience with Jesus Christ, which no person can ever refute.

Apologetics is a rational defense of the Christian faith, including the validity of Scripture. If the person who raises this objection can give an example of something in Scripture they think is an error or inconsistency, address it if you have an answer. If you don't know the answer, tell them so, then ask if you can look into their concern and have a subsequent discussion. The presentation must continue to be respectful and gentle no matter how harsh the criticism. While a reasonable approach, the use of apologetics doesn't work in my experience because the person's objections against the Bible aren't a matter of intellect but an insincere heart.

"A loving God wouldn't allow evil and suffering." The first step is to understand that the definition of evil is theological and to dissociate it from suffering. We must understand that evil isn't whatever is currently considered "morally bad" since that changes over time with moral relativism. Evil is the antonym of good, and good is defined in absolute terms as referring to God's character, will, and declarations. Anything not in line with God's being, character, purity, and rules is evil. It is sin. Sin and evil are intertwined.

We also need to understand that some things are not evil themselves but a consequence of sin and evil. Is a tornado that kills hundreds evil? Is *Streptococcus pneumoniae,* the most common cause of bacterial pneumonia, evil? No! These are downstream maladies from living in a world cursed by God for sin and rebellion against Him. The same can be said for human suffering. Heinous actions instigated by evil in human hearts can certainly cause suffering, but suffering is the outcome of evil rather than evil in itself.

A response to this objection is to gently emphasize that responsibility for evil rests entirely on the shoulders of humankind (see Romans 5:12). God originally created humankind to be in fellowship with Him, but He also gave Adam and Eve free will to do good or evil. What did the first man and woman do with their free will? They rebelled against God and sinned (Genesis chapter 3). Thereafter, humankind was hopelessly corrupted, dead in sin.

None of us can fully realize how repugnant sin is to God. We are so focused on God's kindness to us through His mercy and grace that we become alarmed and incredulous at evil, pain, and suffering. God's pronouncement of punishment for sin was also full of mercy and grace. The human race was not obliterated. Even so, that first sin set things in motion. The ground had to be cultivated for food. Hardships had to be endured, including heat, cold, pain, suffering, disease, and physical death.

God is not and has never been the sponsor of evil. The author of Job vehemently declares, "Far be it from God to do wickedness, and from the Almighty to do wrong" (Job 34:10). On the contrary, God hates evil (see Proverbs 6:16-19) and brings great punishment on evildoers (Isaiah 31:2; Micah 2:1). The Bible admonishes us to follow His example.

> Hate evil, love good, and establish justice in the gate! Perhaps the Lord God of hosts may be gracious to the remnant of Joseph (Amos 5:15).

"The church is full of hypocrites." The lives of some people affiliated with the institutional church can sometimes be indistinguishable from worldly behavior. Joining a local organized church doesn't make a person legitimately born again. The evil one uses such counterfeits to blaspheme the gospel message. Jesus doesn't call us to follow counterfeit Christ-followers, He calls us to follow Himself. Careful inspection of any church will reveal sin, including among legitimately born again Christ-followers. This is because we are all sinners. The process of sanctification is slow and often messy. For this reason, Christ-followers are called to have forbearance for each other as we grow in holiness.

"Religions are just a psychological crutch." Some will argue that Christianity is just an emotional crutch people resort to out of angst over the meaning of life and fear of what will happen when they die. This may be true of human-constructed religions. Many people experience anxiety about this life and fear as to their fate in a possible afterlife. The human heart has a yearning for emotional contentment. Through the millennia, it has sought relief in countless ways, including alcohol, nicotine, opioids and other substances, sexual addiction, other forms of pleasure-seeking (hedonism), and excessive work.

But this doesn't disprove a Creator who loves us and wants a relationship with us. God designed us for a relationship with Him, which is the only thing that can fulfill our heart's yearning and give true contentment. The human heart can only be completed by union with Jesus through the Holy Spirit. Seeking alternate solutions for emotional contentment doesn't invalidate the faith of Christ-followers or prove it is just a psychological crutch. In contrast, it shows that true joy, peace, and contentment can only come from a relationship with God.

"Miracles can't be possible." Throughout Scripture, we see phenomena that defy natural laws. Moses parted the Red Sea for the exodus of the Israelite nation to the Promised Land (see Exodus 14:21, 22). Jesus turned water into wine at a wedding celebration and raised a dead man back to life (John 2:1-11, 11:17-44). The Holy Spirit raised Jesus back to life after His death on the cross (Romans 8:11). What do we make of these and other miracles described in the Bible?

A substantial part of my work in academic medicine was to perform scientific research. I've heard colleagues who are Christ-followers give beautiful descriptions of what motivates their own pursuit of scientific discovery. They are intrigued by being able to peel back a new layer of understanding in God's design, which Scripture tells us our feeble minds can barely understand.

> For now we see in a mirror dimly, but then face to face; now I know in part, but then I will know fully just as I also have been fully known (1 Corinthians 13:12).

The more we peel back the layers, the more we recognize an intelligence in design that is far beyond our understanding. My biochemistry class as a second-year medical student instilled in me an overwhelming conviction that there is a Designer of everything that exists. The complexity of the proteins synthesized by the liver alone that are required for proper organ function and human survival is staggering.

It takes arrogance to hold to an ideology that the Creator who created all things (see John 1:3) can't suspend His natural laws for His purposes, then reinstitute them when He chooses. If God can make life from nothing, He can certainly reinstitute the life of someone who has died, push back tons of seawater to provide a land bridge, or form additional molecules in water to turn it into wine.

Nicodemus, the Pharisee who visited Jesus by night, testified to His deity because of the things Jesus could do that were beyond human ability (see John 3:2). The true miracle is that such a Supreme Being would care enough to walk among us in human flesh, speak to us about His Father, Himself, and the Holy Spirit, and love us so much He would die a horrific, painful death to reconcile us to Himself (John 1:14).

One additional point should be made when someone raises this objection. God gives us ample evidence of Himself, but He doesn't give us all the evidence. He demands faith without having absolute evidence.

> And without faith it is impossible to please Him, for he who comes to God must believe that He is and that He is a rewarder of those who seek Him (Hebrews 11:6).

"I am too great a sinner for God to forgive me." I have encountered people who sincerely believe God could never forgive them for things they've done in their lives. Several points should be made to such a person. First, there is no spectrum of sin from minor to major. All sin alienates us from God and necessitated His Son going to the cross to redeem us. Second, God wants no one to die but all people to receive salvation (see 1 Timothy 2:4). Also, people sometimes believe God can't forgive them because they have a "good works" understanding of salvation. They need to understand that salvation is by faith in Jesus alone and such faith washes away all sins.

> "Though your sins are as scarlet, they will be as white as snow" (Isaiah 1:18).

> If we confess our sins, He is faithful and righteous to forgive us our sins and to cleanse us from all unrighteousness (1 John 1:9).

For two reasons, it is important to gently caution people of the urgency in making this decision. First, the uncertainty and frailty of life.

Any of us may die within the day from something. Second, the human heart doesn't become more receptive to the gospel over time. Rather, it hardens and becomes more resistant. Any person needs to respond to God's free gift the hour they truly hear His voice.

> Today if you hear His voice, do not harden your hearts as when they provoked Me, as in the day of trial in the wilderness (Hebrews 3:7, 8).

"I don't want to give up things I know God views as sin." Some people honestly acknowledge their reluctance to accept the gospel is because of what they would have to give up. They need to be reminded of Jesus' exhortation that every person should count the cost before deciding to follow Him (see Luke 14:25-33). Part of that cost is a conscious decision to depart from all sin in their life (2 Timothy 2:19). Jesus put it this way.

> "For what does it profit a man to gain the whole world, and forfeit his soul?" (Mark 8:36)

They need gently reminded that God is calling them to do something they may feel like they don't want to do, to repent of their sins and turn to Jesus Christ and accept His free gift of salvation offered in the gospel. Only through the power of Jesus can they break their attraction to sin and be freed of its penalty.

"I don't believe in hell." The person offering this can be asked their understanding of the Bible verse stating that the wages of sin is death (see Romans 6:23). Since we all undergo physical death, this must refer to a spiritual death, which at the very least means separation from God in the life to come. The Bible, however, is more specific.

> But for the cowardly and unbelieving and abominable and murderers and immoral persons and sorcerers and idolaters and all liars, their part will be in the lake that burns with fire and brimstone, which is the second death (Revelation 21:8).

Since Adam and Eve, the default destiny for all people is an eternal lake of fire unless one comes to faith in Jesus for forgiveness of sin and redemption from this destiny. Once we die, our destination to Heaven or hell cannot be altered. Jesus told the story of a poor man who died and went to Heaven and a rich man who died and went to hell (see Luke 16:19-31). Somehow, the rich man was able to see the poor man in Heaven and pleaded for him to be sent to cool his tongue with water. The rich man was informed that the chasm between Heaven and hell was too great. Then the rich man pleaded that someone be sent to warn his five living brothers. He was told that the brothers had Moses and the prophets—i.e., the Bible—as ample warning. If they weren't convinced by this, they wouldn't be persuaded even by someone returning to life from being dead.

"I don't discuss religion or politics lest someone judge me." A longtime acquaintance once shut down a conversation on spiritual matters with the statement that he didn't discuss either religion or politics lest other people use his responses to judge him. My approach in this is to be respectful of their position and trust that God will bring some other person to tap their shoulder for the gospel at some later time.

"I'm a church member." This person needs reminded that joining a church isn't what provides salvation; what does is faith in Jesus (see John 1:12; Ephesians 2:8, 9). Scripture is clear that there will be those who consider themselves righteous who will not be with the Father and Son in Heaven (see Matthew 25:31-46).

THE BLESSINGS OF EVANGELISM

American pastor and professor of theology Jack Miller emphasizes the blessings of presenting the gospel. He expands on the acclaimed quote from D.T. Niles about evangelism being one beggar telling another where to find bread.

> Evangelism is also one hungry beggar eagerly eating the bread and being changed by it, and then telling the other poor beggar to eat of the same bread. Learning that I was a poor beggar who needed to lean daily on the promises of God changed my whole life and ministry. I stood by in awe as I watched streams of living water flow into the lives of the people around me.[1]

Directly witnessing the moment the Holy Spirit convicts someone and they come to faith is a privilege and tremendous blessing. As we said at the outset, evangelism is planting the seed of the gospel in good soil. While going with other Christ-followers on an intentional evangelism endeavor is a good thing, living out evangelism every day is even more effective. Someone knocking on your door offering lawn services, a salesman approaching to make a pitch while you are shopping, an electrician in your home repairing something, or just having coffee with a friend—these are all opportunities to share the gospel.

What does that look like? One effective way is to start with a simple query: "Do you mind if I ask you a spiritual question?" If the person gives permission, consider one of the following as your next question.

- Does God exist? If so, what does He want of us?
- Do you know for sure you are going to Heaven?
- If you were to die tonight and God asked you, "Why should I let you into Heaven?" how would you answer?

Be sensitive in concluding the discussion if the other person becomes uninterested. At our county fair evangelism booth, we quickly observed that a step backward is a hint of disinterest, two steps backward a sure sign of retreat.

LEGACY OF A CHRIST-FOLLOWER

Most people desire to leave a positive legacy. University hallways and conference rooms are filled with life-size portraits of department chairs, deans, and college presidents. Obituaries chronicle what the deceased and their family considered the person's legacy. Typically, this comprises worldly accomplishments or contributions to family and society. What should the legacy be of a Christ-follower? Shouldn't it be what is blessed by God?

In His Sermon on the Mount, Jesus identified those to be blessed by God (see Matthew 5:3-12): the poor in spirit, those who mourn, the meek, those who hunger for righteousness, the merciful, the pure in heart, the peacemakers, those who are persecuted for righteousness. In his great sermon "Surprise,"[2] Haddon Robinson clarifies that the peacemakers are those who reconcile people to God. The apostle Paul counted those who had come to faith in Jesus Christ through his ministry of reconciliation this way:

> For who is our hope or joy or crown of exultation? Is it not even you, in the presence of our Lord Jesus at His coming? For you are our glory and joy (1 Thessalonians 2:19, 20).

It may take longer for some, but most people eventually fade into obscurity and are forgotten by the world. The legacy of Christ-followers should not be one who tries to bring glory to themselves but to God and Jesus Christ through the people they've evangelized and discipled, beginning with their own children and grandchildren. While the Holy Spirit accomplishes reconciliation and sanctification, He gives Christ-followers the privilege of being a worthy vessel in the harvest. This becomes their legacy for eternity.

CHAPTER TWENTY-FIVE APPLICATION

DISCUSSION QUESTIONS

- What are the most common objections by someone when the gospel is presented to them?
- What is the answer to the claim that the gospel is unfair?
- How would you respond if someone states they are just going to be as good as they can? Or they have never sinned? How about the allegation the Bible is full of inconsistencies?
- Some people will offer the existence of suffering and evil to try to argue that God is not loving. How would you respond to this?
- What do you want your legacy to be? What did the apostle Paul say was his legacy?

SELF-EVALUATION

- Are you where you need to be in the practice of evangelism? If not, how do you plan to improve?
- Several excellent evangelism training programs are available if your church does not have one. If living in the United States, one to consider is offered through Don Sunshine Ministries,[3] which conducts seminars throughout the country each year. For those seeking an online course for evangelism training, consider the Billy Graham School of Evangelism Online.[4] In addition, EvanTell has numerous webinars and videos on evangelism.[5]

MEMORY VERSES

And Jesus came up and spoke to them, saying, "All authority has been given to Me in heaven and on earth. Go therefore and make disciples of all the nations, baptizing them in the name of the Father and the Son and the Holy Spirit, teaching them to observe all that I commanded you; and lo, I am with you always, even to the end of the age" (Matthew 28:18-20).

CHAPTER TWENTY-SIX

MAKING DISCIPLES *WHO* MAKE DISCIPLES

"Maturity in Christ is the goal both for ourselves and for our ministry to others."[1]
John Stott

In 1775, a child was born in London to a mother who was a devout Christ-follower. The young boy's father, captain of a merchant ship, spent much time at sea. The mother took the boy to church and immersed him in biblical principles until her untimely death when the boy was seven. Reaching adulthood, the young man followed his father's vocation but became entangled in the African slave trade. This didn't go well. He himself was enslaved by a jealous partner until his rescue by a sea captain who was a friend of his father.

On the journey home, the young man passed the time reading a few available books, including *The Imitation of Christ* by Augustinian monk Thomas à Kempis (1380-1471).[2] As he read, his childhood memories were awakened, and he considered whether the book's claims about Jesus Christ might be true. This thought was punctuated by an exclamation point when a raging storm nearly destroyed the ship. As the damaged vessel limped into harbor, the shaken man made a profession of faith in Jesus Christ.

The young man was John Newton,[3, 4] writer of "Amazing Grace," one of the most celebrated songs of all time. God had reached out to him through a righteous mother, faithful ministers, an Augustinian monk, and a severe storm that nearly ended his life. At age thirty-three, he entered the ministry. Through the remainder of his life, God used Newton to influence many others for God's purposes.

One such person was a boy born into a prominent English family. After his father's death when he was nine, the boy lived for three years with an uncle and the uncle's wife, who was a fervid follower of Jesus Christ. Educated at Cambridge and elected to the British Parliament, he decided to travel through Europe to broaden his perspective. He didn't want to do this alone, so he invited an acquaintance, Isaac Milner (1750-1820), to join him.

To pass the time as they traveled, the two young men agreed to discuss a book by Phillip Doddridge (1702-1751), *The Rise and Progress of Religion in the Soul.*[5] On a second trip, Milner suggested the New Testament as their literary agenda. Through reading and discussing Doddridge's book and the New Testament, the young man was deeply convicted and came to faith in Jesus Christ.

Wanting to serve God with all his ability, the young man was conflicted as to whether he should leave Parliament to become a minister. He met with John Newton for counsel.[6] Newton convinced him that God could use him in Parliament and discipled him throughout Newton's remaining years. What is the impact of the disciple-makers God placed in this young man's path, including his aunt, Isaac Milner, Phillip Doddridge, and John Newton? This young man, William Wilberforce, led Parliament to abolish the slave trade in Great Britain in 1807.[6] These two men, John Newton and William Wilberforce, illustrate the impact of disciple-making on this world when Christ-followers are lifelong apprentices of the Lord Jesus Christ.

JESUS' MODEL FOR DISCIPLE-MAKING

Jesus established the model of shared-life discipleship to launch His church. The Gospels reveal that Jesus focused more on Peter, James, and John. While the remaining nine disciples interacted significantly with Jesus, Peter, James, and John likely helped disciple them. Through this model, Jesus discipled the twelve, although one, Judas Iscariot, would betray Him. Matthias was chosen to replace Jesus (see Acts 1:21-26). Jesus' discipleship model launched His church as these disciples began discipling others, who in turn discipled others (2 Timothy 2:2).

The book of Acts describes, in detail, disciples making disciples. The apostle Paul discipled Priscilla and Aquila, whom he'd met in Corinth, living with them for a time (see Acts 18:2, 3). They accompanied Paul when he left Corinth on his third missionary journey. During that time, they encountered Apollos. It was Priscilla and Aquila who instructed Apollos in the gospel (Acts 18:25, 26). Apollos later co-labored with Paul in the Corinthian church (1 Corinthians 3:6).

Every Christ-follower needs someone more spiritually mature to disciple them. Upon reaching a certain level of spiritual maturity, they are then called to disciple others. I thank God for the people He placed in my life to disciple me. I came to Christ during my training in pulmonary medicine through faculty member Frank Sutton. I was then discipled by Dr. Sutton and another faculty member until I completed my fellowship. After I moved to Charlottesville, Virginia, God placed other men in my life who were instrumental in my spiritual growth. These included two pastors at my church, Skip Ryan and John Q. Hall, as well as Dr. Robert M. Carey, a longtime mentor, colleague, and friend at the University of Virginia School of Medicine.

The most influential disciple-maker in my life has been my wife Karren. While I grew up attending church, I hadn't yet accepted Jesus when we married. Early in our marriage, Karren gently reminded me to clean up my language. Church attendance during my medical residency was infrequent. Karren set the example, and I'm chagrined to say she stood alone to present our children, Katie and Charlie, for dedication one Sunday morning. Karren never complained. She quietly but faithfully walked with Jesus, and I saw this. When I was invited to Dr. Sutton's Bible study, I went because of the people God had placed in my life, including my faithful wife Karren.

There was a faithful servant of God in Charlottesville whose fruit from disciple-making continues to be evident today. Daryl Richman (1934–2019) was a pastor in Fluvanna County in central Virginia. During that time he regularly visited Charlottesville to use the library facilities at the University of Virginia. As he did so, he began interacting with the students and was led by God to form a faith-based ministry at the University of Virginia. One of those impacted was a close friend of mine, Wendall Winn. He met Daryl while in law school at the University of Virginia. Wendall described Daryl as having "a gift for evangelism, a heart for people, and an unassuming way. He loved me."[7] Wendall began attending Daryl's student meetings after they met. After one of the meetings, Wendall recalls that Daryl told him, "Give as much of yourself as you can to as much of God as you understand."[7] Wendall came to faith in Jesus Christ in Charlottesville that evening. Afterward, Daryl discipled him. Wendall frames Daryl's style of shepherding like this: "He was walking with me in my faith."

WHY EVERY CHRIST-FOLLOWER NEEDS A SHEPHERD

If you've followed Christ for some time, you might ask why you still need to be discipled throughout your life. There are two main reasons every Christ-follower needs someone more spiritually mature, an "apostle Paul" as it were, to disciple him or her. First, we must grow in Christlikeness to fulfill the Great Commission and bear good fruit, and we can't disciple someone else above our own level of spiritual maturity.

Second, after coming to faith in Jesus Christ, every Christ-follower is spiritually vulnerable for the rest of their lives on earth. We discussed earlier three ever-present threats that may deceive every Christ-follower at any time—our sinful flesh (see Jeremiah 17:9; Romans 7:11), the world (Mark 4:19), and Satan (Revelation 12:9). It isn't just the spiritually weak and immature who are vulnerable. The evil one is a prowling lion seeking to destroy (1 Peter 5:8), and he knows our weaknesses. We will undergo a barrage of temptations and the potential lust of our flesh as long as we are in our earthly bodies.

As we've already seen, Scripture is filled with examples of seasoned servants of God who made grave errors that compromised them. Moses became angry and disobeyed God by striking the rock for water (see Numbers 20:8-13). For this disobedience, God didn't allow him to enter the Promised Land. King David committed adultery and murder. In consequence, his household was afflicted with strife and death for the rest of his life (2 Samuel chapters 11 to 19).

There are plenty of contemporary examples of high-profile ministry leaders whose willful hidden sin has resulted in disqualification from ministry. Why does this happen? Some may resist being in a discipling relationship for fear the information they disclose might be used to betray them. Pride is usually the underlying sin in forgoing discipleship and accountability, a mindset that insists we are so spiritually mature we don't need either one. King Solomon warned:

> Watch over your heart with all diligence, for from it flow the springs of life (Proverbs 4:23).

Unfortunately, Solomon failed to follow his own admonition, taking as wives women who worshiped false gods. In consequence, he turned away from God and did evil (see 1 Kings 11:1-13). The initial battle we must win is for our own heart, a battle that will continue until our final breath. When the apostle Paul urged the elders at Ephesus to shepherd the flock, he first cautioned them to "be on guard for yourselves" (Acts 20:28).

What does that mean? As we've already discussed, once we accept Jesus, we immediately become a threat to the evil one as part of a great spiritual war against dark spiritual forces (see Ephesians 6:12). God provides Christ-followers with His armor so we can withstand Satan's attacks (Ephesians 6:13-18). The armor represents the means of grace God provides His children for protection, not just from physical attacks but attacks on our mind: worry, fear, and anxiety. These are also spiritual attacks that can disable us or destroy us. God's armor allows Christ-followers to have our minds transformed by the Holy Spirit into a "kingdom view," which dramatically changes how we see ourselves, everyone around us, and the Father, Son, and Holy Spirit.

Writing to the Roman church, the apostle Paul refers to the "armor of light," then instructs, "Put on the Lord Jesus Christ" (see Romans 13:12, 14). Do you see? Growing in Christlikeness is putting on the armor of God. As said earlier, it is sanctification. And putting on armor isn't passive. It requires action (i.e., discipline). A prudent soldier doesn't wait until the middle of a battle to put on his tactical body armor. Similarly, the Christ-follower must put on the full armor of God to stand firm in spiritual battle. This requires intentionally engaging the sword of God's Word, praying, obeying God's commandments, and overcoming sin so we don't squelch the power of the Holy Spirit.

One significant means of grace against vulnerability is the discipline of discipleship and accountability to other mature Christ-followers. No one is above it. No one is exempt from it. A pastor once told me, "Christianity is not a solo sport." There is great wisdom in his counsel. "As iron sharpens iron, so one person sharpens another" (Proverbs 27:17, NIV). Being a sequestered Christ-follower is dangerous. Our spiritual shepherds are provided by God to protect us and help us grow to spiritual maturity (see Galatians 6:1; Hebrews 3:13).

In his book *Instruments in the Redeemer's Hands*, American pastor and conference speaker Paul Tripp describes the role of other believers in our lives.[8] He recalls traveling home with his brother Tedd after attending a marriage conference. Applying what they'd learned, Tedd asked Paul about his relationship with his wife. Through his brother's accountability questions, Paul began to see his blindness in not being where God wanted him in his marriage. On getting home, Paul entered into a Spirit-led discussion with his wife that resulted in the restoration of their marriage.

Authentic spiritual accountability is like the blind spot indicator in your car's side mirrors. Like Paul Tripp, we all have spiritual "blind spots" to which we are oblivious. Accountability questions can be an effective screening tool to uncover issues beneath the façade. Appendix 2, in the rear of this book, gives a basic list that can be used in discipleship groups or even personally for self-evaluation.

SHEEP IN NEED OF SHEPHERDS

In short, it doesn't matter who we are or what position we hold, whether a lead pastor or someone recently born again. We all need a mentor for genuine spiritual accountability. When someone decides they are too spiritually mature to need discipled, they've taken the first step in the deception used by the enemy to bring them down.

Let's face it. Human beings are a lot like sheep. Sheep aren't very smart and are at constant risk from predators, elements of nature, insufficient food or water, disease, and death. Millennium after millennium, sheep have required a human shepherd to flourish. There's a reason Scripture frequently compares people to sheep with God as our ultimate Shepherd (see Psalm 23, 79:13, 100:3; Isaiah 53:5-7; Ezekiel 34:15; Luke 15:2-7; John chapter 10). We may think otherwise, but we're not very smart. We ignore danger, deny God, rebel against Him, deny His goodness, and run away from a relationship with Him.

To look after His people, God provided human shepherds. There were good shepherds like Moses, whom God used to lead His people out of bondage from Egypt (see Psalm 78:52). There were also bad shepherds who either shepherded poorly or were unwilling to shepherd at all. Instead of looking after the flock, they pursued their own interests with no pity for the plight of the sheep (Isaiah 56:11). They failed to strengthen, heal, and bind up the weak or sick. They had no interest in searching for lost sheep (Ezekiel 34:3, 4). They allowed the flock to be scattered and ultimately lost, to be devoured by predators (Ezekiel 34:5; Malachi 2:8). Such shepherds were severely condemned by God (Ezekiel chapter 34).

In the New Testament, Jesus is described as our Chief Shepherd (see Hebrews 13:20, 21; 1 Peter 2:25, 5:4). But He also appoints under-shepherds here on earth to care for His flock. Peter was the first shepherd Jesus appointed after His resurrection, telling Peter to shepherd and feed His sheep (John 21:15-17). So it isn't surprising when Peter, in turn, uses that imagery writing to early church leadership about what kind of leaders they should be.

> To the elders among you, I appeal as a fellow elder and a witness of Christ's sufferings who also will share in the glory to be revealed: Be shepherds of God's flock that is under your care, watching over them—not because you must, but because you are willing, as God wants you to be; not pursuing dishonest gain, but eager to serve; not lording it over those entrusted to you, but being examples to the flock. And when the Chief Shepherd appears, you will receive the crown of glory that will never fade away (1 Peter 5:1-4, NIV).

The Chief Shepherd launched and continues to maintain His church through His relational disciple-making model. His final exhortation to His followers was to be His disciple-makers, guiding His flock to spiritual maturity, teaching them to obey His commandments (see Matthew 28:19, 20) and to be His witnesses to the ends of the earth (Acts 1:8). Just as it was with Peter, it is how we show Jesus we love Him and His sheep. After Jesus ascended to Heaven, we see His under-shepherds, the apostles, filled with the Holy Spirit, quickly and resolvedly engaging in this commandment. This resulted in a great harvest of people who followed Jesus, as described in the Acts of the Apostles.

CHAPTER TWENTY-SIX
APPLICATION

DISCUSSION QUESTIONS

- What are two reasons you need to be discipled by a more mature Christ-follower for the rest of your life?
- Is there ever a spiritual maturity milestone for a Christ-follower when they no longer need to be discipled and held accountable? Is anyone exempt from these two practices? Discuss.
- Who were prominent people in the Bible who fell into sin in the midst of major positions of ministry? What about contemporary examples?

SELF-EVALUATION

- Consider the components of the full armor of God in Ephesians 6:11-18. Are you putting on the full armor? If not, which parts do you feel you are utilizing most? How do you plan to "put on" missing parts?
- Which of the following best describes accountability in your life? Do you have a "Paul" with whom you meet regularly for guidance and accountability? Are you part of a life group? Occasional meetings with Christian friends for advice and prayer? Or are you a solo believer except for Sunday services?
- Review the accountability questions in Appendix 2 in the back of this book. Are there areas in which you have sin you have not overcome? How do you plan to conquer them?

MEMORY VERSE

Watch over your heart with all diligence, for from it flow the springs of life (Proverbs 4:23).

CHAPTER TWENTY-SEVEN

CRITERIA OF A GOOD SHEPHERD

"Be on guard for yourselves and for all the flock, among which the Holy Spirit has made you overseers, to shepherd the church of God which He purchased with His own blood."

ACTS 20:28

The goal of a shepherd is to work with the Holy Spirit in the spiritual maturation of Christ-followers to accomplish the works of righteousness for which they were created to bring glory to God (see Matthew 5:16; Ephesians 2:10). Disciple-making is an integral part of that process. The graphic you see on the next page depicts how someone who has come to repentance and faith in Jesus Christ grows in Christlikeness through the Holy Spirit with encouragement by the shepherd, who oversees, disciples, and mentors. It shouldn't escape notice that all the "one another" commandments are essential actions of an effective shepherd toward the sheep. These were characteristics of how Jesus discipled His flock while on earth.

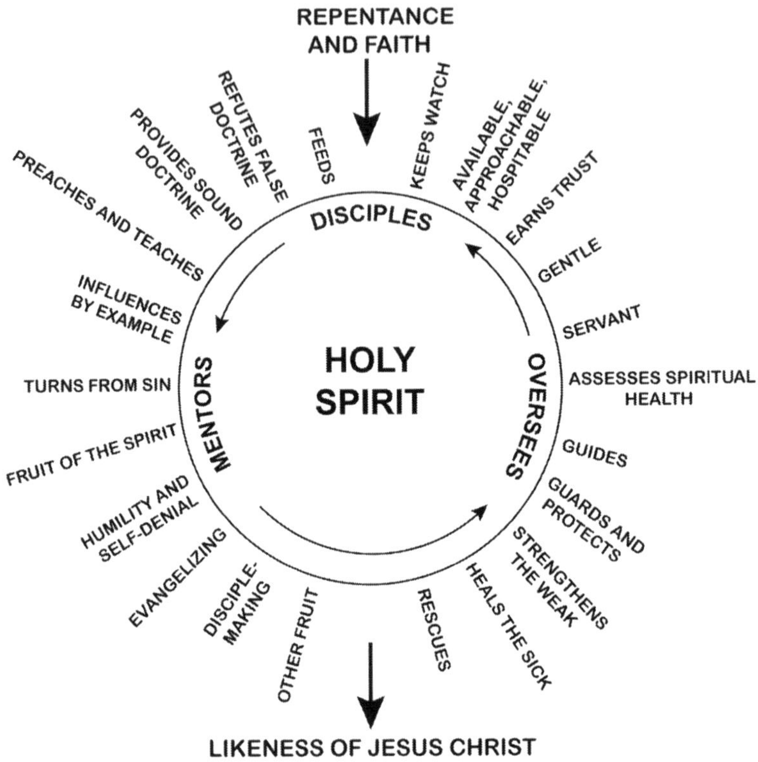

An overseer watches over the sheep of their flock (see Acts 20:28). God situates shepherds in unique spheres of contact and interaction throughout their lives. The shepherd must be available, approachable, and hospitable. They must earn the sheep's trust through gentleness and a servant's heart (Galatians 5:13; Ephesians 4:2). The sheep must know and follow their shepherd's voice. This allows the shepherd to assess his flock's spiritual health. When these interactions are in place, the faithful shepherd can guide, guard, and protect the sheep from danger, strengthen the weak (Acts 20:35), heal and anoint the sick (James 5:14), bind the injured (1 Thessalonians 5:14), and search for and rescue wounded or lost sheep (Ezekiel 34:8-10; Matthew 18:12-14).

The faithful shepherd disciples the sheep, encouraging them to feed in the knowledge of truth and grow in heart transformation and skills. This involves replacing false doctrine with the sound doctrine of the gospel and God's Word through preaching and teaching (see Galatians 1:6, 7; Ephesians 4:14). This leads to walking in the ways of Jesus in holiness through the transforming power of the Holy Spirit. The Christ-follower's initial focus should be on spiritual disciplines that further enhance growth, including prayer, increased hunger for and correct use of Scripture, overcoming sin, replacing pride with humility, seeking God to be in His presence, and manifesting the fruit of the Spirit.

The shepherd also mentors the sheep by example. Paul told the Corinthians, "Be imitators of me, just as I also am of Christ" (1 Corinthians 11:1). He told the Philippians to put into practice what they learned or heard from him (see Philippians 4:9). He implored the Thessalonians to follow his and the other disciples' examples (see 2 Thessalonians 3:7, 9). Good shepherds mentor the flock through what the sheep observe in them, such as turning from sin in obedience, the fruit of the Spirit, humility, and self-denial. The sheep observe and develop skills for evangelism, disciple-making, and other fruits of righteousness. The shepherd influences by example not just when things are tranquil but also during hardship, difficulty, and suffering in their life. Unflappable faith, endurance, perseverance, and love during these times generate hope in the flock.

There must be proximity of shepherd and sheep, sufficient familiarity so that the shepherd knows of events in which the sheep are more vulnerable. These might include a wayward child, death in the family, hospitalization, loss of a job, bad news from a biopsy, severe marriage problems, and other similar events.

BEING CAREFUL WITH DESCRIPTORS

An effective shepherd must be humble. This is critical. And a humble shepherd needs to be careful in his word selection with the flock. After all, a human "shepherd" is no more than an under-shepherd to the Chief Shepherd, Jesus, and will also benefit spiritually from their interactions with the sheep. I once asked a man who'd been in our home Bible study if he'd like to get together every few weeks to grow his relationship with the Lord. I misspoke, and he gently corrected me, saying he didn't want to be someone's "project."

He was right. When Christ-followers meet to grow in our walk with Him, we all grow (see Romans 1:12). Every Christ-follower who is a disciple also needs to be discipled. Ever since, I've changed my invitation to "so we can grow together in our relationship with the Lord." Terms like overseer, shepherd, sheep, mentor, or mentee may also be misinterpreted as an attitude of spiritual superiority and might best be avoided.

Many Christ-followers today who are supposed to be the shepherds and disciple-makers of Jesus' flock are asleep at their posts. Some cop out with the claim that this is the job of pastors and church leaders. But as we already saw, the duty of apostles, prophets, evangelists, pastors, and teachers is to equip the church laity, who are in turn to disciple and build the body of Christ to the "stature which belongs to the fullness of Christ" (see Ephesians 4:12, 13). If you follow Jesus Christ, He has called you to oversee, disciple, and mentor others. That's the Great Commission (Matthew 28:19, 20).

A church is not made up of bricks and boards, sound systems, or LED screens. It is made up of Christ-followers, and it is built up by God's Spirit through faithful declaration of God's Word from the pulpit, steadfast church discipline when necessary, church leadership training laity to grow in spiritual maturity, and by the laity making disciples (see Ephesians 2:19-22; 1 Peter 2:5). Many magnificent church buildings today with splendid architecture and state-of-the-art video and audio technology are filled with people who either don't know Jesus at all or barely follow Him.

THE IMPORTANCE OF ACCOUNTABILITY IN SHEPHERDING

Jesus' church, the *ecclesia*, grows as Christ-followers are built into a holy priesthood by the Holy Spirit with direct relational oversight, discipling, and mentoring by faithful, reliable shepherds (see 1 Peter 2:5). Are you under the care of an authentic shepherd in your church? Ask yourself this question. How often has someone in your church asked you how you are doing spiritually? Or how your prayer life is going? Or whether you are studying the Bible daily and applying it to your life for increased obedience? Is there a sin in your life you can't overcome? Do you struggle with unforgiveness and bitterness? Are you sharing the gospel regularly with others? Are you giving adequate quality time to your family, including your spouse?

These are all vital accountability questions such as you will find in Appendix 2 at the back of this book. I am in my fifth decade as a Christ-follower and can count on one hand the number of people who have ever asked me any of those questions. How can we recognize the authentic shepherds around us? There are three main criteria.

- Shepherds are disciples of Jesus known for their love (John 13:35).
- Shepherds have a flock.
- Shepherds are nurturing their flock to grow spiritually to the likeness of Jesus Christ.

Being a shepherd isn't just getting together with your sheep to attend a sports event, play pickleball, or go fly-fishing. Enjoying a sports event with other Christ-followers can be a valuable part of building relationships. But the shepherd's primary role is to oversee, disciple, and mentor growth of Christlikeness in the sheep so they mature spiritually, evangelize, and themselves become disciple-makers.

QUALIFICATIONS OF A SHEPHERD

A good shepherd (i.e., disciple-maker) cares for their flock with the right motive, agape, and also exhibits a strong love for lost sheep (see Luke 15:7). They should have a solid knowledge of God's Word, holding firmly to correct doctrine (Titus 1:9) and able to teach others (1 Timothy 3:2). Their lives should show no evidence of willful sin, unforgiveness, or bitterness they have not overcome. Their response to hardship and suffering should inspire hope in their flock. They should display excellent oversight of their own family.

Good shepherds are able to receive and respond positively to constructive criticism. They must be warm, gentle, humble, and hospitable, drawing people to themselves through servant leadership rather than rigid authoritarianism (see 1 Peter 5:3). They will have a history of successful, nurturing relationships with other Christ-followers, not a history of hurt or discarded relationships.

Good shepherds need to pray for their sheep. They should be willing to devote the time needed to shepherd each person. Making disciples can't be done from a distance. It involves living lives in close relationships. Age should have no bearing. For senior Christ-followers, the calling to make disciples continues unless there are mitigating health problems, financial issues, or death.

> The righteous man will flourish like the palm tree, he will grow like a cedar in Lebanon. They will still yield fruit in old age (Psalm 92:12, 14).

Lastly, good shepherds should display evidence that they continue striving in their spiritual transformation to the likeness of Jesus Christ. A shepherd will never be able to examine, encourage, empower, and equip the sheep to a level higher than their own level of Christlikeness (see Luke 6:40). Accordingly, a degree of spiritual maturity is requisite before becoming a disciple-maker.

You will appropriately ask what level that is. This book has been prepared with that in mind. The spiritual activities covered in each chapter and the follow-up sections have been written to help Christ-followers grow into disciple-makers, not by simply reading the book but earnestly seeking and growing in these means of grace God has provided under the power of the Holy Spirit.

If you are a Christ-follower, the assessment questions will help you self-determine where you are. Your spiritual mentor, the "apostle Paul" in your life, should have already broached the question about you becoming a disciple-maker. If not, ask him or her. Are you at a level of spiritual maturity to begin shepherding others? If not, on what do you need to focus? You can ask your pastor or small group leader the same question.

ESTABLISHING A FLOCK TO SHEPHERD

Being a shepherd is the calling of every Christ-follower by the Lord Jesus Christ. It isn't easy. It is a life of servanthood to others motivated by *agape* and powered by the Holy Spirit. It is Christlikeness, pouring out costly grace to others (i.e., sacrificial giving of ourselves and our time). That is why many don't undertake it.

Jesus spent three years with His twelve disciples. As with Him, modern shepherds need patience, wisdom, and discernment. Jesus was forthright with those He invited to follow Him that this was not to be a "half-in" engagement. There is no shortcut to making or becoming a disciple. It takes time. The shepherd needs to discern which sheep are serious about a desire to be shepherded to maturity so they can become disciple-makers. Otherwise, the shepherd's effectiveness is diminished.

That said, if you seek to disciple people, God will orchestrate it. It may be through your church and involve people you meet and with whom you worship. The pastors may know someone who needs one-on-one shepherding and ask you to do so. But don't wait until someone approaches you, grabs you by your shirt collar, and demands to be shepherded. That will never happen. You need to be willing to take the initiative.

One way is to form your own discipleship group. I go on the offensive and invite people. I've discipled people from Bible studies, people who worship with me in church, my patients, my neighbors, and my colleagues at work. A simple invitation is enough. With people I'm certain have come to faith in Jesus, I use this invitation: "I am starting a group where we encourage each other to grow in the likeness of Christ to bear good fruit, including making disciples. Would you like to be part of it?" It will likely take minimal time to put together a group of three for your first discipleship group.

If it's not someone I know well or have not confirmed as a Christ-follower, I invite them to have coffee at a local coffee shop or on our home's back deck. At the first meeting, I ask questions that lead to a determination of whether they've accepted Jesus. I frame the invitation as an opportunity to "talk about the big questions in life." Does God exist? If so, does He want something of us? Follow-up questions will allow determination of their need for evangelism. I invite those who profess faith in Jesus Christ to be part of a discipleship group.

THE SHEEP'S RESPONSIBILITY

The shepherds aren't the only ones with responsibilities. Scripture tells us the sheep have their clear responsibilities. For one, we are instructed to submit to the spiritual leaders God has placed in our lives (see Hebrews 13:17). This includes accountability and a willingness to be discipled, mentored, and equipped for ministry. In his commentary, American theologian and pastor Albert Barnes (1798-1870) said of Hebrews 13:17, "It is for your own good that they do this, and you should therefore submit to these arrangements."[1] However, not everyone who attends churches and expresses faith in Jesus is willing to be discipled. Such are the church's unsanctified, the "cheap grace" crowd.

CHAPTER TWENTY-SEVEN APPLICATION

DISCUSSION QUESTIONS

- Is disciple-making the work of pastors and church leaders only, or also of the lay members? Outline the responsibility for each group in disciple-making (see Ephesians 4:11-16).
- What are the three areas in which a shepherd participates in the growth of other Christ-followers to the likeness of Jesus Christ?
- What are the qualifications to be a good shepherd? How can one recognize authentic shepherds of God's flock?
- How can one establish a group of Christ-followers to shepherd?
- What are the responsibilities of Christ-followers who need to be shepherded?

SELF-EVALUATION

- If your local church has no program for encouraging or training you to become a disciple-maker, you are still called to do so. Begin by asking one person to talk about the big questions in life. The person discipling you should be a resource to review your meeting, give suggestions, and pray for you and the person(s) you are shepherding.

MEMORY VERSE

"I am the good shepherd; the good shepherd lays down His life for the sheep" (John 10:11).

CHAPTER TWENTY-EIGHT

MODELS FOR RELATIONAL DISCIPLE-MAKING

"The harvest is plentiful, but the workers are few. Therefore, beseech the Lord of the harvest to send out workers into His harvest."
MATTHEW 9:37, 38

We've discussed that the goal of the disciple-maker is to be a vessel through which the Holy Spirit matures Christ-followers who themselves make disciples. The under-shepherds (i.e., disciple-makers) model the fullness of Jesus Christ to their flocks, nurturing and encouraging their growth with a clear definition of the goal. There are three basic relational models by which a shepherd can disciple the sheep: the life group, discipleship group, and one-on-one disciple-making. All are valid models for evangelism and discipleship in the body of Christ. With every one of these models, it is vital to keep in sight what the goal for the disciple-maker is. The graphics in this chapter represent each model.

Life group: The group size Jesus established with His own disciples (i.e., about ten to fifteen people) is an effective number for a life group.

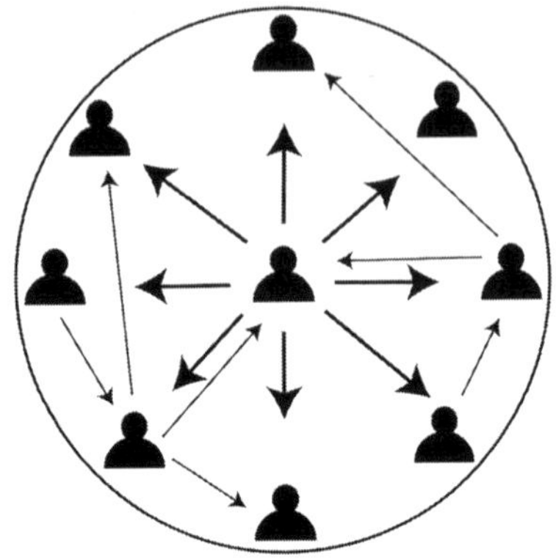

LIFE GROUP

Trusting relationships, which are vital for effective discipleship, are developed most easily within this smaller number.

Often these groups form such tight bonds that many groups tend to continue indefinitely. At the onset of the group, everyone must agree to the goal of participants growing to spiritual maturity, breaking off from the group, and starting their own group to make disciples. As this process happens, those who split off are continuously replaced, producing a healthy life group that grows mature disciples and reproduces itself.

In the dynamics of a life group, the shepherd (in center of graphic) oversees, disciples, and mentors members represented around the perimeter (arrows emanating outward). Maturing members will have discipling impact on each other as well (arrows pointing to each other). This is how small group members are built up—from the shepherd and from each other.

> Therefore encourage one another and build up one another, just as you are doing (1 Thessalonians 5:11).

This first graphic makes one other point. Group members also have discipleship influence that grows the shepherd spiritually (arrows pointing toward the shepherd). As noted before, there is no spiritual retirement. Every Christ-follower must continue growing in sanctification for the entirety of their life, and shepherding others is one means by which that occurs.

Oversight, mentoring, and discipling can occur in a life group, but this is not the preferred model for the sheep to become disciple-makers themselves. Closer interactions are needed to enhance disciple-making skills. These are represented in the following models.

Discipleship group: A discipleship group (see second graphic) focuses more intentionally on growing the sheep into disciple-makers. In this model, there is more personal contact between shepherd and sheep. For this reason, it is wise that men shepherd men and women shepherd women (see 2 Timothy 2:2; Titus 2:4-8). Group members should be invited based on their potential and exuberance for growing in the likeness of Jesus and themselves becoming disciple-makers. The group size should be at most three people besides the disciple-maker. This was the model we see Jesus using with His three most intimate disciples: Peter, James, and John.

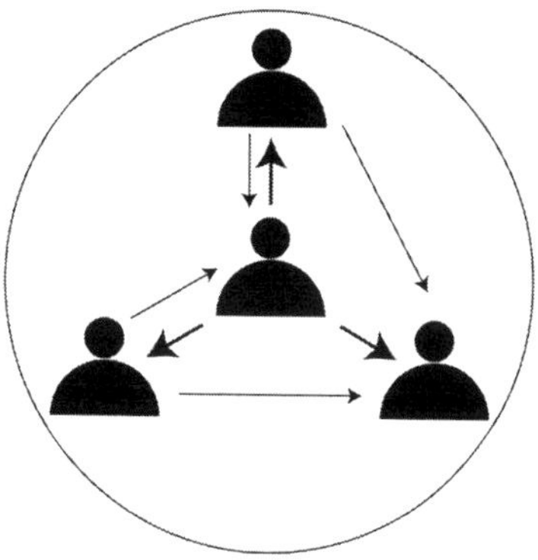

DISCIPLESHIP GROUP

Discipleship groups, ideally, should meet once a week. Every two weeks will work depending on schedules, but every four weeks is the upper limit for frequency. The leader should establish goals and objectives at the outset. The group is not intended to continue indefinitely. The goal is for each person to become a disciple-maker, forming their own discipleship groups once they complete participation in your group. As with the life group, while the leader is most responsible for discipling, group members also disciple each other. Once one group of disciples has developed and graduated, each disciple-maker will form a new group with the same goals.

Individual discipleship: Individual discipleship (see third graphic) is also a helpful model in which the shepherd meets one-on-one with another Christ-follower. I utilize this model to accommodate someone with limited availability that is difficult for others to accommodate. The training is identical to the discipleship group above. That said, the discipleship group is preferable to the one-on-one model for two reasons. It increases the shepherd's efficiency threefold, and the members of a discipleship group get the added benefit of building their peers up through interactions with each other in addition to interactions with the shepherd.

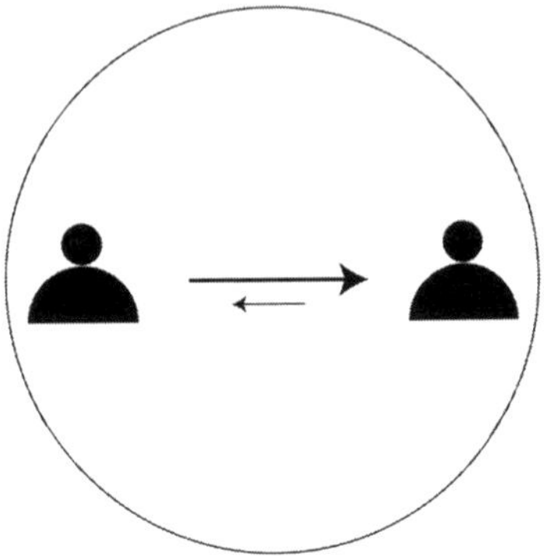

INDIVIDUAL DISCIPLESHIP

DISCIPLESHIP CURRICULUM

For a disciple to become an effective disciple-maker, he or she must grow to model the likeness of Jesus Christ through the power of the Holy Spirit. What does this look like? While the below is not a comprehensive list, it gives a general spectrum of what a disciple-maker should be seeking to instill in disciples so they in turn mature to disciple others.

- A commitment to take up their cross and surrender "self" to pursue Jesus Christ and become like Him through the remainder of their lives.
- Putting on Christ's humility.
- Becoming skilled in the correct interpretation of God's Word, the Bible, availing themselves of it daily and systematically, committing key passages to memory, and sharing it with others.
- Growing in prayer to a point of praying continually and in the Holy Spirit.
- Growing in obedience to God's commandments by overcoming sin with no willful sin remaining in the Christ-followers' lives.
- Abandoning any unforgiveness or bitterness and putting on unconditional forgiveness for all.
- Utilizing trials, hardship, and affliction for spiritual growth.

- Growing in giving not just of financial resources but in sacrificially sharing every aspect of life with others.
- Maturing in Spirit-led *agape* for the Father, Son, and every person.

Clearly, these aren't the only disciplines through which a Christ-follower grows in spiritual maturity. But these represent the basics—boot camp, as it were. When the Christ-follower matures in these likenesses of Jesus Christ, he or she becomes an instrument of honor useful to God to do good works (see 2 Timothy 2:21). They no longer need prodding from their local church through its members or programs. They go on autopilot, so to speak, under the direction of the Holy Spirit. Those good works include, at minimum, the following.

- Faithfully and regularly as a lifestyle sharing the good news of the gospel with others.
- Meeting with and discipling other Christ-followers to grow to spiritual maturity so they themselves are making disciples.
- Bearing other good fruit for which they were created in Christ Jesus, summed up substantially in the "one another" commandments.

Early on in discipleship group meetings, the shepherd should challenge each disciple to identify a person they can begin discipling on their own. After that, the following questions should be asked of each disciple at each subsequent meeting.[1]

- Who are you discipling?
- How is it going, and what questions do you have?
- How can we support you and pray for you?

It is also important that the group review the accountability questions (Appendix 2) together every few meetings.

METRIC FOR GROWTH

If using this book as a curriculum, each disciple should be encouraged to personally use the discussion and follow-up questions to assess their spiritual maturation. It's okay if a disciple volunteers to the group areas where they feel they need improvement. But care needs to be taken that no one is put on the spot or embarrassed. The group leader can encourage each disciple to come to them outside of meeting times to identify areas needing substantial improvement for mentoring and prayer. This is obviously not an issue in one-on-one discipleship. While church leadership can use the questions as metrics to evaluate where their church is in regard to discipleship, discipleship.org has developed a "scorecard" that should be invaluable to churches to assess where they are with disciple-making.[2]

DISCIPLE-MAKING IN THE "REAL WORLD"

In the first-century church, discipleship occurred more on the go than in sit-down meetings. The disciples followed Jesus around, observing and participating in His ministry. Jesus' discipleship was anything but chalkboard instruction in a classroom. After Jesus' ascension and anointing of the disciples by the Holy Spirit, the disciples started out teaching in synagogues as Jesus did. But they also evangelized and discipled from location to location, country to country, living out their ministry.

Paul, Barnabas, and John Mark were together on their first missionary journey (see Acts 13:1-5). Paul and Barnabas separated on the second missionary journey, and Silas went with Paul. On this journey, Paul recruited and began discipling Timothy (Acts 16:1-3). As we've already seen, Paul met Priscilla and Aquila (Acts 18:1, 2), who then accompanied him on his third missionary journey where Priscilla and Aquila discipled Apollos (Acts 18:24-26). The entire book of Acts describes the apostles' on-the-move ministry of evangelizing and discipling with their disciples in turn doing likewise (i.e., disciples making disciples).

This model by Jesus and His disciples emphasizes that it is critical discipleship also be done in the "real world" outside of classrooms, offices, coffee shop meetings, and the like. When eating out with another Christ-follower, I will tell our server we follow Jesus, are about to give thanks for the food, and ask if there is anything we could pray for with them. I've taken men I'm discipling to ask people we meet on downtown sidewalks if we can pray for them. I've invited men to work in our Albemarle County Fair evangelism booth to observe the gospel being presented to others, then to share it themselves.

The shepherd can also take someone on a mission trip or visit someone in the hospital. In a sit-down meeting, the shepherd instructs those he or she disciples. In the field, those being shepherded observe the disciple-maker evangelizing and discipling.

IMPORTANCE OF DISCIPLE-MAKING TO JESUS

Jesus speaks strongly of what will happen in the judgment to those who cared for the hungry, thirsty, sick, strangers, imprisoned, and unclothed—and those who did not (see Matthew 25:31-46). He then lays out clearly why the two groups will reap such different consequences.

> "Then the righteous will answer Him, 'Lord, when did we see You hungry, and feed You, or thirsty, and give You something to drink? And when did we see You as a stranger, and invite You in, or naked, and clothe You? When did we see You sick, or in prison, and come to You?' The King will answer and say to them, 'Truly I say to you, to the extent that you did it to one of these brothers of Mine, even the least of them, you did it to Me.' … 'Lord, when did we [the unmerciful] see You hungry, or thirsty, or as a stranger, or naked, or sick, or in prison, and did not take care of You?' Then He will answer them, 'Truly I say to you, to the extent that you did not do it to one of the least of these, you did not do it to Me.' These will go away

> into eternal punishment, but the righteous into eternal life (Matthew 25:37-46).

Many today continue to be confused as to what leads to the separation of sheep and goats in the final judgment. It is not the positions held in organizations, including the church. It is not the number of publications authored. In the final analysis, as Jesus emphasized above, it is loving and caring for the people that the Father, Son, and Holy Spirit care about. This includes not just their physical needs but their spiritual needs. It includes coming to faith in Jesus Christ. It encompasses growing to spiritual maturity to bear good fruit in a ministry of reconciliation.

Too many in the church continue to misunderstand the good fruit that pleases God. They have blurred vision from world-refracted glasses. As a result, they hurry to be on or chair church committees or become deacons and elders. Their motive is too often prestige and power rather than laboring from an obedient servant's heart. They have little interest in making disciples. A disciple-maker mainly works out of sight. There is little recognition by people, and it is hard work.

CHAPTER TWENTY-EIGHT APPLICATION

DISCUSSION QUESTIONS

- What are the three models for relational disciple-making and the advantages and disadvantages of each? Which are more effective?
- What are the essential components of a curriculum for disciple-making?
- What goals should be explained to every person as they consider becoming part of a discipleship group?

- What is "real world" disciple-making? Discuss its importance.

SELF-EVALUATION

- Are you discipling other Christ-followers?
- If not, what is your plan to get started? This is the calling of every Christ-follower.

MEMORY VERSE

The things which you have heard from me in the presence of many witnesses, entrust these to faithful men who will be able to teach others also (2 Timothy 2:2).

CHAPTER TWENTY-NINE

GOOD SOIL TO BEAR GOOD FRUIT

"Let us not lose heart in doing good, for in due time we will reap if we do not grow weary. So then, while we have opportunity, let us do good to all people."
GALATIANS 6:9, 10

Every person who has ever breathed air on this planet is a fruit bearer, and they will either bear good fruit or bad fruit (see Matthew 7:17-20). We see the fruit of human hearts all around us. Jesus said that a tree is known by its fruit (i.e., a good tree can't produce bad fruit and vice versa). He compares this to what comes from the human heart.

> "For there is no good tree which produces bad fruit, nor, on the other hand, a bad tree which produces good fruit. For each tree is known by its own fruit. For people do not gather figs from thorns, nor do they pick grapes from a briar bush. The good man out of the good treasure of his heart brings forth what is good; and the evil man out of the evil treasure brings

> forth what is evil; for his mouth speaks from that which fills his heart" (Luke 6:43-45).

The unregenerated heart bears hostility, jealousy, anger, bitterness, unforgiveness, malice, racism, violence, murder, and war (see Galatians 5:19-21). If you are careless while driving and inadvertently cut someone off, you can lose your life from road rage. You are at risk of being murdered if you live among people who hate you because of your skin color, ethnicity, religious beliefs, or political ideology. If you state an ideology that offends certain people, you can be marginalized, canceled socially or professionally, or worse. These are all poisonous fruits.

In contrast, Jesus taught that one sign identifying His disciples was good fruit that glorifies the Father (see John 15:8). In his letter to the Ephesians (2:10), the apostle Paul wrote that Christ-followers are created in Jesus to do good works—i.e., to bear good fruit.

What exactly are the good fruit representing good works that God created Christ-followers to bear?

First, they must truly be good. The world's definition of good works is broad. Corporations throw enormous sums of money toward "good" causes. Social gospel devotees are convinced their actions are good works. What is currently "good" according to the world's morally relativistic perspective will likely shift every few years. So to determine what "good works" truly are, we need to consider the spiritual definition of "good," not the world's. Jesus defined what is good when a man approached and called Him "Good Teacher."

> And Jesus said to him, "Why do you call Me good? No one is good except God alone" (Mark 10:17, 18).

In other words, the definition of "good" is not up to us, the created ones. It is defined solely by the Creator. Something truly good is in accordance with God's being, His imperatives, His commandments (the law), His definitions (i.e., His holiness). He tells us what is good in His Word, the Bible.

Second, no one bears good fruit apart from their relationship with Jesus. Christ-followers are united with the True Vine, Jesus, through the Holy Spirit. When the Holy Spirit transforms a person's spirit to love God and love people, that internal change leads to outward actions and deeds—good fruit.

> "I am the vine, you are the branches; he who abides in Me and I in him, he bears much fruit, for apart from Me you can do nothing" (John 15:5).

Good works are the fruit of Holy Spirit-mediated actions. They represent love in action. If the Holy Spirit doesn't empower our actions, they are not in fact good works. God "searches all hearts, and understands every intent of the thoughts" (1 Chronicles 28:9). Many outward acts of the Pharisees such as tithing, public prayer, or giving to charity appeared good, but their motives were corrupt and not based on love for God or others (see Matthew 6:1-8). Accompanying their outward "good" actions were bad fruit, including arrogance, pride, self-promotion, and bankruptcy of love for anyone outside of themselves.

EXHORTATION TO DO GOOD

The Bible contains numerous commandments for God's people to "do good." They are to turn from evil, trust God, and do good (see Deuteronomy 6:18; Psalm 34:14, 37:3). They are not to withhold good from those to whom it is due when it is within their power to act (Proverbs 3:27). Christ-followers are not to become weary but be zealous at all times to do good (see 2 Thessalonians 3:13; Titus 2:14).

Recipients of good works include not only other children of God (see Galatians 6:10) but the enemies of Christ-followers and those who hate them (Luke 6:27). Christ-followers are to do good to all people (1 Corinthians 10:24; 1 Thessalonians 5:15). Who is included in "all people"? Coworkers. Neighbors. Strangers on the side of the road. Sojourners. Foreigners. Divorcees. Ex-spouses. Prostitutes. Political opponents. Personal enemies. Even enemies of God in rebellion against Him.

Bearing the fruit of good works is not optional. Scripture proclaims that Christ-followers must be obedient to God's Word. Hearing the Word and not following in obedience is to delude oneself (see James 1:22). John the Baptist warned the Pharisees and Sadducees to bear fruit in keeping with repentance and not rely on their ancestral relationship to the patriarch Abraham (Matthew 3:8-10). While good works don't result in our salvation, they are an outward sign of the inner faith that saves (James 2:14-22). Anyone who professes faith in Jesus but isn't bearing the fruit of good works should soberly examine themselves to see if they are indeed in the faith (2 Corinthians 13:5; James 2:17).

'ONE ANOTHER' COMMANDMENTS

There are many types of good fruit. Having already covered the good fruit of evangelism and disciple-making, we have to look no further than the "one another" commandments for additional good fruit Christ-followers are called to bear. These are summarized in the graphic on the next page, starting in the center with the Holy Spirit and *agape* and going clockwise from the top.

AGAPE

In Greek, there are separate words to describe different forms of love. *Phileo* is a fondness for another as for a friend. Christ-followers are called to a higher form of love—*agape*, or the kind of sacrificial, unconditional love God shows us. *Agape* is the underlying motive for every "one another" commandment. The apostle Paul in his letter to

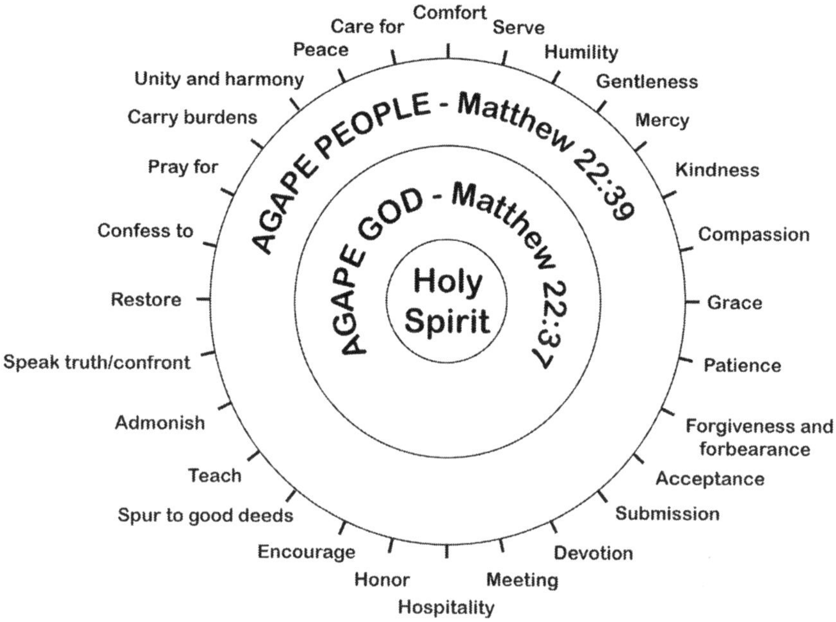

the Corinthians outlines clearly what *agape* is and what it is not (1 Corinthians chapter 13).

There are eight things *agape* is. Seven of them are identified by the apostle Paul (see 1 Corinthians 13:4-8). *Agape* is patient. It is kind. It rejoices with the truth. *Agape* bears all things, believes all things, hopes all things, and endures all things. There is one additional characteristic of *agape*. God is *agape* (1 John 4:8), and He is eternal (Isaiah 57:15). Therefore, *agape* is eternal.

In this same chapter, Paul identifies nine things *agape* is not. *Agape* is not jealous. Jealousy of God comes from pride and leads to rebellion against Him. *Agape* does not brag. Everything we have is a gift from God. When we boast, we are neither remembering that what we are boasting about is from God nor reflecting the glory due Him. *Agape* is not arrogant but humble. *Agape* does not act unbecomingly. It is never rude.

Agape does not seek its own or insist on getting its way. How much disunity has occurred in the church because people are uncompromising and insist on their own way? *Agape* is not easily provoked. It does not easily anger or go into fits of rage. *Agape* does not take into account a wrong suffered. Unforgiveness is an indicator of a heart that needs to grow in *agape*. *Agape* does not rejoice in unrighteousness. A Christ-follower's heart steeped in *agape* will mourn and weep about the wickedness all around them. *Agape* never fails.

From this, we see six attributes central in Christ-followers to *agape* God and people. *Agape* is sacrificial. *Agape* serves. *Agape* submits. *Agape* surrenders. *Agape* is selfless. *Agape* is sustained.

At the center of all good fruit is *agape* (see 1 John 3:23). *Agape* is not within a mortal human's ability but a fruit of the Holy Spirit (Galatians 5:22), as depicted in the center of the graphic above. We must first grow in *agape* for God (Matthew 22:37). Only then can we *agapao* (verb), in the right way, people created in God's image whom He loves (Matthew 22:39). This is another sign that identifies Jesus' disciples.

> "By this all men will know that you are My disciples, if you have love [*agape*] for one another" (John 13:35).

The graphic in this chapter illustrates that the Holy Spirit in the center creates *agape* in a Christ-follower, which spirals out into *agape* for God, then *agape* for other people. The Pharisees and other Jewish leaders missed this point. Their attempts to follow God's commandments were not out of *agape* for God or others. Jesus told the Jewish leaders:

> "But I know you, that you do not have the love [*agape*] of God in yourselves" (John 5:42).

This is the state of all unregenerated hearts, both Jew and Gentile. *Agape* is not just an inner emotional change in someone's soul and spirit but an action. The noun form of *agape* describes it. The verb form, *agapao*, validates it. Words are empty unless accompanied by action. The apostle Paul revealed that those who come to a faith in

God owe no one anything except "to *agapao* one another" (Romans 13:8).

While we get an idea of what *agape* looks like from the apostle Paul's letter to the Corinthians, what is the intensity of such *agape*? The apostle Peter instructed:

> Since you have in obedience to the truth purified your souls for a sincere love [*phileo*] of the brethren, fervently love [*agapao*] one another from the heart (1 Peter 1:22).

What Peter is saying is that, in obedience, the Christ-followers to whom he was writing had developed a fondness or friendship for their brothers and sisters in Jesus. But Christ-followers are called to a higher form of love: *agape*. Moreover, they are called to practice that form of love fervently. What is in your life that you do fervently with great zeal, exuberance, and intensity? That is how Christ-followers are to *agape* one another.

CHAPTER TWENTY-NINE APPLICATION

DISCUSSION QUESTIONS

- What is the definition of "good fruit"?
- What would you answer to complete the phrase, "No one bears good fruit apart from . . . "?
- Are the fruit of good works optional for a Christ-follower?
- What is at the center of all "one another" commandments? What does it mean to do so fervently?
- Describe the eight things *agape* is, and the nine things it is not.
- What are the six attributes of *agape*?

SELF-EVALUATION

- After reviewing the six attributes of *agape*, do you recognize any of them in your life? What is your plan to improve?
- Do you *agapao* people? How do your actions show this?
- Are you fervent in your *agape* for God and His image-bearers?
- For further insight into how Jesus loved, read Paul Miller's book *Love Walked Among Us.*[1]

MEMORY VERSE

Since you have in obedience to the truth purified your souls for a sincere love of the brethren, fervently love [*agapao*] one another from the heart (1 Peter 1:22).

CHAPTER THIRTY

ADDITIONAL GOOD FRUIT

"Who [Christ Jesus] gave Himself for us to redeem us from every lawless deed, and to purify for Himself a people for His own possession, zealous for good deeds."

TITUS 2:14

While God has given every Christ-follower the means to bear good fruit through the Holy Spirit, this is a lifelong discipline. We must seek God's presence with every ounce of our strength, communicate with Him in prayer, be in His Word, increase in obedience, grow in suffering, and interact with and be accountable to other brothers and sisters who are His followers. This means freeing ourselves of worldly values and being cleansed by the Holy Spirit so we become useful vessels for God's special purposes to do the good works He assigns us (see 2 Timothy 2:20, 21).

The pinnacle of good works is unconditional, fervent *agape* for God and people. This type of love is central to good fruit. But there are additional good fruits birthed out of *agape* that are essential in a

Christ-follower if an onlooking world is to know we are Christ's disciples by the fruit we bear.

Humility with gentleness: An essential fruit in serving one another in love is humility (see Ephesians 4:2; Colossians 3:12-14). Lest we become prideful, every Christ-follower needs to remember that it is not us bearing fruit but the Holy Spirit through our connection to the True Vine, Jesus Christ (John 15:1-8). The apostle Paul made clear that neither circumcision nor uncircumcision had/has value, but only faith expressing itself through agape (Galatians 5:6). Christ-followers are to serve one another humbly with gentleness (Philippians 4:5). Jesus modeled this to the disciples when He washed their feet (John 13:12-16). Andrew Murray wrote that humility is God's power for the Christ-follower to "serve one another in love."[1]

Mercy and grace: Giving mercy is to show kindness and compassion, render clemency, and be lenient even when people don't deserve it (see Micah 6:8; Zechariah 7:9). If we do not show mercy to others, we will not receive it from God.

> So speak and so act as those who are to be judged by the law of liberty. For judgment will be merciless to one who has shown no mercy; mercy triumphs over judgment (James 2:12, 13).

Patience, forgiveness, and forbearance: Christ-followers are to be patient, forgiving each other just as God forgave us with forbearance in love for all (see Ephesians 4:2, 32; Colossians 3:12, 13). We are to accept one another just as Jesus has accepted us. Doing this brings praise to God (Romans 15:7).

Submit, meet, encourage, spur on, honor: Christ-followers are to submit to one another because doing so shows reverence for Jesus (see Ephesians 5:21). This is an act of devotion to each other (Romans 12:10). For this to happen, we must share our lives by meeting and showing genuine hospitality to one another (Hebrews 10:25).

Meeting with each other in small groups allows the formation of close personal, trusting relationships. This was the model of the first-century church (see Acts 2:42). It is through close personal contact that Christ-followers honor one another, encourage one another, and spur one another on toward good works (Romans 12:10; 1 Thessalonians 5:11; Hebrews 10:24). In short, we are to value others above ourselves. Instead of looking after our own personal interests, we are to look after the interests of others (Philippians 2:3, 4).

Teach, admonish, exhort, restore: Jesus' church is not a building or denomination but the *ecclesia*, i.e., the collective body of the "called-out ones." In the first century, the *ecclesia* often met in each other's dwellings, "devoting themselves to the apostles' teaching and to fellowship, to the breaking of bread and to prayer" (Acts 2:42). Teaching wasn't only from the leaders. Christ-followers are to teach and admonish one another (see Colossians 3:16) by speaking the truth in agape (Zechariah 8:16; Ephesians 4:15).

This includes gently confronting brothers and sisters in agape about sin (see Matthew 18:15; Hebrews 3:13) and restoring, if possible, those who may be "caught in a sin" (Galatians 6:1). While Jesus cautioned His followers to refrain from judging (Matthew 7:1), Christ-followers are also exhorted to warn each other lest we be deceived and our hearts hardened by the deceitfulness of sin (Hebrews 3:13).

Confess to, pray for, carry burdens: Christ-followers are to confess to each other and pray for each other fervently (see James 5:16). We are to pray for our enemies and those who persecute us (Matthew 5:44). We are to stand in the gap for one another, carrying each other's burdens (Galatians 6:2). Praying for others is not optional even when they may be living in disobedience. When Israel rebelled and demanded a king, the prophet Samuel told them:

> "As for me, far be it from me that I should sin against the LORD by ceasing to pray for you" (1 Samuel 12:23).

Harmony, unity, peace: Christ-followers are to be diligent in living with one another in harmony, unity, and peace (see Romans 12:16;

Colossians 3:14). The apostle Paul wrote to the Ephesians from prison about the importance of unity (see Ephesians 4:1-4).

Paul then follows this admonition with a warning of things that grieve the Holy Spirit: bitterness, wrath, anger, clamor, and slander (see Ephesians 4:30, 31); and an exhortation to be kind to one another, forgiving each other just as we were forgiven by God (Ephesians 4:32). Disunity among Christ-followers grieves the Holy Spirit living in them.

There is a well-known quotation referencing unity among Christ-followers: "In essentials, unity. In non-essentials, liberty. In all things, love."[2] *Agape* must always be pervasive among the body of believers in Jesus. There should be liberty for beliefs or practices that are non-essential. It is only on essential issues that a relationship may have to be broken. Scripture is the primary source for those essential truths that cannot be compromised (see Appendix 3 at the back of this book).

In 1982, a formation of four of the Air Force's precision team, the Thunderbirds, flew their Northrop T-38 jets into the ground while practicing a diamond formation at Indian Springs Air Force Base in Nevada. Three pilots crashed into the ground almost simultaneously with their leader. The Air Force concluded that the crash was due to a malfunction of the lead pilot's plane rather than pilot error. The other pilots trusted the lead pilot and were entirely focused on maintaining the precision formation.

There is a lesson in this for Christ-followers. If a pastor or leader in a local church or denomination becomes apostate in doctrine, church or denominational members may follow them into apostasy. A notable example is the schism today over the issue of sexual immorality, clearly described as an abomination throughout God's Word. A plea for unity is never a call to endorse or tolerate major theological or doctrinal errors or to endorse sin and abandon the pursuit of holiness. Sometimes Christ-followers may find it necessary to separate ourselves from persons, churches, or denominations who have become apostate. Even then, we must do so in *agape*, humility, and kindness.

Care for one another: Fighting injustice and advocating for the cause of the destitute, poor, and needy are also good works (see Jeremiah 22:16). People in these situations often have little or no ability to help themselves or express a voice in their plight (Proverbs 31:8, 9). God condemns people who think their pious actions such as fasting please Him. Instead, true fasting to God is to free the oppressed, provide food to the hungry, shelter to those who wander, and provide clothing to the naked (Isaiah 58:6, 7). Jesus tells us that inasmuch as we have done this for others, we have done it for Him (Matthew 25:37-40).

It is critical to clarify that these Scriptures are not confirming the social or "woke" gospel. Such counterfeit doctrines lead many to believe they can receive salvation by their humanitarian works in opposing injustice and oppression rather than through faith in Jesus Christ. Actions against injustice or oppression alone can never provide salvation or transform a person's heart to the likeness of Christ.

In my profession, many giants in health care have advanced medicine. Some of them have had tremendous influence on those who trained me and some a direct impact on me. Human suffering and premature death have decreased through their influence on medical practice and the development of innovative diagnostic techniques, medicines, and vaccines. But humanitarian efforts alone, no matter how great and for how many people, are only works. As Scripture warns, such works do not serve as atonement for our sins to God (see Romans 3:20).

Comfort: God comforts us so we can comfort others (see 2 Corinthians 1:3, 4). In the mid-nineteenth century, Dr. Edward Livingston Trudeau (1848-1915) compassionately cared for his brother, who lay dying of tuberculosis. In doing so, he contracted the disease that took his brother's life. Effective medicines for tuberculosis didn't become available until the mid-twentieth century. The only treatment at the time was rest and nutrition. As Dr. Trudeau slowly convalesced, God inspired him to establish the first institution to care for patients afflicted with tuberculosis, and it was founded near Lake Saranac, New York. Through his tireless efforts, countless tuberculosis patients were cared for.

While Dr. Trudeau couldn't heal many patients with advanced tuberculosis, he could certainly comfort them. He coined a phrase that continues to be used today in the classrooms and hallways of medical schools to describe the duty of a physician: "To cure sometimes, to relieve often, to comfort always."

What Dr. Trudeau refers to are attributes of God. God cures sometimes and relieves often, but He and His followers comfort always. The American Thoracic Society honored Dr. Trudeau's exemplary care for his patients with their highest award, the Edward Livingston Trudeau Medal. In a statement about his life, Dr. Trudeau said:

> I have indeed had a full life ... full of the aspirations and ceaseless strivings of the spirit for expression in worship, ever groping to know God, and ever sustained through long periods of gloom by too swiftly fading glimpses of the Heavenly Vision.[3]

Community: God has given us our brothers and sisters in Christ as a means for spiritual health and protection. They are our authentic family. I'm now in my fifth decade of leading small groups of Christ-followers. Getting people to commit to a small group, attend regularly, and do their part to nurture fellow believers is a struggle. Reasons for complacency vary. I've heard many. It rained. It might rain. It's too cold. There is a basketball or football game I want to see. Family is coming over. I'm tired. I'm too busy.

We are called to a Christlike "one another" *agape* for others that serves, submits, surrenders, is selfless, is sacrificial, and is sustained. But that means having both a "one" and an "another."

One terrifying weapon employed in ancient times was flaming arrows. Archers dipped their arrows in pitch and ignited them before launching them. These arrows set afire anything they penetrated. The Roman soldiers defended against this with a shield called the *scutum*.[4]

This was made of leather and canvas, approximately thirty by forty inches, and weighed around twenty pounds. A single soldier could not defend himself with the scutum in all directions. So the Romans devised the *testudo* to use these shields in protecting an entire formation of soldiers. On the front, rear, and both flanks of the formation, the soldiers along the periphery held their shields to protect from arrows coming in at ground level. Soldiers inside the boundary positioned their shields overhead to protect from flaming arrows arching in from above. This array resembled a tortoise shell, covering the entire formation in all directions.

As Christ-followers living in biblical relational community, we use our collective shields of faith in the same way to protect each other from the flaming arrows of the evil one (see Ephesians 6:16). There lies the danger of being a solo Christ-follower. The flaming arrows will come for all of us. The wise person of faith in Jesus prepares for this by being in a close community of fellowship with other Christ-followers.

In the world around us, people desperately desire to be loved, an attribute increasingly absent in secular relationships. The results would be astounding if Christ-followers were faithful to the "one another" commandments the way God intends. When the world sees the wonder of people loving and serving each other with good works the way God intends, they will flood into churches to get into a right relationship with God and His children.

Speaking truth to one another by standing in opposition to evil: We live in a society that is increasingly abandoning God and His commandments in a vicious spiral of depravity (see Romans 1:28-32). There is widespread rebellion against God's kingdom and followers through attempts to replace His truth with lies. Too many church pew-warmers are silent. They may remain quiet because they don't believe the Bible, or they believe, incorrectly, that speaking up violates the "speaking truth in love" commandment (Ephesians 4:15). If our motivation is for salvation of a person, group, or society, calling out evil is an act of love. But many are mute out of fear of persecution.

Meanwhile, God's truths are under siege, and God's followers marginalized, attacked, and even murdered. The psalmist asked:

> Who will stand up for me against evildoers? Who will take his stand for me against those who do wickedness? (Psalm 94:16)

Who indeed? God is asking the same question to every Christ-follower in this present time. This current time is our watch! Standing in opposition to evil is a good work.

> Do not participate in the unfruitful deeds of darkness, but instead even expose them; for it is disgraceful even to speak of the things which are done by them in secret. But all things become visible when they are exposed by the light (Ephesians 5:11-13).

THINGS CHRIST-FOLLOWERS *DON'T* "ONE ANOTHER"

When we come to faith in Jesus, we become children in the family of God (see John 1:12). Jesus has bought us with such a price (1 Corinthians 6:20) and given us such a high calling (Philippians 3:14) that there must in turn be a great difference in how we *agape* our brothers and sisters in God's family. We are not to slander or lie to one another (Colossians 3:9; James 4:11). We are not to pass judgment on one another (Romans 14:13). We are not to provoke, envy, or put a stumbling block in the way of one another (Romans 14:13; Galatians 5:26). We are not to grumble against one another (James 5:9). If a fellow brother or sister sins against us, we are to go to them and point it out, not gossip to others (Matthew 18:15). There is a strong warning for those who are not obedient to these exhortations.

> If you bite and devour one another, take care that you are not consumed by one another (Galatians 5:15).

Christ-followers are light to the world and called to shine God's truth and light on the dark, evil deeds of a depraved world (see Matthew 5:14, 15). Such actions must be done for the right motive: *agape* empowered by the Holy Spirit with gentleness. We are never to be angry, rude, disrespectful, or violent. However, we should in love call out sinful actions condemned by God. Opponents will throw up accusations of disrespect even when the truths spoken are God's commandments in the Bible. Christ-followers cannot compromise on this.

CHAPTER THIRTY APPLICATION

DISCUSSION QUESTIONS

- Why are followers of Christ created (see Ephesians 2:10)? Discuss.
- Review each of the "one another" commandments, and the things Christ-followers are not to "one another."
- How many of the "one another" commandments are involved in evangelizing and disciple-making? Discuss.
- Is the scriptural imperative for unity among Christ-followers a call to tolerate major biblical doctrinal errors or sin, or to ignore or even approve continued willful sin in the lives of people in the church?
- How does being part of a small group of Christ-followers promote "one anothering"?

SELF-EVALUATION

- Which of the following best describes the *agape* you have given to others in the past twelve months? Every morning you pray for the Holy Spirit to allow you to fervently *agapao* all around you? You are growing in agape for others and "one anothering" them? You are growing in agape but still put yourself over others? Your life is too busy, so you are just focusing on yourself?

- Did you identify any of the "one another" commandments you are not keeping? If you are like me, there will be areas needing improvement. Don't get down on yourself. Remember, it is the Holy Spirit who gives us the power to do these good works. But do create a plan for specific improvement.

MEMORY VERSE

You also, as living stones, are being build up as a spiritual house for a holy priesthood, to offer up spiritual sacrifices acceptable to God through Jesus Christ (1 Peter 2:5).

APPENDIX ONE

RESOURCES FOR DISCIPLESHIP GROUPS

The following titles are excellent resources to be used for personal discipleship or to study with a discipleship group. I have categorized them for ease of choice according to topic and included my own assessment of their contents.

FAITH ALONE IN JESUS

- Dallas Willard, *The Great Omission: Reclaiming Jesus's Essential Teachings on Discipleship* (New York, NY: HarperCollins Publishers, 2006). This is an excellent outline of the problem of complacency in carrying out the Great Commission.
- Dietrich Bonhoeffer, *The Cost of Discipleship* (New York, NY: Macmillan Publishing Co., Inc, 1959). Bonhoeffer calls out the issue of "cheap grace" in the institutional church.

SANCTIFICATION

- A.W. Tozer, *Discipleship: What It Truly Means to Be a Christian* (Chicago, IL: Moody Publishers, 2018). This superb resource outlines what it means to be a disciple who surrenders to and follows Jesus Christ.

- C. John (Jack) Miller, *Repentance: A Daring Call to Surrender* (Fort Washington, PA: CLC Publications, 2009). Jack Miller details repentance and its importance both in being born again and for growing into the likeness of Jesus Christ.
- Haddon Robinson, "Surprise!!", Fall Preaching Convocation and Workshop, Kyle Lake Center for Effective Preaching, George W. Truett Seminary, Baylor University, Sept. 22, 2009. https://edge.baylor.edu/f/97547-720. This is an outstanding message that will likely expand your understanding of good fruit.

INTERPRETING GOD'S WORD

- Alistair Begg, "The Bible. An Overview. Seeing the Unfolding Story of God's Kingdom" (Truth for Life, March 14, 2004), https://www.truthforlife.org/resources/sermon/the-bible-an-overview/. This is an excellent resource for understanding the origin of the Bible.
- Gordon Fee and Douglas Stuart, *How to Read the Bible for All Its Worth* (Grand Rapids, MI: Zondervan, 2014). This is a very useful resource for studying and interpreting Scripture.
- Walter A. Henrichsen and Gayle Jackson, *Studying, Interpreting, and Applying the Bible* (Grand Rapids, MI: Zondervan, 1990). This is an important reference book for principles on the interpretation of Scripture by a layperson.

PRAYER

- Watchman Nee, *Let Us Pray* (New York, NY: Christian Fellowship Publishers, 1977). This is an essential resource for every Christ-follower early in their faith journey.

- Warren W. Wiersbe, *Prayer 101: Experiencing the Heart of God* (Colorado Springs, CO: David C. Cook, 2016). This resource on prayer is highly valuable for every Christ-follower.

OVERCOMING SIN

- John Owen, *The Mortification of Sin in Believers: The Necessity, Nature, and Means of It* (London: The Bible in Newgate-Street, 1721). This Puritan pastor emphasizes the critical importance of overcoming sin and growing in holiness.

HUMILITY

- Andrew Murray, *Humility. The Beauty of Holiness* (New York, NY: Fleming H. Revell Company, 1910). It is critical that every Christ-follower read this short book on humility. This is a highly valuable resource that will be instrumental in any person's spiritual journey and growth to the likeness of Jesus Christ.

FORGIVENESS

- Joel Kim and Nathan W. Bingham, "Should We Forgive Someone Who Has Not Repented?" (Ligonier Ministries, September 9, 2021), https://www.ligonier.org/podcasts/ask-ligonier/should-we-forgive-someone-who-has-not-repented. This is an excellent resource on understanding the scriptural mandate for unconditional forgiveness by God's people.
- John Piper, "Can I Forgive Someone Who Doesn't Confess Wronging Me?" (Desiring God, May 10, 2017), https://www.desiringgod.org/interviews/can-i-forgive-someone-who-doesnt-confess-wronging-me. This is an equally superb discussion on Scripture emphasizing unconditional forgiveness by Christ-followers.

PAIN AND AFFLICTION

- D.A. Carson, *How Long, O Lord? Reflections on Suffering and Evil.* Second Edition (Nottingham, England: Inter-Varsity, 2006). This is an excellent resource on the causes of pain and suffering and the discipline of God for the good of the Christ-follower.
- John Ortberg, "A Life of Endurance," in *The Life You've Always Wanted: Spiritual Disciplines for Ordinary People* (Grand Rapids, MI: Zondervan, 2002). This book emphasizes the importance of endurance in suffering and affliction.
- A.W. Tozer, *The Crucified Life: How to Live Out a Deeper Christian Experience* (Bloomington, MN: Bethany House Publishers, 2011). This is an equally valuable resource on the calling of every Christ-follower to take up their cross and follow Christ even through the valley of suffering and affliction.

GIVING

- Randy Alcorn, *Money, Possessions & Eternity* (Carol Stream, IL: Tyndale House Publishers, 2003). This book on generosity is an outstanding resource on Christian stewardship.
- Steve Corbett and Brian Fikkert, *When Helping Hurts: How to Alleviate Poverty without Hurting the Poor ... and Yourself* (Chicago, IL: Moody Publishers, 2012). This is an excellent resource on the factors that must be considered in addressing and relieving poverty.

EVANGELISM

- Rico Tice, *Honest Evangelism: How to Talk About Jesus Even When It's Tough* (Charlotte, NC: The Good Book Company, 2015). This is an excellent resource on evangelism.

- A.W. Tozer, *The Crucified Life: How to Live Out a Deeper Christian Experience* (Bloomington, MN: Bethany House Publishers, 2011). In this timeless work, Tozer proclaims that the Christ-follower must progress from the question "What is a Christian?" to "What think ye of Christ?" to "And what are you going to do with Christ?" It should be read by every Christ-follower as it will dispel any notion of "cheap grace."

BEING DISCIPLED AND MAKING DISCIPLES WHO MAKE DISCIPLES

- John Stott, *The Radical Disciple: Some Neglected Aspects of Our Calling* (Downers Grove, IL: InterVarsity Press, 2013). Stott strongly emphasizes the role of discipleship in sanctification.
- Discipleship.org and Exponential.org, "National Study on Disciple-Making in USA Churches" (March, 2020), https://discipleship.org/shop/national-study-on-disciple-making-in-usa-churches/. This downloadable eBook reports the results of a 2019 questionnaire survey of a thousand lead or senior pastors in USA Protestant churches regarding disciple-making in their churches.
- Allen Parr, "The ONE Thing Every Christian Should Be Doing But Most Are Not!" (The Beat, May 12, 2019), https://www.youtube.com/watch?v=slK6HI8tUTY. This short video concisely emphasizes the importance of disciple-making.

LOVE

- Paul Miller, *Love Walked Among Us* (Colorado Springs, CO: NavPress, 2001). This is a must read for every Christ-follower, for it provides glimpses of how Jesus loved.

ONE ANOTHERING

- Haddon Robinson, "Cultivating a Good Memory That Forgets" (Chapel, Gordon-Conwell Theological Seminary, October 31, 2007), https://www.youtube.com/watch?v=0ncTQt2FBTU. This excellent sermon discusses the characteristics of love (1 Corinthians 13).
- Jim Halla, *One-Anothering: An Aspect of Progressive Sanctification* (Greenville, SC: Ambassador International, 2022). This is an excellent book which extends insight into the "one another" commandments.

APPENDIX TWO

ACCOUNTABILITY QUESTIONS

- Are you growing in your pursuit of the likeness of Jesus Christ through the power of the Holy Spirit?
- Is there still pride in your life you are not overcoming?
- Are you systematically reading God's Word and applying it to your life?
- How is your prayer life? Are you praying continually in the Spirit?
- Is there sin in your life you are struggling with? If so, what is it?
- Is there someone you haven't forgiven or toward whom you harbor bitterness?
- Do you use hardship and affliction in your life for spiritual growth?
- Are you where you need to be in giving to God and others, not just with your financial resources but with your time?
- Do you love other people? Define how this is shown.
- Have you manifested a spirit of divisiveness in your interactions with other Christ-followers?
- Are you sharing the gospel regularly with others?

- Are you giving adequate quality time to your family, including your spouse?
- Do you have a "Paul" in your life who is discipling you?
- Do you have "Timothys" in your life you are discipling?
- Are you in a small group of Christ-followers that comprises authentic community?
- Are you being a shepherd and overseer to others? How?

APPENDIX THREE

ESSENTIAL SCRIPTURE TRUTHS

Theological discussions, church doctrinal statements, Christian education institutions, scholars, and ministry leaders may offer vastly differing opinions on Scripture passages, teachings, cultural context, biblical history, or unclear parts of Scripture such as creation, prophecy, or end times. An aspect of spiritual maturity is being willing to disagree on secondary issues so as not to cause dissension within the body of Christ.

But there are also essential doctrines and spiritual truths clearly stated in Scripture on which there can be no compromise if the church is to remain faithful to God's authority and His Word. Below is a list of what I would consider the most essential truths that must be adhered to for a church to claim it is teaching biblical Christianity.

- Inspiration, inerrancy, and final authority of Scripture (see 1 Thessalonians 2:13; 2 Timothy 3:16, 17).
- The virgin birth of Jesus Christ (see Luke 1:34, 35).
- The literal incarnation, absolute humanity, and deity of Jesus Christ (see Hebrews 1:2-14; 1 John 4:2).
- Resurrection of Jesus from the dead (Acts 26:22, 23; Romans 8:11).

- That Jesus is alive and our Great High Priest (see Hebrews 4:14, 15, 7:25).
- Substitutionary atonement for our sins by Jesus through His death on the cross (see 1 Peter 1:18, 19; 1 John 2:2).
- Salvation by faith alone in Jesus alone (see Ephesians 2:8, 9).
- No other way for salvation except by Jesus (see John 14:6; Acts 4:10-12).
- No other gospel than that of Jesus (see Galatians 1:6-9).
- The call of every Christ-follower is to holiness by overcoming sin in their life (see Colossians 3:8-10; 2 Timothy 2:19-21; 1 Peter 1:14-16; 1 John 2:4, 5).
- The call of every Christ-follower is to fulfill the Great Commission to evangelize and make disciples (see Matthew 28:18-20).

ENDNOTES

CHAPTER ONE

1. A.W. Tozer, Discipleship. *What It Truly Means to be a Christian* (Chicago, IL: Moody Publishers, 2018). Reprinted with permission.

2. Gregory A. Smith et al., "About Three-in-Ten U.S. Adults Are Now Religiously Unaffiliated" (Pew Research Center, December 14, 2021), https://www.pewresearch.org/religion/2021/12/14/about-three-in-ten-u-s-adults-are-now-religiously-unaffiliated/.

3. Stephanie Kramer et al., "Modeling the Future of Religion in America," (Pew Research Center, September 13, 2022), https://www.pewresearch.org/religion/2022/09/13/modeling-the-future-of-religion-in-america/.

4. In Matthew 1:1, Jesus is referred to as "the Messiah." The Hebrew word for Messiah is "Mashiach," and means "anointed one." It is in reference to the future arrival of a righteous Savior in Isaiah 53:1-12 who would provide the ultimate sacrifice for the sins of humanity. "The Greek word for Messiah is "Christos." In the English Bible, "Christos" is represented by the English word "Christ." Jesus the Messiah and Jesus Christ are interchangeable terms. The Messiah's name used during His life was likely the Aramaic word "Y'shua." In the English Bible, it is represented by "Jesus." Jesus is a common name in the world today. Going forward, the use of the word "Jesus" is always meant to refer to Jesus Christ.

5. Dr. Edmund P. Clowney (1917-2005) was a pastor and President of Westminster Theological Seminary in Philadelphia from 1966 until 1984. Afterward, he served as theologian-in-residence at Trinity Presbyterian Church in Charlottesville, Virginia, in addition to an adjunct professorship at Westminster Seminary California and Associate pastorate in Houston, Texas. He has authored a number of important books and hymns.

6. Reprinted with permission from Edmund P. Clowney, *The Church* (Downers Grove, IL: InterVarsity Press, 1995).

7. Samuel Wilberforce, "Sermon XIX. Man's Life Ruined by Sin," in *Sermons Preached on Various Occasions by the Right Reverend Father in God, Samuel,*

Late Lord Bishop of Winchester (London: James Parker and Co., 1877): 226-227. https://archive.org/details/sermonspreachedo0000wilb/page/n3/mode/2up?view=theater&q=redemption.

8. Andrew Murray, *Humility. The Beauty of Holiness* (London: Fleming H. Revell Company, 1910), https://archive.org/details/humilitybeautyof00murr/page/n3/mode/2up.

9. James Montgomery Boice, *The Parables of Jesus* (Chicago: Moody Press, 1983): 80, 81.

10. Philip Graham Ryken, *The Message of Salvation* (Nottingham: Inter-Varsity Press, 2001): 68, 69.

CHAPTER TWO

1. Harvey Goodwin, "Sermon II. Personal Responsibility of Man as Entrusted with a Revelation," in *Personal Responsibility of Man. Sermons Preached during the Season of Lent* (London: James Parker and Co., 1869), https://archive.org/details/personalrespons00wilbgoog/page/n8/mode/2up?q=trifled.

2. Reprinted with permission from *Powerful Evangelism for the Powerless* by C. John Miller, copyright © 1997, P&R Publishing, Phillipsburg, NJ.

3. Dietrich Bonhoeffer, *The Cost of Discipleship* (New York, NY: Macmillan Publishing Co., Inc., 1959).

4. Reprinted with permission from *The Heart of a Servant Leader: Letters from Jack Miller* by C. John Miller, copyright © 2004, P&R Publishing, Phillipsburg, NJ.

CHAPTER THREE

1. *Agape* is the Greek word for a love empowered by the Holy Spirit. It is unconditional, sacrificial, and selfless and, therefore, is motivated and accompanied by deep humility.

2. The church is not a building or denomination, but rather the *ecclesia*. After the apostle Peter's statement of faith that Jesus was the Messiah, Jesus said, "I also say to you that you are Peter, and upon this rock I will build My church [*ecclesia*]; and the gates of Hades will not overpower it" (Matthew 16:18). *Ecclesia* refers to the number of "called out ones" who followed Jesus. Acts 9:31 describes this: "So the church [*ecclesia*] throughout all Judea and Galilee and Samaria enjoyed peace, being built up; and going on in the fear of the Lord and in the comfort of the Holy Spirit, it continued to increase." When Paul and

Barnabas arrived in Antioch, they "gathered the church [ecclesia] together" (Acts 14:27)

CHAPTER FOUR

1. Andrew Murray, *Humility. The Beauty of Holiness* (London: Fleming H. Revell Company, 1910), https://archive.org/details/humilitybeautyof00murr/page/n3/mode/2up.

2. Dietrich Bonhoeffer, *The Cost of Discipleship* (New York, NY: Macmillan Publishing Co., Inc., 1959).

3. A.W. Tozer, *Discipleship. What It Truly Means to be a Christian* (Chicago, IL: Moody Publishers, 2018). Reprinted with permission.

4. C.H. Spurgeon, "Sermon No. 1971, The Blood Shed for Many," in *The Metropolitan Tabernacle Pulpit. Sermons Preached and Revised by C.H. Spurgeon During the Year of 1887, Vol. XXXIII,* (July 3, 1887), https://app.logos.com/books/LLS%3AMTPSERMS33/references/page.373.

5. Discipleship.org and Exponential.org, National Study on Disciple Making in USA Churches: High Aspirations Amidst Disappointing Results, March, 2020, https://discipleship.org/shop/national-study-on-disciple-making-in-usa-churches/. Used with permission.

6. Reprinted with permission from Edmund P. Clowney, *The Church* (Downers Grove, IL: InterVarsity Press, 1995).

CHAPTER FIVE

1. The Holy Trinity refers to three persons of God: the Father, the Son Jesus Christ, and the Holy Spirit. The Gospel of John provides insight. In the first chapter of the Gospel of John, he proclaims, "the Word was with God, and the Word was God" (verse 1), and "all things came into being through Him" (verse 3). This means that the creation of the "heavens and the earth" in Genesis 1:1 was the person referred to in John 1. The apostle John then proclaims, "The Word became flesh, and dwelt among us, and we saw His glory, glory as of the only begotten from the Father, full of grace and truth" (John 1:14). John is referring, of course, to Jesus Christ. The Holy Spirit is described in the first chapter of Genesis (see Genesis 1:2). Scripture tells us that the Christ-follower has fellowship with the Father, Son, and Holy Spirit (see 1 John 1:3; Philippians 2:1). Scripture also proclaims the degree of union between the three persons of the Holy Trinity. Jesus stated, "I and the Father are one" (John 10:30). He proclaims, "He who has seen Me has seen the Father" (John 14:9). The Puritan

minister John Owen emphasized the implications of this. The gifts to the Christ-follower are from all three persons of the Holy Trinity. Our communion is with all three persons of the Trinity. When we pray, we pray to all three. For further insight, read the 17th-century Puritan theologian John Owen's book on *Communion with God.*

CHAPTER SIX

1. A.W. Tozer, *The Pursuit of God* (Chicago, IL: Moody Publishers; 2015), https://www.moodypublishers.com/the-pursuit-of-god/?variation-Code=978-1-60066-912-5, Nook ebook. Used with permission.

2. Aidan Remple, "How Fast Is The Earth Moving?" (WorldAtlas, December 14, 2022), https://www.worldatlas.com/space/how-fast-is-the-earth-moving.html.

CHAPTER SEVEN

1. Gordon Fee and Douglas Stuart, *How to Read the Bible for All Its Worth* (Grand Rapids, MI: Zondervan, 2014): 21-35.

2. A.W. Tozer, *The Crucified Life. How to Live Out a Deeper Christian Experience* (Bloomington, MN: Bethany House Publishers, 2011). Reprinted with permission.

3. J.I. Packer, *Knowing God* (Downers Grove, IL: InterVarsity Press, 1973): 23.

4. Bible Hub, https://biblehub.com/.

CHAPTER EIGHT

1. Olive Tree Bible Software, https://www.olivetree.com.

2. YouVersion Bible App, https://www.youversion.com/the-bible-app/.

3. Bible Hub, https://biblehub.com/.

4. Blue Letter Bible, https://www.blueletterbible.org.

5. Fighter Verses, https://www.fighterverses.com.

CHAPTER NINE

1. Taken from *My Utmost for His Highest®* by Oswald Chambers, edited by James Reimann, © 1992 by Oswald Chambers Publications Assn., Ltd., and used by permission of Our Daily Bread Publishing, Grand Rapids MI 49501. All rights reserved.

2. Reprinted with permission from Watchman Nee, *Let Us Pray* (New York, NY: Christian Fellowship Publishers, copyright © 2014), Kindle.

3. Thomas Watson, "Discourse VIII. Chapter IV. Showing the Character of a Godly Man," in *The Select Works of the Rev. Thomas Watson. Vol. 1* (Glasgow: Blackie, Fullarton & Co., 1829): 459, https://books.google.com/books?id=IOdLAAAAYAAJ&dq=the%20godly%20man%27s%20picture%20watson&pg=PA383#v=onepage&q&f=true.

4. Reprinted with permission from *The Heart of a Servant Leader: Letters from Jack Miller* by C. John Miller, copyright © 2004, P&R Publishing, Phillipsburg, NJ.

5. Excerpted from *Prayer 101* © 2006, 2016 Warren W. Wiersbe. Used by permission of David C. Cook. May not be further reproduced. All rights reserved.

6. A.W. Tozer, *The Set of the Sail. Spiritual Guidance for the Christian Life* (Chicago, IL: Moody Publishers, 1986). Reprinted with permission.

CHAPTER TEN

1. Reprinted with permission from Watchman Nee, *Let Us Pray* (New York, NY: Christian Fellowship Publishers, copyright © 2014), Kindle.

CHAPTER ELEVEN

1. Phillips Brooks, "Sermon XVIII. Going Up to Jerusalem," in *Twenty Sermons* (New York, NY: E.P. Dutton & Company, 1886): 330, https://archive.org/details/twentysermons00broogoog/page/n341/mode/2up?q=tasks.

2. Reprinted with permission from Watchman Nee, *Let Us Pray* (New York, NY: Christian Fellowship Publishers, copyright © 2014), Kindle.

CHAPTER TWELVE

1. A.W. Tozer, *Discipleship. What It Truly Means to be a Christian* (Chicago, IL: Moody Publishers, 2018). Reprinted with permission.

2. C.H. Spurgeon, *Sermon No. 2133.* "Lama Sabachthani?" in *The Metropolitan Tabernacle Pulpit. Sermons Preached and Revised During the Year 1890.* Volume 36. (London: Passamore and Alabaster, 1891), https://archive.spurgeon.org/index/c36.php.

3. The late Haddon Robinson (1931-2017) was the Harold John Ockenga Distinguished Professor of Preaching at Gordon-Conwell Theological

Seminary. Over his career he taught at the Dallas Theological Seminary and was President of the Denver Seminary. He authored the definitive textbook on preaching, *Biblical Preaching*, published by Baker Academic in 2001. During his life as a seminary professor, he trained many pastors in expository preaching.

4. Haddon Robinson, "Surprise!!", Fall Preaching Convocation and Workshop, Kyle Lake Center for Effective Preaching, George W. Truett Seminary, Baylor University, Sept. 22, 2009. Used with permission. https://edge.baylor.edu/f/97547-720.

5. John Owen, *Of The Mortification of Sin in Believers: The Necessity, Nature, and Means of It* (London: The Bible in Newgate-Street, 1721), https://archive.org/details/bim_eighteenth-century_of-the-mortification-of-_owen-john_1721/mode/2up.

CHAPTER THIRTEEN

1. C.S. Lewis, *The Screwtape Letters* (New York, NY: Macmillan Publishing Co., Inc., 1996).

CHAPTER FOURTEEN

1. John Stott, "Pride, Humility, and God," in *Alive to God. Studies in Spirituality*, eds. J.I. Packer and L. Wilkinson (Downers Grove, IL: InterVarsity Press, 1992): 119.

2. In severe lung disease with inadequate oxygenation, a tube is often inserted through the patient's mouth into their trachea (windpipe); this is known as an endotracheal tube. This allows for administration of higher concentrations of oxygen and to assist ventilation through an inflatable bag or a mechanical ventilator.

3. Oxygen saturation is the percentage of hemoglobin that is oxygenated. It is measured by an external pulse oximeter device placed on the patient's finger or earlobe. The range for oxygen saturation adequate to meet the patient's oxygen needs is 90 percent or above.

4. Jarrod M. Mosier et al., "Tracheal Intubation in the Critically Ill," A*m. J. Respir. Crit. Care Med. 201* (April 1, 2020): 775-788, DOI: 10.1164/rccm.201908-1636CI.

5. A.W. Tozer, *The Crucified Life. How to Live Out a Deeper Christian Experience* (Bloomington, MN: Bethany House Publishers, 2011). Reprinted with permission.

6. Andrew Murray, *Humility. The Beauty of Holiness* (London: Fleming H. Revell Company, 1910), https://archive.org/details/humilitybeautyof00murr/page/n3/mode/2up.

CHAPTER FIFTEEN

1. Patrick Koppenburg, "Physicists Just Found 4 New Subatomic Particles That May Test the Laws of Nature," *Science Alert* (March 5, 2021), https://www.sciencealert.com/scientists-just-discovered-four-new-subatomic-particles-all-tetraquarks.

2. William Ernest Henley, *A Book of Verses*. Fifth Edition (New York, NY: Charles Scribner's Sons, 1897): 56-57, https://archive.org/details/bookofverses0000henl/page/n9/mode/2up?q=Horror.

3. Andrew Murray, *Humility. The Beauty of Holiness* (London: Fleming H. Revell Company, 1910), https://archive.org/details/humilitybeautyof00murr/page/n3/mode/2up.

CHAPTER SIXTEEN

1. Andrew Murray, *Humility. The Beauty of Holiness* (London: Fleming H. Revell Company, 1910), https://archive.org/details/humilitybeautyof00murr/page/n3/mode/2up.

2. Benjamin Franklin, *The Autobiography of Benjamin Franklin* (Philadelphia: Henry Artemus, 1895): 163, 164, https://archive.org/details/autobiography00fran/page/164/mode/2up?q=disguise.

3. A.W. Tozer, *The Pursuit of God* (Chicago, IL: Moody Publishers; 2015), https://www.moodypublishers.com/the-pursuit-of-god/?variationCode=978-1-60066-912-5, Nook ebook. Used with permission.

CHAPTER SEVENTEEN

1. Reprinted with permission from *The Heart of a Servant Leader: Letters from Jack Miller* by C. John Miller, copyright © 2004, P&R Publishing, Phillipsburg, NJ.

2. Ivan Mesa, "Broken: The Power of Conversion in Louie Zamperini's Life" (The Gospel Coalition, Oct. 24, 2014), https://www.thegospelcoalition.org/article/broken-louie-zamperini/.

3. Claire Musters, "How I Forgave the Racist Man Who Murdered My Wife" (Premier Christianity, May 27, 2020), https://www.premierchristianity.com/real-life/how-i-forgave-the-racist-man-who-murdered-my-wife/2198.article.

4. Frank Sutton, email to author, February 16, 2023.

5. Joel Kim and Nathan W. Bingham, "Should We Forgive Someone Who Has Not Repented?" (Ligonier Ministries. September 9, 2021), https://www.ligonier.org/podcasts/ask-ligonier/should-we-forgive-someone-who-has-not-repented.

6. John Piper, "Can I Forgive Someone Who Doesn't Confess Wronging Me?" (Desiring God, May 10, 2017), https://www.desiringgod.org/interviews/can-i-forgive-someone-who-doesnt-confess-wronging-me.

CHAPTER EIGHTEEN

1. Abraham Lincoln, *Abraham Lincoln's Second Inaugural Address*, March 4th, 1865, Veterans of Foreign Wars, https://archive.org/details/abrahamlincolnss01linc/page/n5/mode/2up.

CHAPTER NINETEEN

1. A.W. Tozer, *The Crucified Life. How to Live Out a Deeper Christian Experience* (Bloomington, MN: Bethany House Publishers, 2011). Reprinted with permission.

2. Andrew Murray, *Humility. The Beauty of Holiness* (London: Fleming H. Revell Company, 1910), https://archive.org/details/humilitybeautyof00murr/page/n3/mode/2up.

3. American Colony, Horatio Gates Spafford, and Anna T Spafford, *American Colony in Jerusalem Collection: Part I: Telegram from Anna Spafford to Horatio Gates Spafford re: being "Saved alone" among her traveling party in the shipwreck of the Ville du Havre. December 2, 1873.*Telegram from Anna Spafford to Horatio Gates Spafford re being "Saved alone" among her traveling party in the shipwreck of the Ville du Havre (Library of Congress, December 2, 1873), https://www.loc.gov/resource/mamcol.011/?r=-0.264,-0.209,1.6,0.784,0.

4. D.A. Carson, *How Long, O Lord? Reflections on Suffering and Evil*, Second Edition, (Nottingham, England: Inter-Varsity Press, 2006).

5. Loren Grush, "Astronauts' Spinal Muscles Shrink and Weaken After Long Stays in Space" (The Verge, October 25, 2016), https://www.theverge.com/2016/10/25/13392824/astronauts-back-pain-health-space-spinal-muscles.

CHAPTER TWENTY

1. Andrew Murray, *Humility. The Beauty of Holiness* (London: Fleming H. Revell Company, 1910), https://archive.org/details/humilitybeautyof00murr/page/n3/mode/2up.

2. A.W. Tozer, *The Crucified Life. How to Live Out a Deeper Christian Experience* (Bloomington, MN: Bethany House Publishers, 2011). Reprinted with permission.

3. D.L. Moody, *The Overcoming Life — and Other Sermons* (New York, NY: Fleming H. Revell Company, 1896): 101, https://archive.org/details/overcominglife0000dlmo/page/100/mode/2up?q=rake.

4. U.S. Congress, House, Hon. Christopher H. Smith, "In recognition of Watchman Nee," 111th Cong., H. Rep., https://www.govinfo.gov/content/pkg/CREC-2009-07-31/html/CREC-2009-07-31-pt1-PgE2110-2.htm.

5. Watchman Nee, *The Normal Christian Life* (Carol Stream, IL: Tyndale House Publishers, Inc., 1977).

6. Watchman Nee, *Let Us Pray* (New York, NY: Christian Fellowship Publishers, Inc., 2014). Kindle.

7. Watchman Nee, *Sit, Walk, Stand* (Carol Stream, IL: Tyndale House Publishing, Inc., 1977).

8. Johan Gous, conversation with author. Johan is President of Hope Builders Ministries, Greenwood, VA. Through this ministry, Johan and his wife Lida train and equip indigenous missionaries to evangelize and make disciples in countries in the southern African continent. https://www.hbmin.org.

9. D.A. Carson, *How Long, O Lord? Reflections on Suffering and Evil*, Second Edition, (Nottingham, England: Inter-Varsity Press, 2006).

CHAPTER TWENTY-ONE

1. Gospel Fellowship Association Missions, "Robert Moffat" (GFA Missions, June 14, 1999), https://gfamissions.org/robert-moffat/.

2. A.W. Tozer, *I Talk Back to the Devil: The Fighting Fervor of the Victorious Christian* (Chicago, IL: Moody Publishers, 1990) Reprinted with permission.

CHAPTER TWENTY-TWO

1. Reprinted with permission from Elisabeth Elliot, *Suffering Is Never for Nothing* (Nashville, TN: B&H Publishing Group, 2019).

2. Randy Alcorn, *Money, Possessions & Eternity* (Carol Stream, IL: Tyndale House Publishers, 2003).

3. Credit Suisse Research Institute, "Global Wealth Report 2022," https://www.credit-suisse.com/about-us/en/reports-research/global-wealth-report.html.

4. Worldometer, "Northern American Population. 2023," https://srv1.worldometers.info/world-population/northern-america-population/.

5. Ken Elzinga, "Stewardship and Giving: Implications for Daily Life," 2023. Used with permission.

6. Steve Corbett and Brian Fikkert, *When Helping Hurts. How to Alleviate Poverty without Hurting the Poor ... and Yourself* (Chicago, IL: Moody Publishers, 2012).

CHAPTER TWENTY-THREE

1. Johan Gous, conversation with author. Johan is President of Hope Builders Ministries, Greenwood, VA. Through this ministry, Johan and his wife Lida train and equip indigenous missionaries to evangelize and make disciples in countries in the southern African continent. https://www.hbmin.org.

2. Harry Lee Poe, *The Making of C. S. Lewis. From Atheist to Apologist* (1918-1945) (Wheaton, IL: Crossway, 2021).

3. The Pocket Testament League (https://www.ptl.org).

CHAPTER TWENTY-FOUR

1. Gilbert K. Chesterton, "Chapter V. The Unfinished Temple" in *What's Wrong with the World* (New York, NY: Dodd, Mead and Company, 1910): 48, https://archive.org/details/whatswrongwithwo0000ches/page/48/mode/2up?q=difficult.

2. Rico Tice with Carl Laferton, *Honest Evangelism: How to Talk About Jesus Even When It's Tough* (Charlotte, NC: The Good Book Company, 2015).

3. Glenn Stanton, "FactChecker: Misquoting Francis of Assisi" (The Gospel Coalition. July 10, 2012), https://www.thegospelcoalition.org/article/factchecker-misquoting-francis-of-assisi/.

CHAPTER TWENTY-FIVE

1. Reprinted with permission from C. John Miller, *A Faith Worth Sharing: A Lifetime of Conversations about Christ* (Phillipsburg, NJ: P&R Publishing, copyright © 1999).

2. Haddon Robinson, "Surprise!!", Fall Preaching Convocation and Workshop, Kyle Lake Center for Effective Preaching, George W. Truett Seminary, Baylor University, Sept. 22, 2009. Used with permission. https://edge.baylor.edu/f/97547-720. .

3. Don Sunshine Ministries, https://donsunshine.org.

4. Billy Graham School of Evangelism Online, Billy Graham Evangelistic Association, https://soe.billygraham.org.

5. EvanTell, https://www.evantell.org.

CHAPTER TWENTY-SIX

1. John Stott, *The Radical Disciple. Some Neglected Aspects of Our Calling* (Downers Grove, IL: InterVarsity Press, 2012).

2. Thomas à Kempis, *The Imitation of Christ* (London: George Routlege and Sons, 1888), https://archive.org/details/imitationofchris00thomuoft/page/n3/mode/2up.

3. Josiah Bull, *John Newton of Olney and St. Mary Woolnoth. An Autobiography and Narrative* (London: The Religious Tract Society, 1868), https://archive.org/details/johnnewtonofolne00bull/mode/2up.

4. Josiah Bull, *Letters By the Rev. John Newton* (London: The Religious Tract Society, 1869), https://archive.org/details/lettersbynewton00newtuoft/page/2/mode/2up.

5. Phillip Doddridge, *The Rise and Progress of Religion in the Soul* (Boston, MA: Kimball and Johnson, 1831), https://archive.org/details/riseprogresso00dodd/page/n3/mode/2up.

6. Robert Isaac Wilberforce and Samuel Wilberforce, *The Life of William Wilberforce* (London: John Murray, 1838), https://archive.org/details/lifewilliamwilb02wilbgoog/page/n12/mode/2up.

7. Wendall Winn, conversation with author, July 13, 2023.

8. Paul David Tripp, *Instruments in the Reedemer's Hands* (Phillipsburg, NJ: P&R Publishing Co., 2002).

CHAPTER TWENTY-SEVEN

1. Albert Barnes, *Notes, Explanatory and Practical, on the Epistle to the Hebrews* (New York, NY: Harper & Brothers, Publishers, 1855): 331, https://archive.org/details/notesexplanator21barngoog/page/n334/mode/2up?q=arrangements.

CHAPTER TWENTY-EIGHT

1. Personal communication with Johan Gous, founder and President of Hope Builders Ministry (https://www.hbmin.org). Johan developed these questions for encouraging disciple-making in his ministry. Used with permission.

2. Discipleship.org and Exponential.org, "III. Develop New Measures of Success." *National Study on Disciple Making in USA Churches: High Aspirations Amidst Disappointing Results,* March, 2020, 16-17, eBook, https://discipleship.org/shop/national-study-on-disciple-making-in-usa-churches/.

CHAPTER TWENTY-NINE

1. Paul Miller, *Love Walked Among Us. Learning to Love Like Jesus* (Colorado Springs, CO: NavPress, 2001).

CHAPTER THIRTY

1. Andrew Murray, *Humility. The Beauty of Holiness* (London: Fleming H. Revell Company, 1910), https://archive.org/details/humilitybeautyof00murr/page/n3/mode/2up.

2. Rod Benson, "Origin of the phrase, 'In necessariis unitas'" (Idigress, March 27, 2018), https://rodbenson.com/2018/03/27/origin-of-the-phrase-in-necessariis-unitas/.

3. Edward Livingston Trudeau, *An Autobiography* (Garden City, NY: Doubleday & Page Company, 1916, copyright Lea & Febiger, 1915), https://archive.org/details/autobiography00truduoft/page/n9/mode/2up?q=aspirations.

4. Evelyn S. Shuckburgh, *The Histories of Polybius. Translated from the Text of F. Hultsch. Vol. I* (London: Macmillan and Co., 1889), 379, 477, https://archive.org/details/polybius-shuckburgh-1889/page/n329/mode/2up?q=shield.

SUBJECT INDEX

ABOUT THE AUTHOR

C. Edward Rose, Jr., MD founded Good Soil Good Fruit Ministries, which encourages Christ-followers to grow in the image of Jesus Christ and become disciple-makers. Ed has been a ruling elder and part of medical mission teams to India, Bolivia, and Honduras. He continues to lead and teach Bible studies and discipleship groups. His passion is to share the gospel and disciple men and women to become mature Christ followers to bear fruit becoming disciple-makers.

Dr. Ed Rose is Professor Emeritus of Medicine at the University of Virginia School of Medicine, where he was a pulmonary and critical care medicine professor for more than forty years. Ed continues to practice medicine in a free clinic in Lynchburg, Virginia. He and his wife, Karren, reside in Charlottesville, Virginia. They have two children and six grandchildren.

To learn more about C. Edward Rose, Jr., MD and Good Soil Good Fruit Ministry visit www.GoodSoilGoodFruit.com